The Handbook for
SMART
School Teams

Second Edition

Revitalizing Best Practices
for Collaboration

Anne E. Conzemius & Jan O'Neill

Foreword by Stephanie Hirsh

Solution Tree | Press

a division of

Solution Tree

555 North Morton Street

Bloomington, IN 47404

800.733.6786 (toll free) / 812.336.7700

FAX: 812.336.7790

email: info@solution-tree.com

solution-tree.com

Visit **go.solution-tree.com/schoolimprovement** to download the reproducibles in this book.

Printed in the United States of America

17   5

Library of Congress Cataloging-in-Publication Data

Conzemius, Anne, 1953-

 The handbook for SMART school teams : revitalizing best practices for collaboration / Anne E. Conzemius, Jan O'Neill ; foreword by Stephanie Hirsh. – Second edition.

     pages cm

 Includes bibliographical references and index.

 ISBN 978-1-936764-78-5 (perfect bound) 1. School improvement programs. 2. School environment. 3. Group work in education. I. O'Neill, Jan, 1955- II. Title.

 LB2822.8.C67 2014

 371.2–dc23

                    2013036044

Solution Tree

Jeffrey C. Jones, CEO

Edmund M. Ackerman, President

Solution Tree Press

President: Douglas M. Rife

Publisher: Robert D. Clouse

Editorial Director: Lesley Bolton

Managing Production Editor: Caroline Weiss

Senior Production Editor: Joan Irwin

Copy Editor: Sarah Payne-Mills

Proofreader: Elisabeth Abrams

Text Designer: Jenn Taylor

Text Compositor: Rian Anderson

Cover Designer: Amy Shock

For Quinn William and Edilfanta James Van de Grift
—Anne E. Conzemius

For Betty Ward
—Jan O'Neill

Acknowledgments

In 2002, moved by the dedication to continuous, never-ending improvement our friends and colleagues demonstrated every day in the course of their work, we wrote *The Handbook for SMART School Teams*. We are grateful for the number of people who use the handbook—district administrators, school principals, classroom teachers, educational consultants, and even college professors. Their feedback about what is most useful in practice informs this second edition. In addition, our professional colleagues who work with teachers and administrators in the field have provided invaluable input. Conferring with our colleagues and clients has shaped our choices about what to continue to include, what to add, and what to modify.

As always, the birth of a book—even a second edition—requires guidance, support, and wisdom from a supportive team. There are many people to thank, but two deserve special mention: Terry Morganti-Fisher, whose passion for continuous learning and commitment to integrity is a constant wind beneath our wings, and Mark Zimmerman, editor extraordinaire, whose great sense of organization and gift for words (not to mention sense of humor!) made the process of revising this book a pleasure.

We are grateful to our Solution Tree family for their many years of support and encouragement. The first edition of *The Handbook for SMART School Teams* was a bit of an experiment for them. The format, with lots of white space for writing, lighthearted cartoons, and an emphasis on practical, user-friendly tools and processes was different from their other published works. We so appreciate their taking a chance on it; it's an honor to work with them again to bring a second edition to practitioners.

Finally, we are always humbled by the passion, brilliance, and stamina that educators bring to their work. There is no tougher job and no higher calling. Our greatest hope is that *The Handbook for SMART School Teams (Second Edition): Revitalizing Best Practices for Collaboration* will become dog-eared and rumpled—proof that the tools and processes herein are useful and used.

Anne E. Conzemius
Jan O'Neill
www.smartlearningcommunity.net

Table of Contents

Reproducible pages are in italics.

Visit **go.solution-tree.com/schoolimprovement**
to download the reproducibles in this book.

About the Authors... xv

Foreword..xix

INTRODUCTION
SMART Thinking for (Still) Critical Times 1

    Linking Learning and Improvement......................... 3

    Thinking in a SMART Way................................. 5

    Making SMART Schools 7

    Becoming a SMART School 8

        Focus... 9

        Reflection... 10

        Collaboration 11

        Leadership Capacity............................... 12

    Embedding Learning Within a SMART System 14

    Pulling the Pieces Together............................. 15

PART ONE:
Building Effective Teams................ 17

CHAPTER 1
Cornerstones of Collaboration
and Teamwork 19

    Three Cornerstones of Productive Collaboration.......... 19

People 19

Tasks 20

Processes 21

The Dynamic Interaction of People, Tasks, and Processes 21

Barriers to Collaborative Learning and Improvement 22

Final Check: Cornerstones of Collaboration and Teamwork . 25

CHAPTER 2

Fundamentals for Getting Started

Fundamentals for Getting Started 27

Ongoing Teams 27

Governance Teams 28

School Improvement Teams 29

System-Level Improvement Teams 30

Professional Learning Teams 31

Ad Hoc Groups 33

Steering Committees 33

Study Circles 34

Process Improvement Project Groups 35

Committees and Task Forces 37

Getting Teams Started 37

Step One: Identify Members 38

Step Two: Identify Stakeholders 40

Step Three: Define Functions 41

Step Four: Identify Goals 43

Step Five: Develop a Charter, Schedule the Work,
        and Determine Roles and Responsibilities 43

Step Six: Discuss Assumptions 46

Step Seven: Agree on Guidelines for Behavior 46

Supporting Ongoing Teams and Ad Hoc Groups 49

Final Check: Fundamentals for Getting Started 49

CHAPTER 3

Teamwork Basics

Teamwork Basics 51

Team Growth and Development 51

Stage One: Forming 52

Stage Two: Storming 53

Stage Three: Norming 54

Stage Four: Performing 55

Stage Five: Transforming. 56

Going Through the Stages 57

Communication: Pay Attention to What Is Said

    and How 58

Sharing 59

Discussion 60

Dialogue. 61

Active Listening 62

Mental Models and the Ladder of Inference 65

Decision Making: Decide How to Decide 67

Team Authority. 68

Four Decision-Making Options 69

Conflict Management 74

Conflict Management Techniques 74

Giving and Receiving Feedback 76

Use of Data. 80

The Data-Logic Chain. 83

Cohesiveness 84

Techniques for Building Team Cohesiveness 85

Continuously Improving Your Team's Work 85

Final Check: Teamwork Basics 87

PART TWO:
Using Tools and Processes for Effective Teamwork 89

CHAPTER 4
Tools for Productive Meetings 91

Elements of Meeting Design. 92

Purpose. 92

Participants 93

Time. 93

Methods and Tools 93

Types of Meetings 94

Turbo Meetings 94

Decision-Making Forums. 95

Dialogue Sessions 95

The SMART Meeting Process 96

The Meeting Plan 96

   Purpose and Objectives 97

   Logistics 97

   Agendas 98

   Communication Strategy 98

The Meeting Process 100

   Check In 100

   Review Agenda and Ground Rules 101

   Discuss, Decide, and Present 102

   Identify Next Steps 102

   Develop Next Agenda 102

Studying the Meeting Process 103

   Checkout 103

   Evaluation 103

Action Between Meetings 104

Meeting Records 105

Managing Team Meetings 106

   Functional Roles for Effective Meetings 106

Final Check: Tools for Productive Meetings 109

CHAPTER 5

Group Process and Planning Tools 111

Group Process Tools 112

   Dialogue 112

   Brainstorming 112

   Affinity Diagrams 113

   Multivoting 118

   Decision Matrices 119

   Consensus Decision Making 120

Process-Mapping Tools 125

   Basic Flowchart 126

   Top-Down Flowchart 127

   Deployment Flowchart 128

   Detailed Flowchart 131

Planning Tools 134

   Tree Diagrams 134

   Responsibility Matrices 138

   Gantt Charts 139

Final Check: Group Process and Planning Tools 141

CHAPTER 6

Tools for Understanding Perceptions and Opinions 143

Collecting and Analyzing Perceptual Data 143

Sampling 144

Stratification 145

Disaggregation 147

Questioning 148

Quantifying 150

Methods for Obtaining Perceptual Data 150

Interviews 150

Focus Groups 153

Surveys 155

Final Check: Tools for Understanding Perceptions and Opinions 158

CHAPTER 7

Data Tools for Understanding More Than Problems 161

Cause-Analysis Tools 161

Five Whys Analysis 162

Cause-and-Effect Diagram 164

Relations Diagram 167

Numerical Data Tools 168

Snapshot Tools 169

Moving Picture Tools 186

Final Check: Data Tools for Understanding More Than Problems 194

PART THREE:

Implementing Effective School Improvement 197

CHAPTER 8

Systems Thinking for Coherent School Improvement 199

Aspects of Systems Thinking 201

Patterns of Behavior..................................201

Systemic Structures...................................205

Mental Models......................................207

Strategies for Improving Processes and Systems.........208

A Problem-Solving Process............................211

Step One: Identify and Define the Problem...........212

Step Two: Analyze the Problem.....................214

Step Three: Establish Specific Goals
for Improvement................................215

Step Four: Study and Decide on Solutions............216

Step Five: Plan for Implementation..................217

Step Six: Implement on a Small Scale................218

Step Seven: Monitor and Continuously Improve.......219

Functional Analysis Process............................219

Step One: Clarify Mission, Values, and Recipients of
Our Service.....................................220

Step Two: Create a System Flowchart................221

Step Three: Identify Core Processes.................221

Step Four: Identify Responsibilities for
Core Processes..................................223

Step Five: Learn Recipient Needs...................223

Step Six: Prioritize and Flowchart Processes..........224

Step Seven: Make Improvements to Processes........224

Step Eight: Check Results, and Hold Gains...........224

A Process for Solving Complex Problems.................224

Step One: Identify the Original Problem Symptom.....224

Step Two: Map Out All the Quick Fixes..............225

Step Three: Identify the Impact....................225

Step Four: Identify Fundamental Solutions............226

Final Check: Systems Thinking for Coherent School
Improvement...................................226

CHAPTER 9

A Schoolwide Improvement Process 229

Guidelines for Your SMART Leadership Team.............231

Historygram Process to Prepare Your School
for Change.......................................233

Core Questions for SMART Schools....................235

Core Question One: Where Do We Want to Be?.........235

Core Values......................................236

    Vision. 239

    Mission 245

  Core Question Two: Where Are We Now? 251

    Needs Assessment 252

    Friendly Observers 254

  Core Question Three: How Will We Get There? 256

    The SMART School Improvement Process. 257

  Core Question Four: What Are We Learning? 274

  Core Question Five: Where Should We Focus Next? 276

  Final Check: A Schoolwide Improvement Process 277

APPENDIX A

Tools for SMART Schools. 279

APPENDIX B

Reproducibles 299

  Random Number Table. 300

  Template for Organizing Staff Research Findings. 302

  Template for Planning Professional Development 303

  The SMART Schools Self-Assessment. 304

  Team Charter 307

  Meeting Agenda Template 308

  Meeting Evaluation Form 309

  Meeting Record. 310

  Meeting Skills Self-Assessment 311

  Decision Matrix 313

  Responsibility Matrix 314

  Worksheet for Computing Control Limits 315

  Collaborative Action Research Guide. 316

References. 317

Index. 323

About the Authors

Anne E. Conzemius is president and cofounder of SMART Learning Systems, LLC, a Madison, Wisconsin, based company specializing in strategic professional development for educators throughout the United States. She is the coauthor of five books that provide the framework and tools educational leaders at all levels of the preK–12 system need to continuously improve both adult and student learning. Her work has also been published in local, state, and national educational newsletters and journals.

Most recently, Anne led the management team of QLD Learning, a school improvement company she cofounded with Jan O'Neill in 1998. From 1990–1995, Anne served as the executive assistant to Wisconsin's superintendent of public instruction. In that capacity, she advised the state superintendent on educational policy and led the department's organizational strategic planning and restructuring initiative.

Prior to her appointment at the state education department, Anne was a senior associate with Howick Associates, a human resource training and consulting firm. In her consulting practice, she worked with organizations representing diverse industry groups including government, education, manufacturing, finance, and health care.

From 1985–1988, Anne served as director of employee development and training for the state of Wisconsin. In that capacity, she led the state's efforts in designing and delivering continuous improvement training and in developing training policy for more than sixty thousand state employees. In addition, Anne worked in the public schools for eight years as a school psychologist and for four years as a professional development consultant with the Department of Public Instruction.

Anne earned two master's degrees from the University of Wisconsin–Madison, one in educational psychology and the other in industrial relations, human resource management. Her work experience in higher education includes instructor in the Masters of Educational Leadership program for Cardinal Stritch University and lead program developer and instructor for the Academy for Continuous Improvement, University of Wisconsin–Madison and the Institute for the Development of Effective Administrative Leadership, University of Wisconsin–Milwaukee.

To learn more about Anne's work, visit www.smartlearning community.net.

Jan O'Neill began her career teaching elementary and middle school students and has diverse experience in early childhood education, special education, multicultural education, and the Montessori method. As an independent consultant, she pioneered the systemwide application of quality principles in municipal and state governments and in health care. She has developed and implemented numerous training and improvement efforts for public and private sector clients.

With Anne, Jan cofounded Quality Leadership by Design (QLD) and coauthored three books: *Building Shared Responsibility for Student Learning*, *The Handbook for SMART School Teams*, and *The Power of SMART Goals*. Additionally, she codeveloped the school improvement training program *Creating Meaning Through Measurement*.

Jan holds a master's degree in public policy and administration from the La Follette School of Public Affairs, University of Wisconsin–Madison. She is a community coach with the *County Health Rankings & Roadmaps* program, a collaboration between the University of Wisconsin Population Health

Institute and the Robert Wood Johnson Foundation. As part of a team that develops online tools to connect communities to evidence-informed strategies, delivers technical assistance and training, and recognizes and celebrates health improvement, Jan provides strategic guidance to communities that want to put the *Rankings* into action for community health improvement. Jan's commitment to education, begun more than thirty years ago, continues in her broader context, where quality education is a key factor determining the quality and length of life for both youth and adults.

To book Anne E. Conzemius or Jan O'Neill for professional development, contact pd@solution-tree.com.

Foreword

Conceptually, who would disagree that our schools and school systems should create a culture of continuous improvement? The idea makes great sense from many perspectives. In a culture of continuous improvement, everyone involved is a learner every day. Everyone agrees on the outcomes he or she needs, studies what is happening in the workplace, builds individual and group capacity to get improved results, and monitors progress. Participants in such a culture don't give up when they don't meet their goals, and they push one another to tougher goals when they do meet them.

Yet, creating such a culture of continuous improvement in school systems isn't as easy as it is logical. For one thing, the demands on schools and the people who work in them are urgent and constant. For another, school systems haven't historically had structures in the workday to support the kinds of activities and tasks that support the creation of a continuous improvement culture.

Developments in school systems, however, take us closer to the widespread possibility of continuous improvement. More and more school districts have embraced the concept of collaborative teamwork and professional learning communities. You can read news articles every week about another school system that has approved a schedule change so that teachers can meet weekly to explore student learning challenges and solutions.

The schedule changes and the more common embrace of collaborative learning are exciting. Learning Forward's Standards for Professional Learning call for such structure and cultural changes if schools and school systems want professional learning to have its intended results—improved educator practice and student results.

Time for collaborative professional learning and widespread agreement that such learning is critical aren't enough, however. Collaborating effectively isn't easy, particularly in high-stress, high-stakes environments, where those participating have deep expertise and diverse perspectives. School systems can't take for granted that those who most need to collaborate already have the knowledge, skills, and tools to make productive collaboration happen. Without deliberate attention to the development of those knowledge and skills, school and district leaders may find that the energy they've spent on creating time for learning is wasted and that the results are disappointing.

The Handbook for SMART School Teams (Second Edition): Revitalizing Best Practices for Collaboration comes at a time when school systems need it the most. The book offers not only the knowledge base for developing the skills to collaborate but also ready-to-use tools. Grounded in the framework that has made SMART goals the standard for goal setting in school improvement, this handbook helps readers understand first the basics of meaningful teamwork and then how to refine and advance teams to serve the many perspectives and purposes that 21st century education challenges require.

Professional learning will reach its full potential for school- and systemwide improvement only when educators are supported with the full range of resources necessary for continuous improvement. This resource will help those planning and leading professional learning as they implement meaningful collaboration at all levels.

—Stephanie Hirsh

SMART Thinking for (Still) Critical Times

When we think about the complexity of the educational enterprise of the 21st century, with its growing demands on the resources and energy of educators, it's easy to see why people feel tugged and pulled in all directions. Consider the enormity of the task.

- **We must educate the whole child:** Teachers must ensure that students can read, write, and compute; know basic scientific facts and processes; are knowledgeable about history, geography, social, civic, and economic issues and events; learn and apply creative expression through art, music, and dance; and are physically, socially, and emotionally healthy.

- **We must attend to students' daily needs:** Educators are responsible for feeding and transporting students, providing a safe environment in which to learn, disciplining them, teaching them, and even attending to their most basic physical needs when they are not yet skilled to do so for themselves.

- **We must prepare students for all possible futures:** Teachers prepare students to be good workers, good parents, good citizens, and good people. They need to learn technology skills, employment skills, problem-solving and critical-thinking skills, organizational skills, communication skills, conflict-resolution skills, and teamwork.

- **We must meet the needs of all students:** Students represent a full spectrum of abilities, ages, attitudes, interests, economic conditions, and experiences. Teachers must educate and care for all of them, including those who speak different languages and come from diverse cultural backgrounds.

- **We must meet the needs of multiple stakeholders with differing expectations:** Schools must satisfy the needs and desires of parents, grandparents, community members, social service agency employees, politicians, journalists, higher education and business members, and taxpayers.

- **We must be accountable to our government:** Teachers must meet the continuous onslaught of new initiatives and requirements that come from state and federal mandates (mostly unfunded) whether we believe they are in the best interests of the students or not.

When we view these demands collectively, it's no wonder educators feel attacked. Considering the enormity of the challenge, it's also a testament to educational practices that we have been able to accomplish as much as we have. Additionally, the list demonstrates why there is growing interest in finding new and better ways to educate students (Bellanca & Brandt, 2010; Zmuda, 2010). The ability to meet these demands—and do them all well, at the same time, and for a sustainable period—is well beyond the capacity of most traditional educational systems and certainly well beyond the capacity of individuals working in isolation.

However, many U.S. schools and districts have discovered new ways for educators to work together that fundamentally increase their capacity to learn and grow. One of the most powerful changes is the creation of professional learning communities (PLCs). Informed by the research and teaching of educational thought leaders (DuFour & Eaker, 1998; Eaker, DuFour, & DuFour, 2002; Hipp & Huffman, 2010; Hord, Roussin, & Sommers, 2010), this model engages the entire school in becoming a community of learners. By developing a shared mission, vision, values, and SMART goals, all members of the school community accept responsibility for the success of *all* students. The mission defines what we exist to do; the vision defines what we aspire to achieve; and the core values reveal what we care about most deeply. There is a clear priority on improving student results by working collaboratively to examine data, research best instructional practices, implement and assess new school-based strategies, and continuously learn what is working and what needs to change. As a result, professional learning communities are resilient in times of change because they never stop learning and improving.

Linking Learning and Improvement

This book is about professional learning as the key driver of improvement. The principles that underlie all of the methods, tools, and processes we describe in the book are simple.

- Make learning something that an entire school does as a natural part of the daily life of educators and their students.
- Apply new learning to achieve ongoing, continuous improvement of both the system of learning and its results.

To some people, continuous improvement in education means that test scores go up every year. That is one way to look at it, but it is just a small part of the picture. For schools to become effective learning organizations, they must look beyond static test scores that symbolize whether learning has or has not taken place to creating systemwide structures and supports that embed professional learning into everything that happens.

In its broadest sense, continuous improvement is a state of mind—the belief that no matter what we do well, there's a way to do it better next time. When we think this way, everything we do is fair game. Improvement becomes something that applies to both things our schools are currently doing poorly and things we think we are doing well.

The only way to continuously improve is to continuously come up with new and better ideas that produce better results. The only way to come up with those ideas is through learning.

Nothing is more motivating and energizing for educators than learning something new and useful—especially if what they learn has a potential impact on their teaching and students' learning. Learning happens when:

- Theory and practice interact
- Past experience and new knowledge meet
- Data confirm or negate perceptions
- Separate, isolated events or facts emerge into patterns, trends, or new ideas
- Two or more individuals' creative potentials collide

The PDSA model of continuous improvement illustrates the link between learning and improvement.

- **Plan** a change or action.
- **Do** the change or action (on a small scale at first).
- **Study** the results to learn what did and did not work.
- **Act** by refining the idea or by implementing it on a broader scale.

PDSA is most often depicted as a wheel (see figure I.1) to capture the idea that learning is ongoing.

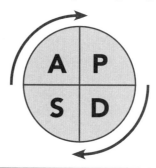

Figure I.1: PDSA wheel.

PDSA is a process of learning by trying out approaches on a small scale, reflecting on the results, and then either abandoning the approach if it does not work well or institutionalizing it if it does. Walter Shewhart (1939) first developed the process, and W. Edwards Deming (1982) later adapted and taught it.

You will find PDSA thinking embedded throughout this book. It influences everything from how to hold effective

> You don't just learn knowledge; you have to create it. Get in the driver's seat, don't just be a passenger. You have to contribute to it or you don't understand it.
>
> —W. Edwards Deming

meetings (page 91) to developing, implementing, and monitoring school improvement plans (page 229). When an entire school community is thinking PDSA, learning and improvement become second nature. Schools quickly implement successes on a broad scale so that all can benefit from the new methods or approaches; they see mistakes as learning by *failing forward*, another opportunity to do better the next time around. With PDSA, schools can move rapidly up the learning curve to understand how and why they are (or are not) making progress.

Thinking in a SMART Way

Believing that learning and improvement should be explicitly linked is one thing; finding tools and methods that let you act on that belief is entirely different. SMART goals are very effective tools for making this translation. These goals are:

Strategic and specific

Measurable

Attainable

Results oriented

Time bound

Strategic goals are linked to strategic priorities that are part of a larger vision of success for the entire school district (see chapter 9). *Strategic and specific* means that these goals will have both broad-based and long-term impacts because they are focused on the specific needs of the students for whom the goal is intended.

Measurable means being able to know whether actions made the kind of difference we wanted: being able to measure a change in results because of those actions. Measurement can and should occur in a number of different ways using a variety of different tools and strategies. Seeing results across measurements that yield consistent patterns gives us greater confidence that our actions truly have made a difference.

A goal needs to be *attainable* (within the realm of our influence or control) and doable (given current resources). To know whether a goal is attainable, you must know your starting point (baseline), how much time you have to accomplish the goal, and what kinds of resources you have to make the necessary changes. Setting a goal that is attainable then becomes an art of balancing the degree of stretch that will make the goal compelling without making it unattainable.

SMART goals are *results oriented*—aimed at specific outcomes that schools can measure or observe. Results-oriented goals define not only what is expected but also desired as an end point. Results could come in the form of student achievement in a particular area, a percentage of students who improve in a certain area, or as a demonstration of learning that teachers can define and measure. (Refer to page 259 for more information on results versus process goals.)

Finally, SMART goals are *time bound*. Specifying a time frame for achieving the goal helps in two ways—first by providing a reference point for determining attainability, and second, by helping to keep the goal a priority. It makes the goal more compelling by giving it some urgency. Having a time limit as part of a goal makes it imperative that we periodically check how well or swiftly we are progressing toward the goal. This helps to keep the goal a dynamic part of the improvement process.

In short, SMART goals let us monitor which of our efforts are making a difference and by how much. For example, here's a SMART goal from an intermediate school: "Within the next two years, increase by 50 percent the number of fourth- and fifth-grade students who are able to demonstrate proficiency or mastery of reading and mathematics standards. Currently, only one-third of students are able to do so." This goal is:

- **Strategic and specific**—It deals with students in grades 4 and 5 and with reading and mathematics skills, both of which are strategic priorities in the district.

- **Measurable**—The district knows how many students have scored at the desired levels in the past and, therefore, can easily compute whether that figure increases by 50 percent.

- **Attainable**—It is neither so conservative to be uninspiring nor so high that people will think it is impossible to achieve.
- **Results oriented**—It describes the *outcome* (better readers and mathematicians), not a test score or a process or activity that might contribute to that goal, such as implementing a new reading or mathematics program.
- **Time bound**—It gives a time frame to achieve the goal: within the next two years.

Because SMART goals provide a basis for assessing progress and a tool for ensuring that teams focus efforts on strategically important targets, they become the engine that drives continuous improvement and learning.

Making SMART Schools

Having a single team that uses SMART goals will not increase a school's capacity for improvement, but applying this thinking *throughout* a school can have enormous impact.

In SMART schools:

- Everyone knows what the priorities and expectations are and can align efforts to achieving them (because they have agreed on strategic and specific and attainable goals).
- Everyone knows how the school defines success and how and when teachers will measure it (because they have agreed on what is measurable).
- As a part of the overall results-oriented strategy, everyone is involved in finding a way to achieve the priorities (within the context of his or her own work) and collectively learns what is and is not working.
- New initiatives have a better chance of success and being sustained and continuously improved over time when they are based on well-informed decisions and targeted resources.

Now that's SMART!

SMART schools build shared responsibility for continuous learning and improvement. They create an environment where specific actions are aligned with strategic intent and are continuously monitored for effectiveness using multiple measures over time. SMART schools use teams as vehicles for collaborative goal setting, problem solving, and decision making, thus ensuring that strategies are mutually agreeable and attainable. SMART schools have a results orientation; they use good processes to target high-priority needs in a timely way.

Becoming a SMART School

In SMART schools, continuous improvement is not an event—it is a way of thinking and being. Individuals, teams, schools, and entire school districts engage in the ongoing process of learning. You may have heard this referred to in the contemporary literature as a *learning organization* or as a *professional learning community* (Drago-Severson, 2009; Drago-Severson, Blum-DeStefano, & Asghar, in press; DuFour, DuFour, Eaker, & Many, 2010). It doesn't really matter what you call it, as long as it results in everyone sharing responsibility for the improvement of student learning.

How do schools become communities of continuous learners? Across the United States, you will find hundreds of models representing the basic elements of continuous improvement. This book is built on a simple framework for becoming SMART (see figure I.2), incorporating the best of continuous improvement within a culture of shared responsibility.

Here is a brief overview of this framework; we discuss each element in more detail in the following section.

- **Focus** means being clear about where you want to go.
- **Reflection** means using data and information to understand where you are now and what impact your actions have.
- **Collaboration** means working together to create learning and improvement.
- **Leadership capacity** grows as the other three elements work together. People develop the skills

Source: QLD Learning, LLC © 2013. Reprinted with permission.

Figure I.2: Framework for becoming SMART.

and knowledge to take effective action and have the authority to act on ideas that are consistent with the organization's vision and plans.

Schools that use a framework like this achieve the results that are most important to them. They know their priorities, know how they are progressing toward achieving their goals, and continuously monitor and adjust what they are doing for the sake of improved results.

Focus

Focus helps us think clearly about what we are doing and why. Focus helps schools and school districts decide not only what is most important to do but also what not to do or what to stop doing. Working toward focus helps separate the daily urgent issues from the important priorities that teams need to nurture on a longer-term basis. Focus helps schools and individuals stay centered on the purpose of what they're doing, no matter what it is.

Focus is absolutely essential in a learning community. In many ways, focus is what defines the community—what it is, who it serves, its values, and its reason to exist. Without focus, a community attempts to be all things to all people and ends up doing very little with any depth.

Creating focus is SMART because it helps schools know their true priorities. Many schools create focus by developing statements that capture the essence of a school's mission, vision, values, and goals (see chapter 9). All of these work together to create focus. As a community matures, its vision and goals will change because continuous learning will shape and inform new ideas. What remains intact, however, are the values and the purpose (mission) that define the uniqueness of that particular community.

The essence of focus is captured in a concept known as the *Pareto principle*. Vilfredo Pareto, an economist who studied the distribution of wealth, discovered that 20 percent of the people held 80 percent of the wealth (Pareto, 1935). From this basic principle, corporate leaders made financial and business decisions based on targeting a small percentage of the population while influencing a large percentage of the wealth. Renowned management expert Joseph Juran (1964)

Framework for Becoming SMART

The words in brackets show the link between the statement and the framework for becoming SMART (see figure I.2).

"A strong professional community consists of (a) the staff sharing clear goals for student learning [focus], (b) collaboration and collective responsibility among staff to achieve the goals [collaboration], (c) professional inquiry by the staff to address the challenges they face [reflection], and (d) opportunities for staff to influence the school's activities and policies [leadership capacity]."

Source: Newmann, King, & Youngs, 2000.

An Example of Pareto Thinking

A team of elementary teachers became concerned about the safety of students on the playground. The teachers believed that a lack of playground supervision was leading to fights that caused an increasing number of injuries, ultimately resulting in students losing instructional time. They asked their principal to try to secure funds to hire another playground supervisor. Wisely, the principal suggested that they gather some data to determine the following.

- When and where injuries were occurring
- What types of injuries students were suffering
- What was causing the injuries (fights, playground equipment, bad weather, and so on)
- How much instructional time was lost as a result of students missing class due to injuries

The data showed that while fights were up slightly over the previous year, the majority of class time lost was due to falls and cuts from aging equipment and poor overall playground conditions. Once the teachers were able to

Continued➔

applied the principle to management practices and came up with the following simple tenets.

- **Use the 80/20 rule:** 80 percent of the trouble comes from 20 percent of the problems.
- **Focus on the vital few:** Only a few (20 percent) of the causes account for the majority (80 percent) of the problems (losses, failures, time spent, or errors). Focus on improving the few that will achieve the greatest gain. Although often low in visibility, the 20 percent are high in leverage.
- **Avoid the trivial many:** Because 80 percent accounts for a large number (volume, frequency, occurrences, or incidence), it often seems overwhelming and critically important. Although, large in number, these trivial many are low in impact. More often than not, they are symptomatic of the fewer underlying causes (the 20 percent). Addressing the vital few can solve, eliminate, or reduce the trivial many.

In short, Juran (1964) shows us that we should focus on improving the few that will achieve the greatest gain.

Reflection

Reflection encompasses everything that schools and individuals do to understand where they are now and what they can learn from previous or current practices. Reflecting well requires the blending of objective data and feedback with more subjective (but equally valid) knowledge, experience, and observations. In that way, reflection helps us go beyond our best guesses or informed hunches about what is or is not working.

Like focus, reflection generates both enthusiasm and clarity. By taking time to reflect on what we are learning about our practice, we can actually accelerate the improvement process. Reflection at the school and classroom levels gets to the heart of the teaching and learning process. When we reflect on data and monitor progress over time, we can determine whether the strategies we are using or the changes we are making are having a positive impact on students.

Data play an essential role in a school's ability to be reflective. Unfortunately, too often when people hear the word *data*, they automatically associate the use of data with inspecting what is happening in a classroom or school. It is important not to confuse *reflection* with *inspection*.

- Reflection exists within a culture whose core values—what we care most deeply about—are learning and improvement; inspection exists within cultures that seek to assign blame.
- Reflection is a growth-driven process; inspection is a defects-driven process.

Within the SMART school context, teams use data solely to learn and to improve the system, not to punish people or distort results. Therefore, we have a choice about how we use data. We can use data as the basis for learning and inquiry to discover better methods for doing our work, or we can use data as an extrinsic motivator to reward or punish people.

We can do one of three things to show that results are improving.

1. **Distort the data:** Look for a story line that we prefer.

2. **Distort the system:** Stop teaching things that are not on the test.

3. **Improve the system:** Use data to inform decisions and measure the impact of improvements on learning.

Obviously, only the last option leads to deep learning and lasting improvement. However, it takes hard work to create an environment that truly supports the open use of data, no matter what those data tell you.

Collaboration

Collaboration is a core value and a critical component of learning communities. Schools cannot do the work of continuous improvement in isolation. Collaboration is most effective when everyone contributes skills, knowledge, and experience in pursuit of improved results.

narrow their investigation to the few causes for the majority of lost class time, their recommendation to the principal changed—fix the playground equipment and repave the surface to eliminate surface cracks.

Chapter 9 (page 229) provides more details on how your school can identify its vital few priorities. You can derive these priorities by comparing where your school is now in relation to your vision. Additional guidance appears in chapter 7, where you will find different data tools (including a Pareto chart) that can help you determine the areas in need of greatest attention or work.

The greatest value of collaboration is the diversity of thought and perspectives that it brings to the creative process. Without a collaborative approach, focus and reflection can easily lead us to conclusions that support what we think we already know.

Collaboration for its own sake is not enough. Collaboration is a process we use to achieve shared goals. Having people share their knowledge, expertise, and experience gives us a better understanding of the challenges we face. The end result of collaboration is a better solution, program, or idea and a greater commitment and capacity to implement that solution, program, or idea. Collaboration builds community, fuels motivation, renews the spirit, and enhances innovation. When people come together around a common purpose, with each person contributing his or her unique perspective and skills, and ultimately achieve a mutually defined goal, there is an infusion of energy into the school that a single initiative or program cannot match.

This book focuses on one particular vehicle for collaboration: *teams*. The first lesson to learn about teams is that they require an environment of focus and reflection to reach their fullest potential.

Unfocused collaboration—teamwork devoid of data and purpose—is counterproductive. Teams in these situations produce superficial content, have vague notions about what needs to be done to improve results, and are often engulfed in unresolved conflict and shotgun approaches to problem solving.

Teams are more than just groups of people coming together to accomplish something. They serve a unique purpose, and when they are performing at high levels, they are generative—they create new knowledge, stimulate energy, and promote improvement in ways that individuals acting in isolation could not achieve.

Leadership Capacity

Leadership in a SMART school looks and feels much different from leadership in traditional schools. In a SMART school, leadership is not about official positions of authority. Rather, it is about the school's or district's ability to engage

Synergy for Improvement

The elements of the framework for becoming SMART are most useful in combination. Teams, individuals, schools, and whole school districts can apply these ideas in all of their improvement efforts. Skillful collaboration develops interdependent relationships, where everyone is focused on a common purpose and set of goals, where people need each other to achieve those goals, and where teams use data to reflect progress toward the goals. Skillful collaboration results in synergy: the effectiveness of a group exceeds what the individuals can accomplish on their own.

the entire school community in broad-based and skillful participation in learning and improvement. In this sense, the real target is increased *leadership capacity*, which allows a school to create and fulfill a vision focused on student learning. Schools achieve leadership capacity when there is a dynamic interaction of focus, reflection, and collaboration.

When a school or a district has high levels of leadership capacity, everyone takes responsibility for improving every aspect of the organization. Teams of teachers, support staff, administrators, and parents and students work together on system and process improvements, school improvement, and ongoing improvement of student results.

SMART schools have high levels of leadership capacity. One of the key characteristics of schools with high levels of leadership capacity is that leadership and learning are inextricably linked. There are some basic assumptions that support the link between leadership and learning (DuFour & Marzano, 2011; Honig, Copland, Rainey, Lorton, & Newton, 2010).

- The opportunity to lead is inherently self-motivating.
- Everyone is capable of developing and exercising leadership.
- Leadership is expressed in a variety of ways.
- There are many domains within which leadership can be exercised.
- A school's culture either supports or diminishes the ability to develop shared leadership.

Although we distinguish *leadership* from the formal role of *leader*, leadership capacity is not intended to be a replacement of those in formal leadership positions. In fact, one of the most important things a leader can do is promote a different vision of leadership where everyone plays a role in improving the success of the whole school. A strong positional leader is most effective in building leadership capacity when he or she:

- Engages others in the work of leadership
- Leads by example

> Predict the rough water and provide time to learn, reflect, and shape. Get the people to say, "I helped build it. I feel safe here."
>
> —Patrick Dolan

- Has and adheres to a vision of success for all students and staff
- Acts with integrity and honor
- Is a learner, committed to continuously growing in knowledge and skill
- Facilitates the learning of others
- Makes difficult decisions on behalf of kids
- Is consistent, fair, and swift to act when team members or stakeholders compromise the values of the school community

Embedding Learning Within a SMART System

Teams maximize the effectiveness of the SMART framework in a culture that supports and celebrates continuous learning. Four critical factors are necessary for successful implementation of the framework. They are:

1. Coherence
2. Leadership
3. Incentives
4. Feedback

Coherence means that the significant systems of teaching and learning (that is, curriculum, instruction, and assessment) are in alignment with the vision and goals of the system. *Leadership* is the set of actions that clear the way, find the time, and provide the support for professional learning communities as they work to achieve improved results. The *incentives* are intrinsic, emanating from the experience of achieving worthy goals that teams have identified and pursued collaboratively in a professional environment. Finally, a system of goal management that runs both vertically and horizontally throughout the organization provides continuous *feedback* to the system so that teams can monitor progress and adjust practices on an ongoing basis. In chapter 9, we share a process for implementing the framework that builds in the four factors.

Pulling the Pieces Together

This book addresses all aspects of the SMART framework—focus, reflection, collaboration, and leadership capacity—in three parts: (1) Building Effective Teams, (2) Using Tools and Processes for Effective Teamwork, and (3) Implementing Effective School Improvement. In some cases, the tools and methods we present will fall clearly into one of the corners of the framework. In other cases, especially as we move to more systemic tools and protocols, we will address multiple portions of the framework. Together, the nine chapters of this book provide both theory and practical advice on how to create SMART teams in SMART schools.

PART ONE

Building Effective Teams

CHAPTER 1

Cornerstones of Collaboration and Teamwork

Productive collaboration does not come easily. Most of us have belonged to a team in which everyone got along, but nothing got done. Sooner or later, busy people lose patience with teams that do not seem to accomplish much of anything. Productive collaboration takes both purpose and skill to be effective; teams need to be clear about why they exist (purpose) and have the ability to create and implement a plan for getting it done (skill). We can't create productive collaboration just by telling people to work together. Teams that have skill and purpose save time and develop effective solutions that they can implement smoothly. Without skill and purpose, collaboration is a waste of time—yet, ironically, time is one of the most frequently cited reasons for why people do not collaborate (Kanold, 2011; Loehr & Schwartz, 2003).

This chapter discusses the components needed to add purpose and skill to collaboration and ways that you can set the stage for productive collaboration.

Three Cornerstones of Productive Collaboration

The three cornerstones of effective collaboration and teamwork are *people*, *tasks*, and *processes* (see figure 1.1, page 20). When teams incorporate the characteristics of all three cornerstones synergistically, collaboration will be highly productive and enjoyable.

People

Teams operate with two influences: (1) individual members' interests and background knowledge, and (2) the

---

Is Collaboration Worth the Effort?

Since the birth of the human relations movement in the 1920s, social scientists have been exploring the relationship between participation and productivity in the workplace. Social science researchers study the structures and opportunities that people have to interact and to collaborate in their work.

The result? When people are taught the skills to work together collaboratively, they:

- Have clearly defined and shared expectations as a group (task)

- Are given time and resources to engage in collaboration targeted at a specific task or outcome (process)

- Realize improved performance, higher-quality solutions, and greater innovation

- Are happier workers

What could be better?

Source: Weisbord, 1987, 2012.

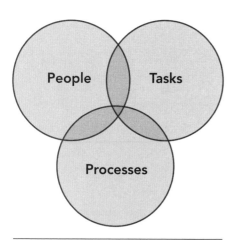

Figure 1.1: Three cornerstones of effective collaboration.

whole group's combined knowledge and creativity. Teams are comprised of *individuals*, which is important to remember because sometimes people think they must give up who they are in order to be effective team players. Not true. In fact, high-performing teams tap into the unique talents and skills of their individual members and value the diversity that those individuals represent. Successful teams acknowledge people's contributions—their leadership, commitment, knowledge, and skills.

Consider what it takes for us as individuals to be successful team members.

- We must be committed to developing skills that help us work effectively with others (communicating, listening, participating, and resolving conflicts).

- We must be committed to increasing our professional knowledge and experience so that we can help the team make good decisions.

- We must be aware of our own behaviors and work-style preferences and their impact on others, so we can adjust our behavior and help the group address all team members' needs.

- We must bring our background and experiences to the table and share them. Helping our group tap into what people know and have done is an essential part of building a successful team.

- We must be willing to work together to become clearer about our common purpose and goals to develop a shared sense of responsibility and commitment to achieving the group's mission—what we aspire to achieve—and goals.

These conditions are the same for everyone on a team, and we cannot forget that effective teamwork is a balancing of individual and group needs. Creating an environment where team members can contribute their individual creativity to a collaborative effort increases the success rate of the team.

Tasks

Teams exist for a purpose; they must accomplish certain goals within a given time frame. That is why an essential part of effective collaboration is organizing the team's tasks by identifying its functions and developing plans and timelines to fulfill those functions in order to achieve the desired results.

Chapter 3 provides guidance on how a team can identify and organize its tasks. The basic principles are the following.

- Be clear about the purpose and goals of the work.
- Identify tasks that move the team toward those goals.
- Clarify roles and responsibilities around those tasks.
- Develop skills to work together effectively.

Processes

Try to recall a major decision a team to which you belonged faced. How did the team make that decision? Did your group talk about how it would make the decision before making it? If the answer is no, you are not alone. Even when a committed group of skilled and highly motivated people comes together around a clear and common purpose, conflicts often emerge when the group has not discussed how to work together. In too many cases, team processes such as decision making, problem solving, communicating, and having meetings are informal or undefined.

Knowing what to expect as you set out to solve a problem or make a decision can help your team minimize conflict and confusion. A team that has not agreed on how it will solve problems or make decisions can easily get mired in unproductive conflict. Using well-defined collaborative processes is the best way to achieve full success as a team.

The Dynamic Interaction of People, Tasks, and Processes

Both the beauty and the challenge of teamwork can be found in the dynamic interplay of people, tasks, and processes. High-performing teams understand the complexities of this dynamic interaction and consciously manage the processes in ways that maximize the talents of the people to creatively and effectively complete their common tasks.

Is Teamwork Time Consuming?

Based on our experiences, time can be the most challenging barrier to teamwork in schools. Ironically, the confines of traditional school systems have limited the effectiveness of teamwork because they are not fundamentally designed to support it. Where in the busy school day can we find time not only to develop team skills but also to use them in collaborative settings? Time—even more than money—is a school's most precious commodity, and effective teamwork takes time.

However, the perception that teamwork is time consuming is part truth, part fiction. Some of what we perceive to be time consuming is actually the spin put on teams and time. Here are some of the reasons we might consider teamwork to be time consuming.

- Teams treat time as an add-on, not as a different way to accomplish better results.

- Teams view time as the enemy ("We only have an hour to do this!") as opposed to viewing it as an ally ("We have an hour together—let's see how much we can do.").

- New learning always takes time. However, because of the

Continued➜

Successful teams continuously assess their own performance in all three spheres: people, tasks, and processes. They expand their knowledge in each area—getting to know one another as individuals outside of the team environment, expanding their task knowledge and professional competencies together, and learning new process techniques and applying them in new ways, as well as expanding their collective understanding of how all three areas are working together.

Barriers to Collaborative Learning and Improvement

Many schools would say that they are committed to the cornerstones of productive collaboration (people, tasks, and processes), but there are many barriers that prevent them from acting on that commitment. Institutional barriers are relatively easy to identify; social barriers are less obvious and present even greater challenges because they are not so visible. Table 1.1 shows institutional and social barriers to collaboration.

Schools that have successfully implemented a collaborative approach have built structures for teamwork into their everyday lives and have made it a high priority. It is up to the leaders to create an environment that encourages teamwork. One method for doing this is to explicitly address the symbolic, cultural, and structural barriers to teamwork. Figure 1.2 (pages 24–25) illustrates some ways your school can work to eliminate or reduce the impact of institutional and social barriers.

Collaborative teamwork is a perfect venue for sharing learning. As teams search for new and better ways of achieving their goals, individuals will be reading, researching, asking others for input, and studying the impact of their strategies. In chapter 3, we describe the basics of effective teamwork.

Table 1.1: Examples of Barriers to Collaborative Learning and Improvement

Institutional Barriers	Social Barriers
Departments, units, and grade levels operate in individual "silos"—each one performing well to meet its goals but not working well collaboratively to meet school goals.	Individuals have mental models and assumptions about teamwork that make it difficult to work collaboratively.
The school day is scheduled into fragmented units of learning.	Individuals have limited skills working as teams.
Contractual guarantees segment and define the school year, leaving little flexibility for innovation or collaboration.	Leadership roles and responsibilities are not clearly defined.
Time for collaboration and teamwork is rarely built into the schedule of the day or year.	The team's purpose is not clearly defined.
Policies and procedures reinforce individual approaches, rather than collaborative approaches.	An individualistic approach is reinforced by the way in which people are recognized and rewarded for their work.
A team's purpose, roles, and responsibilities are unclear, and structure suffers as a result.	A school culture that celebrates individual accomplishments diminishes the value of teamwork.
Space limitations make it difficult for people to work easily in groups.	Teamwork is not sustained because previous attempts were not well received.

pressure to perform, teams seldom get past the threshold of the learning curve to a point where members can perform effectively together.

- What seems urgent almost always draws us away from what is most important. Thus, teams tend to devote time to managing a crisis, leaving little time to address the root cause of the crisis.

- Educators have the do-it-all-to-perfection disease. Rather than testing new ideas on a small scale before full implementation, they want to get it all right and then implement it on a full scale.

- Systems have limited capacity. Systems that weren't designed for teamwork are more limited than those that were. It's almost a catch-22: the best way for systems with the least capacity to increase that capacity is to find time for collaborative efforts. However, they feel the most squeezed in trying to find that time.

- It takes time to make time. In SMART schools, educators and staff learn to use whatever time is available to them to make incremental gains. Doing less, but in focused and targeted ways, yields more in the long run.

Expose and Address Institutional Barriers

1. Review current policies and procedures to see how they either encourage or hinder people working collaboratively.

2. Examine your priorities, and shift how you spend your time so that your priorities get the most time and attention.

3. Examine schedules to identify opportunities to combine individual planning time into team time, to establish blocks of time for teachers to collaborate: such as arranging specials so that each grade is at specials together or modifying academic start time.

4. Examine the duration of team tasks taking into account time needed to accomplish both short- and long-term objectives.

5. Examine the composition of teams (for example, grade level, vertical grade level, departmental, cross-curricular, leadership, and so on) to determine if the participants are best-suited to meet the team's purpose and fulfill its objectives.

6. Examine meeting objectives and agenda to determine if these fulfill the team's needs and expectations.

7. Create learning forums (for example, study teams, action research teams, focus groups, community planning groups, and so on) as part of the real work of the school.

8. Embed professional learning in real work, bringing successful best practices into alignment with emerging best new evidence-based practices.

9. Make data accessible, and use the data regularly to inform decisions.

10. Consider all the stakeholders and ways in which they can be brought together to address schoolwide issues (for example, safety, discipline, playground or study hall supervision, community involvement, and so on).

Expose and Address Social Barriers

1. Explore the mental models, assumptions, and beliefs people have about teamwork.

2. Celebrate team accomplishments.

3. Model effective teamwork yourself.

4. Sponsor skill-building sessions for teams.

5. Speak in terms of *we*.

6. Manage personal and team meeting time more effectively.

7. Challenge how faculty, department, and grade-level meetings currently work.

8. Create opportunities for diverse groups to come together to challenge assumptions, learn new perspectives, and share ideas.

9. Encourage innovation teams to find new and better ways to meet emerging student needs.

Figure 1.2: Addressing barriers to collaborative learning and improvement.

*Visit **go.solution-tree.com/schoolimprovement** for a reproducible version of this figure.*

Final Check: Cornerstones of Collaboration and Teamwork

Teamwork will be more productive when the school environment supports collaborative efforts. Review the following checklist. What have you and your colleagues done to:

☐ Encourage people to contribute their individual skills and talents to a collaborative effort? (People)

☐ Identify the work that teams need to accomplish? (Tasks)

☐ Help teams learn and identify the processes they will use to accomplish their tasks? (Processes)

☐ Remove barriers that make it difficult or impossible for teachers, staff, students, parents, and other community members to work together? (Processes)

☐ Make sure everyone is using time effectively so that people are able to participate fully in team efforts? (Processes)

☐ Build formal learning into everyone's daily work? (Processes)

CHAPTER 2

Fundamentals for Getting Started

Collaboration occurs in a variety of ways, depending on the purpose or need that is driving the collaboration. For example, two teachers might meet over lunch to discuss a class exercise they both will be using. Collaboration here is brief and informal; creating a team would be more trouble and more time consuming than it is worth.

On the other hand, a collaborative effort that is focused on a more complex or long-range task is more likely to be successful if the collaboration is formalized or has a clearly defined structure. Designing a new response to intervention (RTI) system is an example of a situation calling for a structured collaborative effort. In the case of grade-level or departmental teams, which have an official designation of responsibility that establishes the mission of the team, a formal team structure makes great sense. Professional learning teams are an excellent example of this type of structure. In both contexts, formalizing the structures and processes will increase understanding and ensure shared accountability for success.

Generally speaking, if it is important to include diverse points of view, there is a lot of work to do, and the nature of the task is challenging or long-term, a structured collaboration is needed. The best vehicles for structured collaboration are ongoing teams and ad hoc groups.

Ongoing Teams

Ongoing teams are responsible for the continuing and emerging success of one or more aspects of the system. They are a part of the organizational structure of the school or district and have an enduring purpose. Ongoing teams may be distinguished by where they exist within the organization (such as grade level or department) or they may be

---

Structured Collaborative Efforts

Some situations may call for a more structured collaborative effort. Schools should consider creating teams if the situation meets the following characteristics.

- There is a clear purpose for the team.
- Informal collegiality will not accomplish the purpose.
- The resulting decisions or actions of the team will have broad impact.
- Several meetings will be required.
- Diverse points of view are needed and should be accommodated.
- Broad-based changes are anticipated or required.

classified by function (such as governance, improvement, or professional learning). Table 2.1 shows the characteristics and types of ongoing teams typically found in schools and districts.

Table 2.1: Characteristics and Types of Ongoing Teams

Characteristics of Ongoing Teams	Types of Ongoing Teams by Function
• They are part of the school's or district's organizational structure. • They have a broad, ongoing mission. • Their existence is open ended. • Their membership is relatively stable or rotated based on a long-range plan. • They often include members sharing similar perspectives or functions. • The members usually feel a strong allegiance to the team.	• Governance teams • School improvement teams • System-level improvement teams • Professional learning teams

Governance Teams

Governance teams can include school management teams, site-based decision-making teams, leadership teams, and faculty councils. These teams meet regularly, perhaps monthly or quarterly. The content of the meetings fluctuates in response to situations that have arisen for which a policy or procedure is unclear or inappropriate. If the team's function is more managerial, agendas will reflect schoolwide operational concerns.

Purpose and Function

As the name of the team indicates, its primary purpose is to *govern* the school. Sometimes governance teams set school policies and allocate resources. In other cases, they are more managerial, making decisions that traditionally have been the responsibility of the school principal.

Your school and school district must determine the role and function of your school's governance team. Because governance is not traditionally a site or school function, the philosophy of the district will influence whether these teams even exist. When they do exist, the broader district vision of governance will shape their role (whether advisory or for decision making) and the scope of their influence (for example, schedules, budgets, curriculum innovations, or staffing).

Membership

The school principal leads the governance team, which may include teachers, support staff, and parents. Students may also be governance team members, notably at the middle or high school levels. Students are included if the role of the team is to make decisions about policies and procedures that address curricular offerings, behavioral expectations, and extracurricular programs and events.

Of special note is the process for selecting team members. Except for the team leader (typically a principal), members are usually voted onto a governance team by the constituents they represent and serve, and terms are on a rotating basis.

School Improvement Teams

School improvement teams are sometimes called *school effectiveness teams*. As ongoing teams, they meet frequently throughout the year—at least quarterly and possibly more often. The natural cycle of the school year influences their meeting agendas. For example, at the beginning of the year, the team will review the school's mission, vision, and progress on schoolwide improvement goals.

Purpose and Function

School improvement teams are stewards of the school's mission, vision, and values. They monitor achievement, climate, and satisfaction data to ensure that the learning environment is producing results consistent with the school's stated goals. In some schools, school improvement teams serve as the bodies responsible for leading and monitoring the cultural transformation of the school into a professional learning community.

However, the school improvement team is *not* an official watchdog of accountability nor is it responsible for achieving improved results. That is the work of everyone in the school. The school improvement team is responsible for identifying where gaps in performance exist and when, if at all, the mission, vision, and values of the school are being compromised. It also monitors progress toward school goals, and it may identify processes that are in need of improvement. Notably, the school improvement teams can serve an important role in monitoring and reinforcing the school's vision and core values. For example, they may conduct a climate survey to assess how effectively the core values are being adhered to (such as, "On a scale of 1 to 5, to what extent do you feel that our school offers students, teachers, and parents a sense of community?") Another approach is to convene dialogue sessions to learn how people are feeling about progress toward the school's vision.

Membership

Like a school governance team, the school improvement team should be representative of the school population. The most effective school improvement teams include teachers, parents, administrators, and support staff, as well as students where appropriate. The team often decides on the leadership—it is not necessary for the principal to be the school improvement team leader. The team may decide to rotate the leadership role on a scheduled basis. In this way, more team members have opportunities to show or develop leadership skills.

System-Level Improvement Teams

The mission of system-level improvement teams is to continuously improve key aspects of the system in which they are working. The focus of system-level improvement teams encompasses the full range of district services including both academic areas (such as curriculum, instructional programs, assessment, and professional learning) and non-academic areas (such as business services, human resources, public relations, and facilities). They usually meet on a quarterly basis to address both the content and the processes that affect their areas of focus. An example of an academic system-level improvement team is a K–12 curriculum team that would review current standards and resources within a particular content area (such as science) as well as assess and improve the process by which professionals in that content area develop, communicate, and use the standards. An example of a nonacademic system-level improvement team is a recruitment and hiring team that reviews the processes and policies used to attract and retain minority teachers.

Purpose and Function

System-level improvement teams serve much the same function as school improvement teams, except their scope is systemwide. They usually have a specific but ongoing purpose in topics like curriculum, staff development, student services, community relations, or technology integration. These teams serve as stewards of the district's vision in that they help design, improve, and coordinate the delivery systems that support school and district success in high-priority areas.

Membership

Usually the team leader is a central office person in charge of the specific area the team is studying (for example, the director of curriculum). As a districtwide team, membership includes representatives from each site and various disciplines such as content areas, grade levels, student services, and so on.

Membership is typically limited to staff; however, in some cases, it makes sense to include parents and community members on the team. This is especially true when the outcome of the team's work is likely to require community support (for example, in the form of referenda or a tax increase) or involves any decision having significant impact on student learning such as program additions or deletions or school closings.

Professional Learning Teams

Professional learning teams meet weekly or daily so that they can closely monitor implementation and shape day-to-day instructional decisions. Sometimes known as collaborative planning teams, these teams set goals based on their analysis of student performance on common assessments. They also examine current approaches to differentiating instruction based on the data from those assessments. They use their time together to learn what is and is not working for students and to make collaborative decisions about the best ways to adjust their teaching. Collaborative, professional learning teams exist within the broader community of learners known as professional learning communities (PLCs). Their goals and actions are guided by and are in alignment with the school's mission, vision, and SMART goals.

Their meeting agendas include both standard and responsive items. A standard item is something they do every time they meet, such as a quick check of where they are on a timeline for pacing instruction or a review of the previous day's or week's progress on unit objectives. A responsive item is something the team addresses in response to a new requirement or request for information that may have come up since their previous meeting.

Purpose and Function

Professional learning teams determine the goals, guide the work, and monitor progress for the area they represent (such as the music department, fourth-grade teachers, pupil services, or cross-grade or cocurricular initiatives). These teams are responsible for service and program delivery and, as such, are much more hands-on than other ongoing teams. They manage the day-to-day teaching and learning of students in their areas.

Membership

All staff within a particular area participate in the professional learning team. Even in large schools, regular departmental, course, or grade-level meetings that include all staff occur for the purpose of improving student learning. Teams can appoint, elect, or rotate their leader, depending on the team's focus. In some districts, the team leader receives additional pay, while in other districts leadership rotates on a volunteer basis.

The principal is usually an *ex officio* member of the team by virtue of his or her responsibility as the instructional leader in the school. Therefore, communication strategies that keep the principal informed of key discussions and decisions are a vital element of the success of professional learning teams.

Ad Hoc Groups

Ad hoc groups come together around specific problems or challenges and then disband when the specific challenge is met. Examples include action research projects, process improvement projects, textbook adoption groups, and study circles focused on one or a limited number of topics. Table 2.2 describes the characteristics and identifies types of ad hoc groups.

Table 2.2: Characteristics and Types of Ad Hoc Groups

Characteristics of Ad Hoc Groups	Types of Ad Hoc Groups
<ul><li>The groups have terms with specific start and end dates.</li><li>Members may come and go.</li><li>The groups have a specific and usually fairly narrow mission and limited set of goals.</li><li>The groups often include members of various disciplines, functions, or perspectives.</li><li>Members often feel a first allegiance to other parts of the organization.</li></ul>	<ul><li>Steering committees</li><li>Study circles</li><li>Process improvement project groups</li><li>Committees and task forces</li></ul>

Steering Committees

The steering committee exists for as long as it takes to launch the selected initiative. Functioning in an advisory capacity, the committee handles start-up and planning and disbands when its tasks have been completed, even though the program may be ongoing.

Purpose and Function

Steering committees are typically created to launch major initiatives. They are aptly named: their purpose is to steer a program or process by advising a staff group or some other team on important aspects of design, implementation, and strategies for evaluation. It is not appropriate for the steering committee to do the actual implementation or evaluation. That becomes the work of other teams or individuals, depending on the nature of the program or process being implemented.

For example, a school or district might choose to engage in a strategic planning process. The role of the steering committee in this case is to work with either the school's governance team or its school improvement team to design the process and to determine the budget, timelines, and participants for strategic planning to occur.

Membership

Individuals who represent the process or initiative the committee is directing will serve on it. For initiatives that will have broad impact, such as a technology initiative on selection of a districtwide student data system, the steering team must include wide representation. Because steering committees have responsibility to initiate programs or processes, members should have experience in program development and evaluation.

Steering committees benefit from access to someone with budget-making expertise. Because such groups are advisory, that person need not be a full-fledged member. Nonetheless, the committee will have the benefit of access to financial advice and direction when it is concerned with budget decisions that have affected or could affect the implementation of the process or initiative.

Study Circles

Although the learning is ongoing, a study circle usually disbands once it meets a well-defined objective, such as selecting a new teaching strategy or completing a book. Study circles exist to serve a broader purpose, so their work is incomplete until they share their results with others. For example, the group may be part of a needs-assessment process (results shared with a broader community of planners) or a professional development or action research study (results shared within their department, grade level, or unit). Study circles usually have a process they agree to follow; sometimes they are required to complete their work within a specified time frame. In other ways, however, they tend to be less structured than other teams. Leadership in study circles is broad based and often informal. For example, when a study team comes together to explore a particular topic through research, reading, or observations, its agenda may be just one item—dialogue.

Purpose and Function

The purpose of study circles is to develop a deep understanding of an issue or process and then share it with others in the school or district. Their specific purpose depends on the broader context in which they exist. If the study circle is part of a needs-assessment process within a school or district planning initiative, its focus is the organization or the community. If the study circle is part of a school improvement process, its purpose is to learn about best instructional practices and share that information with colleagues. Study circles may also simply reflect a more collegial approach to shared learning in the context of collaborative action research or professional development around a particular topic.

Membership

Individuals usually decide to participate based on interest. In some cases, those who set and pursue goals will determine membership. A study circle convening to inform school improvement study, for example, would research best schoolwide practices, and membership would depend on the focus of the goal—academic subject, school climate, assessment practices, or student behavior.

Process Improvement Project Groups

To be successful, these ad hoc groups must structure their work around a well-defined improvement process (see chapter 9). Typically, the improvement process is developed schoolwide or systemwide and includes vision statements, mission statements, needs assessments, action plans, and evaluation procedures. The depth of study—and duration of the process improvement team—depends on the complexity of the issues associated with the targeted process. If the targeted process has proven resistant to improvement, the group may need to engage in a more detailed improvement process such as problem solving (see chapter 8, page 199).

Purpose and Function

Process improvement project groups exist to improve any process in the school or system that, because of inefficiencies or unnecessary bureaucracy, is currently diverting or has the potential to divert resources away from the district's core mission of student learning. For example, existing practices designed to schedule collaborative planning time might be so cumbersome that the amount of time it takes to create and revise the schedules exceeds the amount of planning time ultimately made available for planning. By examining and improving the process, ongoing scheduling challenges can be eliminated or reduced, thereby creating additional time to devote to collaboration, such as the introduction of technology resources to assist with scheduling and communication.

Membership

The members should be individuals who are directly involved with the process that needs improving. If the potential pool of members is relatively small, leaders may find it necessary to include the entire faculty on the team. Alternatively, if there are far more people working on the process than you can include on the team, the leader will have to select representatives to work on different parts of the process. Ideally, process improvement groups have six to eight members.

For example, if the team wants to improve the process of accounting for activity fees, members could be anyone involved in collecting and documenting fees. If the process has five main steps, one person from each step of the process would be a member of the improvement group.

Committees and Task Forces

Committees and task forces are transitory, even more so than other ad hoc groups. Their focus is narrowly defined; consequently, the groups tend to be short-lived, disbanding once they achieve their objective. One of the challenging areas for committees and task forces is closure. Committees and task forces that are very clear about their specific objective and stay on target with that objective find it much easier to disband than those that don't. Without a specific objective, committees and task forces simply have a hard time knowing when they are done. To avoid needless continuation, leaders can create a charter that clearly specifies the team's purpose, tasks, timelines, and expected outcomes, along with a plan that identifies the group's exit strategy and projected completion date (see chapter 5).

Purpose and Function

Committees and task forces exist to achieve a predetermined product (a set of recommendations, a document or survey, and so on) or to implement a particular event (for example, grandparents' visiting day, a class trip, or an all-school assembly). When the group has successfully executed the event, it no longer has a purpose.

Membership

Membership is often a function of personal interest or expertise. Boards of education sometimes create task forces to handle sensitive political issues. In such cases, balanced membership becomes very important; the board or superintendent therefore usually determines who participates. The same may be true of a school task force that the principal or school governance team convenes.

Getting Teams Started

Getting off to a good start is important regardless of team structure. The process for getting started answers three important questions of teamwork: (1) *Who* are the participants? (2) *What* is the task, and *why* is it necessary? and (3) *How* will the team accomplish the task? This process has seven steps that enable a team or group to get off to

> The team is the cornerstone of the learning organization. What really matters is how people make decisions and take action—how the team thinks and acts together.
>
> —Peter Senge

an organized, efficient start. Based on the type of structure being initiated, some steps might have been predetermined; in other cases, the group or team will need to decide how to proceed through the steps. The steps for getting started are the following.

- **Step one:** Identify members.
- **Step two:** Identify stakeholders.
- **Step three:** Define functions.
- **Step four:** Identify goals.
- **Step five:** Develop a charter, schedule the work, and determine roles and responsibilities.
- **Step six:** Discuss assumptions.
- **Step seven:** Agree on guidelines for behavior.

Step One: Identify Members

Membership will depend on what the team needs to accomplish and, therefore, the knowledge, experiences, and authority members must have. Schools can determine membership in a variety of ways.

- **Volunteering:** Individuals volunteer when a high level of member interest is of primary importance.
- **Election:** Peers elect members when representation is of primary importance.
- **Appointment:** The principal, superintendent, or board appoints members when the stakes are high.

Parent and Community Involvement

The trickiest consideration may well be whether to involve parents and community members. These stakeholders provide a number of benefits.

- Broader perspectives and new ideas
- Diverse expertise, which contributes to better results
- Strengthened commitment to the recommendations
- Enhanced communication
- Stronger school-community relationships

However, some will argue that the challenges are greater than the benefits warrant. This is usually because the team views parents and community members as invited guests rather than as true group members. As a result, the team compromises the dynamics of the group, and there is a pervasive tension that keeps it from becoming truly effective. Three of the most obvious and easiest remedies involve (1) roles, (2) logistics, and (3) language for parents and community members.

Roles for Parents and Community Members

When parents and community members volunteer or accept an invitation to be a part of an ad hoc group, they will have the same kinds of questions about their roles and their involvement as any other member would. They are likely to wonder such things as:

- What perspective am I expected to bring? Am I here as the parent of my child or as a representative of a parental point of view?
- Am I an equal member with the right to share my opinions even though I've never been a professional educator? Do I have a vote?
- Will I be expected to attend all meetings and to do work between meetings?
- What happens if I disagree? Will my child suffer any consequences?
- Do I have anything unique or valuable to offer?

There is only one way to find the answers to these questions: talk about them. Early on, parents and community members may not feel comfortable asking these kinds of questions, so it's important that the group be proactive in addressing them as part of the start-up process.

Logistics for Parents and Community Members

Logistics include both where and when the meetings are held. Making a concerted effort to hold meetings at times and places that are accessible to a variety of parents and community members sends an important message that their involvement really is important. This may mean some compromises on the part of school staff, but in the long run, the results will be worth the necessary accommodations.

Language for Parents and Community Members

Like most disciplines, education has its own language. Even within the educational system, the language differs from one discipline to the next. This use of specific language is intimidating to those outside the system. The group should take time during the first couple of meetings to identify terms that are likely to cause confusion and work together to develop agreed-on definitions, especially if group members come from the community or different disciplines, grades, or schools. That way, individuals who may not know the meaning of the terms do not feel left out or uninformed.

Step Two: Identify Stakeholders

A team's work ultimately affects more than just its members. Additionally, external groups or individuals who have something at stake in the process affect the group's work. To operate efficiently and effectively, the team or group needs to know who has authority over or ultimate responsibility for its actions, as well as which people are interested in and likely affected by its work—the stakeholders.

Typical stakeholders include parents, community members, board members, teachers, other school staff, and students or graduates. Although nonsupervisory stakeholders have little formal authority over a team or group, their support and buy-in can be critical to implementation.

Typically, an administrator (school or central office) will have advisory or supervisory responsibility for overseeing the work of the group or team. Because this individual has the authority to allocate time and resources and to approve or deny the group's or team's solutions and actions, it is critically important to keep him or her informed and involved. The administrator, a special kind of stakeholder, can play an advocacy role, especially if the team needs to address barriers. The administrator also plays an important role as a communication link to the rest of the school system.

Step Three: Define Functions

Every group or team member has an important function to perform in achieving the team's mission and accomplishing its goals. Ideally, leadership is a shared function; everyone accepts responsibility for making sure the work goes well. Different members, depending on their particular knowledge or experience, will step into a leadership role when their expertise is needed. Three main team functions are (1) leader, (2) member, and (3) facilitator.

Leader

The leader is responsible for seeing that the team accomplishes the work. This person doesn't do all the work himself or herself but provides the guidance, support, and structure that allow all members to contribute. The leader shapes meeting agendas to ensure the team addresses critical issues at appropriate stages in the project or effort, using initial meetings to identify goals and define roles and ground rules and subsequently scheduling regular reviews so that the team or group can check on and improve its work.

Leaders also play a pivotal role in linking the team's or group's work with the rest of the school, district, or community. They apprise the administrative stakeholder of progress and seek support and guidance from that person as needed. For example, a principal who will ultimately be held accountable for overseeing the implementation and results of a team's recommendations is the administrative stakeholder in this situation. They make sure to communicate progress to all stakeholders.

Member

Members are essential to the team's success—they carry out the work. Members bring expertise, experience, and knowledge that sustain the team's efforts. To do so effectively, they must be fully engaged by attending all meetings, voicing opinions, offering input and advice, and volunteering to perform specific tasks. Meeting commitments on time is an important aspect of a member's participation. He or she must carry out assigned or voluntary tasks on time or communicate with the leader when tasks cannot be completed on schedule. Effective members are open to learning from others. Their willingness to share information, respect contrasting points of view, and strive for consensus is critical to the team's smooth functioning.

Members reflect the diversity of skills, talents, and expertise needed to perform team functions. As individuals, they add value to the team's effectiveness by willingly sharing their perspectives, experience, and knowledge. As team members, they commit to taking responsibility for their share of the work, fully engaging in the research, analysis, and development of solutions as well as working respectfully with others to get the job done.

Facilitator

A facilitator is a special advisor who is an expert in group dynamics and collaborative methods and tools. This person makes sure the members work together as effectively as possible. He or she can help structure activities to achieve desired goals, provide alternative discussion techniques when the team or group is stuck, help the members work through conflict, and so on. In short, the facilitator's job is to make it easier for the team or group to be successful. In some cases, a facilitator works closely with the leader in all of the meetings; in other cases, a facilitator may be available on call to provide assistance when needed.

The facilitator is usually not a member in the sense that he or she would carry out work like gathering data, studying issues, or making decisions. Rather, the facilitator is an impartial observer who is there to help the group or team accomplish its work. Since the facilitator is outside of the work, he or she does not necessarily have content knowledge associated with the group's or team's mission.

Not every group or team has the luxury of having a skilled facilitator. However, all members can acquire basic facilitation skills, particularly those needed to run meetings efficiently and effectively (see chapter 4, page 91). If basic facilitation skills among members are not adequate to move the group or team through a particularly difficult period, there are a number of places to look within the school district or community for an objective person who can help facilitate. In particular, don't overlook the potential of skilled facilitator

When to Have a Facilitator

A facilitator can be very helpful in the following situations.

- When the school is going through a school improvement planning process
- When there is conflict and strong disagreement
- When a team or group is stuck or floundering
- When there is a mix of strong personalities
- When starting a team or group

volunteers from school support staff, parents, community members, and high school students.

Step Four: Identify Goals

Goals directly related to the mission keep the team focused and on task. Goals can address desired results (for example, improve third-grade reading achievement) and how the members will work together (for example, resolve conflicts quickly and respectfully). Two aspects are of particular importance: (1) the goals collectively lead teams to accomplish its mission, and (2) all members participate in developing the process and tasks to achieve the goals. Developing goals collaboratively helps ensure understanding and commitment to achieving them.

Any goal is better than no goal at all, and SMART goals are better still. Use the SMART guidelines (see pages 5–14) to define goals that are *strategic* and *specific*, *measurable*, *attainable*, *results oriented*, and *time bound*. Building SMART goals helps ensure goals are realistic.

Step Five: Develop a Charter, Schedule the Work, and Determine Roles and Responsibilities

Ill-planned implementation strategies can diminish, or even ruin, the best intentions of a team or group. Careful thought as to how the tasks are organized is necessary to ensure that all the work will not be rendered useless. School-based projects or initiatives can be especially difficult to plan because they are multifaceted, affect a broad range of stakeholders both inside and outside of the school, and may carry some emotional or political baggage.

For these reasons, teams need a good project-management strategy. Given limited time and a bias for action, the temptation is to jump headfirst into doing the work. In the long run, this kind of approach can lead to duplication of effort or missed opportunities. Instead, take time early on to get organized by:

- Making sure everyone understands the scope (size), overall expectations, and time frame for the work
- Dividing the work into manageable pieces

Where Do Goals Come From?

Ideally, your district and school have broad-based school improvement plans that identify both immediate needs and a long-term vision. The team's goals derive from what the district and school have identified as strategic priorities. Review meeting notes, data, surveys, and other resources and background knowledge that provide the impetus for the formation of the group or team.

How to Monitor Effectiveness Using Goals

Goals can be used to monitor effectiveness. You can do this informally by asking, "Is what we're doing contributing to progress toward our goals?" Or, you can chart formal data that provide objective measures of success.

- Defining specific goals and benchmarks for each task
- Assigning individual or small-group responsibilities based on member interest, skills, and knowledge
- Scheduling tasks and time frames for review

Develop a Charter

Simply completing a charter together will help to organize the team or group. A charter is a good place to start defining the parameters of the project. Once members are clear about the materials they'll need to accomplish the tasks and the amount of time available to do so, they can attach names to the various tasks, roles, or responsibilities. This is where the match between interests, skills, and experiences of the members and the needs, roles, and responsibilities of the project becomes critical. If the appropriate start-up work has been done, this should not be a difficult exercise.

Using a standard format to charter the team or group can facilitate getting organized and ensure that everyone is literally on the same page when it comes to the work ahead (see figure 2.1). See also the reproducible "Team Charter" (page 307).

Schedule the Work

A variety of useful tools is available for scheduling complex projects. If you don't have access to online scheduling tools, consider creating a Gantt chart (see page 139). This tool allows the team or group to schedule tasks on a calendar. By creating the chart collaboratively, members will see how the full scope of tasks will progress and have a better understanding of how each person's contributions affect both the work of others as well as the overall timeline.

Determine Roles and Responsibilities

A key aspect of planning work is deciding who is responsible for what. A special type of flowchart called a deployment flowchart (see page 128) can help you visually depict the individuals or groups responsible for specific tasks. When developed collaboratively, the deployment flowchart serves as a tool to guide discussions about individuals' or

Team Members
(List all members.)

_____

_____

_____

_____

_____

Mission
(Write a brief statement of purpose that includes specific end results or outcomes.)

_____

_____

_____

_____

Tasks to Complete
(Sequentially list activities that the team will use to achieve the end results or outcomes in the mission.)

_____

_____

_____

_____

_____

_____

_____

_____

_____

Timeline
(List specific phases or a timeline that the group will follow to achieve its mission. Ad hoc groups will most likely have a stated date for completion; ongoing groups will have a timeline that targets incremental progress within specified time ranges.)

_____

_____

_____

_____

_____

_____

_____

Figure 2.1: Team charter template.

subgroups' responsibilities and to document the agreements that emerge from the conversations. The flowchart communicates the specific tasks, who will perform the tasks, and who will assist or support them in those tasks.

Step Six: Discuss Assumptions

To fully appreciate the value and complexity of teamwork, teams and groups must fully understand the underlying assumptions that influence their performance. Consider the following.

- Teams and groups exist for a purpose. They are a means to an end that individuals working in isolation cannot effectively achieve.
- Skillful teamwork doesn't just happen. Teams and groups must work at becoming effective.
- Team and group development is a dynamic journey, not an event.
- Teams and groups move through predictable stages of development, though each is manifested in unique ways (see chapter 3).
- Team and group development becomes increasingly complex and dynamic over time, requiring increasing levels of personal effectiveness, skill, and trust on the part of the members.

When teams and groups openly discuss these assumptions and expectations, members often indicate a sense of relief in discovering that there's more to teamwork than previously thought. Understanding these assumptions builds a foundation for teamwork in three ways: it (1) sets the expectation that the team or group exists to accomplish real work (while having fun!), (2) helps people accept that teamwork involves specific skills that must be learned and improved, and (3) eases the pressure to feel as though the team or group must be perfect from the beginning.

Step Seven: Agree on Guidelines for Behavior

Developing team or group norms helps members take ownership of their individual behaviors and provides an opportunity to articulate concerns and take action on those concerns. This is often an iterative process, meaning the groups or teams will establish desired norms early on in the formation of the team, which become more specific and more targeted as members work together and discover the need to create or revise based on the dynamics of the group. As the team or group works together, it will continuously use the norms to assess team effectiveness. In this way, norms become a tool for self-accountability for the individuals as well as the team collectively.

Creating Norms

Creating norms collaboratively increases the odds that people will follow them. There are several methods you can use. We describe two methods that enable teams to explore the dynamics of group behavior.

Method One: Pose Open Questions and Discuss Answers

Use the following questions as discussion starters for talking about how the group or team wants to function. You might write down answers to the questions on a flipchart or whiteboard and then discuss the themes that appear in the answers.

- What could this group or team do to ensure that it fails? This question, known as the Cotter Question, is based on the facilitation practices of Maury Cotter from the Office of Quality Improvement at the University of Wisconsin–Madison (M. Cotter, personal communication, 1993). Cotter uses this question to prompt a group's early evaluation of their possible misbehaviors as a team. The question usually generates some laughter. However, after the members begin to really think about it, they discover that some of their previous experiences were bad enough to have been planned that way. Had they thought through the behaviors that they wanted to avoid, those experiences would have been quite different.

Suggestions for Using Norms

- Create them collaboratively.
- Review them often.
- Discuss them with new members.
- Keep them visible at all times.
- Confront behaviors that violate them.
- Revise them as needed.

- What will make us successful?
- What drives us crazy about meetings?
- If we had the chance to create the perfect team or group experience, what would it be like? It's OK to _____. It's not OK to _____.

Method Two: Discuss Various Categories of Behaviors

Another process for creating norms is to identify categories of behaviors and ask people to write one idea per category on sticky notes and post their ideas on a flipchart. Then discuss which of the ideas the members would like to adopt as their own. Table 2.3 shows typical norm topics and examples.

Table 2.3: Norm Topics and Examples

Norm Topics	Examples
Attendance	"We agree to attend every meeting. When someone cannot attend, that person agrees to contact the leader twenty-four hours in advance of the meeting, if possible."
Participation	"We will participate fully both inside and outside meetings. We will not allow substitutes."
Interruptions	"We will attend meetings as though we have driven one hundred miles to attend. We will allow interruptions for emergencies only."
Preparations	"We will come to all meetings with assignments completed, prepared to productively contribute to discussions and decisions."
Timeliness	"We will start the meeting on time if at least 80 percent of the members are here. Since schedules are so important, we will stop all discussion five minutes before the meeting ends so that we can decide on next steps and how to handle unresolved issues."
Decision Making	"We will discuss the best decision-making model for each situation. We will support the group or team's decisions."

Norm Topics	Examples
Conflict Management	"We will deal with conflicts directly, respectfully, and immediately."
Communication	"We will keep accurate meeting records and share them with members within three days following the meeting if at all possible."
Meeting Practices	"We will have an agenda for every meeting and commit to following it."
Jargon Cops	"At each meeting, we will appoint one person to pay attention to jargon. Violators will throw twenty-five cents into the treat fund."

Visit **go.solution-tree.com/schoolimprovement** for a reproducible version of this table.

Supporting Ongoing Teams and Ad Hoc Groups

Ongoing teams and ad hoc groups require different types of support. Ongoing teams usually have a clearer sense of their mission, so they usually do not need to work as much on purpose and goals as an ad hoc group.

Ad hoc groups need to spend time early on defining their mutual interests, clarifying their mission, and establishing their processes for completing tasks on time. Because assignment to an ad hoc group is usually short-term and layered on top of already-busy schedules, ad hoc group members (and others from their work team who are not included) tend to struggle more with issues around time, workload, and the sharing of responsibilities. Ad hoc groups also need clear criteria for knowing when they are done with their work and may need help coming to closure when their tasks have been completed.

> Experience is something you don't get until just after you need it.
>
> —George Carlin

Final Check: Fundamentals for Getting Started

Teamwork and collaboration are challenging and complex. We cannot simply convene a group of people and expect that they will be successful. Teams need planning and communication around myriad dimensions to set them on a strong and confident path. The following checklist provides the key aspects of teamwork that, if addressed early on, can make a world of difference in both the team's experience and the results of its collaboration.

☐ We have concluded that a formal collaborative structure is the best way to address an issue or meet a particular need.

☐ We have matched our purpose to the appropriate type of team or group.

☐ We have selected appropriate members.

☐ We have support mechanisms in place.

☐ Our ongoing teams have a means for identifying and including new members.

☐ Our ad hoc groups have a means for closure.

☐ We have planned, organized, and coordinated work tasks and clearly understand priorities.

☐ We are using timelines effectively.

☐ We have defined norms for our behavior.

CHAPTER 3

Teamwork Basics

Effective schools have a deep capacity for learning and leading and are places where staff, students, and parents are engaged in the work of leadership every day. A commitment to professional learning that increases educator effectiveness and results for all students addresses the importance of building this capacity. Teamwork is at the heart of this capacity (Learning Forward, 2011). However, teamwork involves a complex set of skills and methods not usually included in an educator's preparation. Teamwork requires managing the interactions and development that are a normal part of team dynamics. This chapter discusses a broad range of roles, principles, skills, methods, and techniques that go into learning how to become an effective team, beginning with the predictable (and natural) stages of team growth and development.

Team Growth and Development

No matter how perfectly everyone on a team gets along, or how skilled team members are at group processes and team skills, every team will go through stages as it develops into maturity. Bruce Tuckman (1965) describes five stages of group development, each of which is an inevitable part of healthy team growth. The five stages are the following.

- **Stage One: Forming**—Members are anxious about what their team will be like and preoccupied by how they will fit in.
- **Stage Two: Storming**—Members experience significant conflict concerning leadership, power, and control.
- **Stage Three: Norming**—The team resolves many conflicts, negotiates disagreements, develops norms that contribute to productivity, and develops functional relationships among its members.

- **Stage Four: Performing**—Members focus on performance and results ensuring that all attention is directed toward achievement.
- **Stage Five: Transforming**—Some teams may regress to a previous stage then work their way back to the performing stage. Teams that have accomplished their mission can then evaluate the process, celebrate its results, and achieve closure.

Understanding these stages and moving through them is essential to full functioning as a team. Let's take a deeper look at each stage.

Stage One: Forming

Stage one is an orientation period when members are anxious about what their team will be like and how and if they fit into the team. During this stage, the challenge is for the whole team to address team goals, expectations, membership, and tasks.

Characteristic Group Behavior

During this preliminary stage, the group avoids conflict. The group emphasizes similarities and ignores or glosses over differences and disagreements. Nominal teams—groups that are teams in name only—tend to look for easy answers, quick fixes, and external solutions. They discuss issues in a general way, but people tend not to share their individual experiences or the impact events have on them. Denial is common.

Some find the forming stage exciting; others just find it frustrating. Roles are changing; people are learning new skills; there is a rapid learning curve. Those who have the easiest time during this stage have faith in a collaborative philosophy and are personally committed to helping their team succeed. These people look for small successes, even at this early stage; they share their excitement about the little victories; and they praise the efforts of colleagues. They don't dwell on failures (which are inevitable), and they don't find reasons why this collaborative effort will never work.

Stage One Example

A school is ready to launch a new mathematics initiative, and a K–12 team of teachers and parents is overseeing a pilot study of the new program. At the first meeting, team members are confused about their task—both its scope and purpose. They do not know each other but are polite and engaging. Some may be wondering why they were selected for the team. Team members are anxious to get started but may not know what to do first. Not everyone has the same level of familiarity or comfort with the new program.

Stage Two: Storming

Stage two is a period of frustration and disagreement among the members. There is usually significant conflict around the issues of leadership, power, control, and influence. Members wrestle with the question of how much influence they will exert on the team, as well as who they will allow to influence them. There may be a power struggle between dominant members or different factions. The team must decide on leadership and clarify roles and authorities. The mission of the team needs to be kept at the forefront of all discussions.

Characteristic Group Behavior

In stage two, conflicts are no longer kept below the surface. Longstanding differences erupt into the open, often resulting in intense polarization and fragmentation. Instead of dealing directly with problems, people form cliques or factions; they take sides. In the storming stage, you might see people having meetings after the meeting, perhaps in the hallway or parking lot, where they discuss their version of what is going on with others who share their views. Some people try to flee back into the false safety of nominal community (where politeness substitutes for reality); others leave the conflict altogether and simply stop coming to the meetings. In this stage, people are intent on defending their own positions or turf. They tend to listen to the opposition only long enough to derive ammunition for the next round of debate. Neither side listens to nor appreciates the viewpoint of the other.

Struggle in some form or another is an essential phase in building true teamwork. The problem is not the presence of the struggle, but rather getting stuck in it. People flounder and feel uncomfortable, and their attempts to get away from the discomfort include cutting off debate or discussion. ("Let's just get on with it!" or "Let's just take a vote and be done.") Any mutual trust or sense of safety that had started to develop can degenerate into feelings of animosity and mistrust during this stage. One of the best things you can do is assure people that this stage is normal and that sometimes the only way out is through. Slowing down to really listen to one another is an important way to move through this stage effectively.

Stage Two Example

A principal selected team members from a list of peer-nominated representatives to serve on a high school team and explore whether to move to a block schedule. The team has successfully organized its strategy for studying the subject and surveying staff, students, and parents to get their input and ideas. Members are now faced with the task of interpreting the data and formulating recommendations. It becomes obvious that with each potential scenario at least one program will suffer—enrollment, schedule, number of prep periods, and so on. It's also abundantly clear that most teachers will have to change both what and how they teach. Arguments break out, accusations are made, and factions begin to form. Some teachers go back to their departments to rally the resistance to this change in scheduling. At this point, unless the team engages in a serious dialogue where they can listen to one another's concerns and fears with genuine compassion, this initiative is doomed to failure.

Stage Three: Norming

Stage three is a period when the team resolves many conflicts, negotiates disagreements, establishes norms of behavior that contribute to team productivity, and develops functional relationships among its members. Team members openly identify and address their individual issues, agreeing to let go of their personal agendas for the sake of the team's agenda. Review, renewal, or establishment of new ground rules is a key task at this stage.

Characteristic Group Behavior

People remove their own barriers to communication. They let go of defensive stances (the need to be right, to prevail, or to hold their position); they begin looking for what is best for the system as a whole. They let go of abstractions and speak more personally; they become more willing to share their own experience.

During norming, the group finds a way to channel its storming energy into more productive means of communication and problem solving. Norming involves the decision to be a genuine part of the team and a willingness to let go of old patterns, unfinished business, past hurts and resentments, and the need to control the outcome.

Stage Three Example

A group of school district administrators, staff, and community members has been working on a plan for getting a building referendum developed and publicized. Some dominant members of the team have been taking up huge amounts of time in debates that support their personal agendas (storming). Finally, after heated arguments about budgets, building locations, and boundaries, the facilitator reminds the group of its common purpose: to get an educationally sound and economically responsible referendum out to the citizens in a timely way. The group then reviews and revises its ground rules and puts new ones in place. The team members clarify the issues and agree on a decision-making process.

Stage Four: Performing

In stage four, the team focuses on performance and results. Members are realistic in their expectations; the team has resolved even the major conflicts and continues to clarify its behavioral norms. All attention is directed toward *achievement*: productivity and continued team development are now the primary issues. The team reviews progress on its goals, adjusts strategies and timelines accordingly, and works together to accomplish all aspects of its task.

Characteristic Group Behavior

Competitiveness gives way to a spirit of cooperation. Individuals respect and honor diversity. The group immediately addresses any conflicts that arise so they don't fester and resolves them according to common agreed-on ground rules and guidelines.

A burst of creative energy often appears quite spontaneously as group members discover their sense of community. Barriers that once seemed insurmountable are now manageable. The group becomes clear on both issues and priorities, which leads to efficiency and a bias for action. The members replace self-defeating behaviors with creative and even brilliant solutions: fresh approaches now appear possible and desirable. Leadership is spontaneous and comes from anyone on the team, regardless of role or position. The team generates great self-confidence through its successes. A bond can develop in such teams, which makes them seem invincible.

Stage Four Example

A team of middle school teachers has been working diligently throughout the year to create a career exploration experience for their eighth graders. After months of planning, surveying, and contacting local businesses, everything begins to fall into place. The team *sings* with productivity. Team members divide up the tasks and complete assignments quickly. Most decisions seem like no-brainers; when disagreements arise, the team knows how to work through them quickly. The team's enthusiasm is permeating the rest of the school. There's already talk about improving the career exploration experience to plan for next year.

Stage Five: Transforming

Stage five is a period of significant change that may happen in some groups. Changes that may occur include losing or adding members, redefining a team's primary mission, or breaking up the team. Any of these changes can have a major impact on the team and will force members to address their fundamental expectations, goals, norms, and ground rules.

In the case of new membership, the team must revisit its mission, goals, ground rules, and assignments. If the team has accomplished its specific team mission, the transformation is one of closure. Here the team addresses final details, evaluates its process, and celebrates its results.

Characteristic Group Behavior

In many cases, teams will regress to one of the previous stages and then work their way back to achievement. If membership changes or the scope of the team's mission changes, the team may need to spend some time on forming (or reforming) again in order to re-establish the parameters of the team's work. With new membership or a new mission, a team can experience storming as it struggles to redefine roles and responsibilities. However, with solid team communication and problem-solving and decision-making processes in place from the norming stage, teams can quickly become high performing once again.

Stage Five Example

Under the direction of a new superintendent, a district is beginning its transition into a site-based decision-making model. Until now, school-based leadership teams consisted of staff members only, and the mission of those teams was to oversee planning activities for special events (assemblies, chorus concerts, homecoming, science fairs, and so on). In this new model, the school teams will have the authority to make significant decisions and will manage 80 percent of the school's budget. Parents must constitute 50 percent of the members of the new site teams. In this scenario, both the membership and the fundamental purpose of site-based leadership teams are transforming.

Going Through the Stages

All teams generally go through all of the stages. The speed at which they do this will vary depending on their size, the complexity of the tasks, the personalities of the members, and the circumstances of the situation. Teams can develop faster if they are given the appropriate training, time to deal with issues, and support as they move through the stages.

Maintaining effectiveness for a team is a dynamic challenge because the stages are neither stagnant nor permanent. Developing true teamwork is a discipline that requires constant practice. Moments of struggle will inevitably arise. However, successful teams will recognize the stages they experience, discuss them, and find ways to return to high performance.

The tools and methods in the remainder of this book will help your group or team be aware of and progress more quickly through the difficult stages of development. Here are some specific steps you can take to help manage the transitions from one stage to the next.

- Take time periodically to raise the issue of where the team is in its development and to discuss the signs and the strategies that might move it through its current stage.
- In the early stages, build in time for warm-up activities and icebreakers so that members can begin to become more relaxed and open with one another.
- If you find your team struggling, revisit and revise the ground rules to address new or emerging behaviors that may be contributing to and sustaining the struggle.
- During the stage of high performance, the team should be careful not to become overconfident in its decisions and actions.

Throughout the process, we recommend that you always check with stakeholders outside the team to ensure that the team's decisions support its specific mission.

When team members build their collaboration skills, they increase their ability to successfully navigate the predictable stages of group development. Five areas that, if attended to, will increase a team's likelihood for success are (1) communication, (2) decision making, (3) conflict management, (4) use of data, and (5) cohesiveness.

Communication: Pay Attention to What Is Said and How

Communication in high-performing teams encompasses a broad range of formal and informal ways for people to exchange ideas and information. The underlying theme is that all communication is open and honest. People feel free to express their thoughts, feelings, and ideas, knowing that they will be heard and considered without criticism. They view communication as a vehicle for building relationships, staying informed, obtaining input and feedback on the group's work, and maintaining a level of professional respect that keeps the team confident in its work and its members.

Four types of communication that are particularly important in teamwork are (1) sharing, (2) discussion, (3) dialogue, and (4) active listening.

Sharing

Table 3.1 provides examples of ways to build communication into your team's everyday work.

Table 3.1: Information-Sharing Techniques and Examples

Information-Sharing Techniques	Examples
Maintain accurate records of meetings.	Post logs of decisions and to-do lists in a common space.
Check in with team members between meetings.	Ask, "I was wondering how your research on criterion-referenced tests was going. Do you need any help?"
Share information about team discussions and decisions with colleagues outside of the team.	State, "We're developing some really terrific rubrics for the first-grade art students that I think will be helpful in other grades as well."
Invite feedback as a normal course of interaction on the team.	Ask, "I decided to do _____. What do you think? Did I miss anything?"
Use different ways of communicating to accommodate the different ways in which people listen and learn.	Write discussion points on a flipchart in clear view of the group. Use round robin to share opinions so that the talkers don't overshadow others in the group. Provide written documentation for those who learn better by reading.

Discussion

Much of a team's work happens through discussion. On a personal level, a basic discussion skill is being able to express ideas clearly. As a team, discussion skills include techniques that stimulate thinking in the group and help guide the discussion into productive pathways. Table 3.2 shows a few skills that any team member can use during a discussion.

Table 3.2: Discussion Skills and Examples

Discussion Skills	Examples
Lead Introduce new topics, and keep the discussion moving.	"The next agenda item is about the alternative class schedules we've been exploring." "Has everyone had a chance to give their opinion? Are we ready to make a decision yet?"
Innovate Introduce new ideas and strategies. Push the group to think differently—outside the box.	"Let's think about entirely new ways to evaluate how well the fourth graders are doing on their science projects. Has anyone worked with rubrics before?"
Summarize Restate key discussion points, and review decisions to make sure there is a common understanding about decisions and their consequences.	"It sounds like we've agreed to do a pilot study in Ivan's class before doing anything else. Is that right?"
Clarify Identify when there is confusion and clarify the points of misunderstanding by restating the issue or asking clarifying questions.	"I think we're confusing two different issues here."
Advocate Challenge the underlying assumptions and unstated biases that keep the group from moving toward innovative solutions.	"Do we know for sure that we can't hire a part-time aide to monitor classes twice a month while we hold our meetings? Has anyone asked?"
Extend Bring new information and strategies to the group to help members learn and grow.	"I just learned this great technique for integrating art and history content."
Integrate Merge disparate conversations, ideas, and concepts together into an integrated whole.	"The problems we're talking about remind me of the discussion we had last week about _____."
Initiate Initiate new models of working together and work to implement them.	"Let's do a map of our history curriculum to see if we're missing anything important. Here's a process we can use."

Dialogue

Dialogue is a special way of talking together. Its purpose is to explore meaning—to create mutual understanding, not necessarily to come to an agreement, a decision, or a solution. Dialogue is a balancing act—balancing speaking and listening, reflection and assertion, and advocacy and inquiry.

Speaking and listening in dialogue mode means being very aware of how much "air time" you are taking during a conversation and making sure that you are listening as much as speaking. Speaking involves both asking good questions that help surface assumptions and sharing your own assumptions and theories. In dialogue, the purpose of listening is to understand as fully as possible the other person's assumptions and theories in order to comprehend where they are coming from, not to prepare your own next statement.

Reflection and assertion involve the balance of fully taking in the meaning being created between speakers and stating a perspective or idea to be considered as part of that meaning making. In dialogue, the pace of conversation is slower than in traditional discussion, as speakers pause to reflect on what's been said and what it means. Assertions are made tentatively from a position of wondering whether something may or may not be true, leaving open the possibility that other perspectives may be more accurate.

Advocacy is making one's own thinking or point of view known and visible to others. Advocacy includes stating your assumptions, describing your underlying reasons for your assumptions, and talking about how you feel about the topic or issue, being careful to distinguish the data from your own interpretation of the data.

Inquiry is asking others to make their thinking, perspectives, assumptions, and feelings visible. Inquiry involves asking for and then listening deeply to someone else's point of view and seeking to understand why he or she sees the situation in that way.

The following example demonstrates the balance between advocacy and inquiry in a team meeting. A team member says, "I'm convinced that our students are not being challenged to their fullest potential. Too many students have a lot of ability but don't go on to take more rigorous classes at the high school. That frustrates me." The speaker is stating an

Data Dialogue

There is a special form of dialogue known as *data dialogue*, which focuses the group's discovery process on various forms of data relative to student performance.

—Bruce Wellman and Laura Lipton

opinion (students are not being challenged enough) and advocating a particular position (taking more rigorous classes).

She goes on to ask, "Does anyone else have that same feeling? What do you think is happening? Is my reasoning flawed?" By inquiring of the group, the speaker has opened the topic for discussion.

She then says, "The data show a trend downward in the number of students electing advanced placement classes. At least that's how I read the chart."

The group returns to advocacy, using the data to support their statements.

The speaker follows up by asking, "What else could the data be telling us? Are there other interpretations or possible reasons?"

Once again, the speaker creates an opportunity for true dialogue by making an inquiry.

After engaging in a dialogue session, have the team do an analysis of the experience. This can be a free-flowing exchange or a more structured exchange using the following questions.

- How well did we adhere to the guidelines for dialogue?
- Did this feel different from other discussions we have had? In what ways?
- When is the best time for us to have this kind of conversation? On what topics?
- How did the environment contribute to or detract from our ability to dialogue?

Active Listening

Advocacy and inquiry are two skills that team members can use to articulate clearly when they speak (for a comparison of advocacy and inquiry, see chapter 5, table 5.2, page 114). The complementary skill is *active listening*. On the one hand, listening does not seem to be all that difficult. But active listening—where you really *hear* and *understand* what someone else is saying—is hard work. Why? In part, it is because we usually listen just long enough to hear what we need to fuel our next point of disagreement or agreement.

> Nature has given men and women one tongue, but two ears, that we may hear from others twice as much as we speak.
>
> —Epictetus

This is especially true when we feel that time, other stresses, or the need to be heard pressure us. Some of the more common barriers to listening include the following (Drago-Severson, 2009; Johnston, 2012).

- Stress
- Emotions
- Preoccupation
- Bias or closed-mindedness
- Physical state
- Attitude about the speaker
- Lack of interest in the topic

Changing our listening habits isn't easy; it takes commitment and effort. If you want to become a better listener, focusing on the benefits of listening can help. These benefits include building trust and relationships, creating understanding, reducing erroneous assumptions, and clarifying meaning. If these are the outcomes you desire, then ask yourself these questions.

- "Under what conditions or circumstances am I an effective listener?"
- "When don't I listen effectively?"
- "How would I expect someone else to behave when listening to me?"
- "When I'm not really listening, what am I doing instead?"
- "What gets in the way of my being a good listener?"

There are ways to turn passive listening into active listening. Active listening means that the listener is providing some sort of feedback to the speaker during the communication. There are three strategies for active listening.

1. Paraphrasing
2. Perception checking
3. Probing

Table 3.3 (page 64) defines these strategies and provides actions that listeners can take to improve their listening performance.

Table 3.3: Strategies for Active Listening

Strategy	Definition	Actions
Paraphrasing	*Paraphrasing* is a reality check on the listener's understanding. It improves mutual understanding about what is being said and provides an opportunity to correct or clarify any potential misunderstandings. Note that paraphrasing is not the same as agreeing with the speaker. In fact, good paraphrasing should bring no judgment or evaluation. The need to be heard and understood far exceeds a person's need to have someone agree with him or her.	Listen without distraction. Tune in to both text and subtext (tone of voice, choice of words, pacing, body language, and so on). Briefly summarize what you heard and understood in your own words (you don't want to sound like a parrot): • "What I hear you saying is . . ." • "If I understand correctly, you . . ." Check the accuracy of your paraphrasing: • "Did I catch what you're saying?" • "Am I understanding what you're feeling?"
Perception Checking	*Perception checking* involves a level of interpretation that paraphrasing does not. The listener draws a conclusion or makes an interpretation and then checks with the speaker to make sure that he or she is accurate. The interpretation doesn't express either disapproval or approval.	Listen for the feelings the speaker may be experiencing, as well as the specific ideas being expressed. • "It sounds like you're really frustrated with this project. Is that correct?" • "This doesn't seem like a good time to talk. Am I right?" • "With everything that you've described, it sounds to me like you're pretty overwhelmed."
Probing	*Probing* is a strategy for taking the conversation deeper. The speaker sets the stage in terms of content and initial depth of the conversation. Probing serves a number of purposes. • To expand on ideas • To go deeper in understanding • To get clearer about meaning • To unearth assumptions • To explore applications The role of the active listener is to probe into the meaning that the speaker has initiated, not to take the speaker in another direction.	Watch for signs that the speaker may not be comfortable going deeper, especially if the content of the conversation is personal. In that case, the listener should get permission from the speaker to probe further. • "Do you mind my asking, what led you to that conclusion?" • "If you don't mind telling me, what do you think were the most critical facts that influenced you in this situation?" • "Tell me more, if you are comfortable doing so." • "So what do you think that means?"

Generally, whether paraphrasing, perception checking, or probing, there are some things to keep in mind when working on improving your listening skills.

- **Listen patiently:** Stop talking; don't interrupt; refrain from reactions or comments that would indicate judgment, disagreement, or evaluation; accept silence.

- **Indicate understanding:** Be interested; ask for clarification if you don't understand something; listen for changes in tone and volume; listen for what is not being said.

- **Be objective:** Try not to let your feelings or biases about the speaker influence you; check your tendency to hear only what you want to hear; respect the speaker's comfort zone about personal topics.

Mental Models and the Ladder of Inference

Understanding mental models is key to all types of communication. Mental models are the assumptions, beliefs, and perceptions we bring to all of our experiences; they determine not only how we make sense of the world but also how we take action. Mental models can be simple generalizations, or they can be complex theories, but what is most important is that mental models are active. They shape how we act and, in particular, what and how we communicate.

Figure 3.1 (page 66) shows how we interpret an individual's actions differently and react accordingly depending on our mental model. It's only by checking facts (perhaps by asking) that we can know what the real reasons are. (One possibility that doesn't appear in any of the four interpretations is that the individual has to pick up a child from daycare before a certain time.)

The *ladder of inference* (Senge, Kleiner, Roberts, Ross, & Smith, 1994) provides a series of steps for helping the team think through the various interpretations that individuals make when looking at data, solving a problem, or understanding a given situation. Each step on the ladder is a point

---

Listen with your heart as well as your mind.

—Anonymous

Listening Discussion Items

- I listen best when ...

- I don't listen effectively when ...

- I know someone is listening to me when ...

- When I am not listening, I am most likely doing ... instead.

- I fake listening when ...

- When I am talking and I know I am not being heard, I feel ...

- When I am talking and I know I am not being heard, my reaction is to ...

Fact: Chris regularly gets up and leaves the leadership team meeting approximately one and a half hours after it starts.				
	Person A	**Person B**	**Person C**	**Person D**
Infer Meaning or Interpret Observations	Chris has a lot of important things to do.	Chris has too much to do.	Chris always seems to leave when I'm talking.	Chris leaves after the team discusses the items he is in charge of.
Evaluate and Impose a Value	Chris is very valuable to us.	Chris is unorganized and can't prioritize.	Chris doesn't respect me.	Chris doesn't value anything he's not in charge of.
Create an Assumption	Chris has everything under control.	Chris is out of control.	Chris is heartless and manipulative.	Chris is not a team player.
Draw a Conclusion	Chris should be rewarded.	Chris should be trained.	Chris can't be trusted.	Chris should be reprimanded.
Take Action	Person A gives Chris a promotion.	Person B recommends that Chris attend time management training.	Person C refuses to serve on any more teams with Chris.	Person D reports Chris to her supervisor.

Figure 3.1: Mental models example.

of potential revelation with regard to why a team is being successful or unsuccessful in resolving conflicts. By learning to use the ladder, a team is empowered with a process for analyzing its own communication and thinking patterns that can ultimately help the team come to an agreed-on resolution.

Begin by assembling the facts around a particular situation. Be very careful to discern between fact and perception. The ladder of inference is laden with perceptual information in the form of assumptions, judgments, and inferences, which is the dynamic that the team is trying to understand. That is why it is so important to start with the facts. From there, the team will explore individuals' reactions to the facts in the sequence shown in figure 3.2.

To analyze team actions, start at the bottom of the ladder and go up until you get to the mental model. What mental model (perceptions, assumptions, and beliefs) must have been in place for the facts to match the actions that were taken?

For example, a high school algebra team decided not to tell its students about a regional mathematics competition, believing it would distract them from focusing on a big semester test. Parents learned about this after the fact and became angry, venting their frustration to the principal. The students were upset as well, claiming their school performance would have benefited from the extra time they would have spent on mathematics problems. In order to better understand how this situation had occurred, the algebra team worked through the ladder of inference to re-examine their thinking, asking the following "Why?" questions at each step to determine how they came to the decision, or action, to not tell students about the competition.

- Why? They concluded that many of their students would do poorly on the test.

- Why? They assumed students wouldn't focus on preparing for the test while participating in the competition.

- Why? They judged this year's students as being less interested in learning and achievement than students in previous years. (Evaluation)

- Why? They inferred that students didn't care about tests.

- Why? They assumed the students didn't care about algebra.

- Why? Student test scores were lower than in previous years. (Fact)

As a result of this analysis, the team understood that it had jumped to an assumption about the students not caring about algebra. It resolved to examine other reasons this year's student test scores were low.

Decision Making: Decide How to Decide

There are a lot of ways to go about making a decision. Since a team is a cooperative effort, decision making also

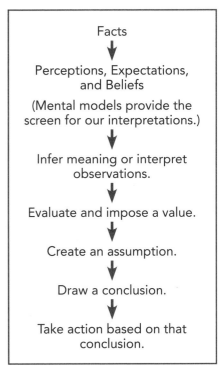

Source: Adapted from Senge et al., 1994, p. 243.

Figure 3.2: The ladder of inference.

The more the team uses the sequence of thought that makes up the steps of *the ladder of inference*, the more natural it will become to insert a question anywhere along the way. For example, let's say that the team has concluded the best way to approach a conflict with a parent is to show him or her the data on the child's behavior. An important question to test this conclusion would be, "What assumptions are we making about this parent?" When in doubt, back up the ladder to test your assumptions, value judgments, and interpretations before committing to action.

needs to be collaborative. The key to good collaborative decision making is for the team to be explicit about its decision-making process—selecting the right decision-making process for the need. Collaborative decision making is highly effective with the following conditions.

- Decisions require diverse, creative ideas.
- Many perspectives help others to better understand the issue or problem.
- A fundamental or significant change is likely.
- Many people or groups share the same problem.

The first step in collaborative decision making is determining the outcomes that your team needs as well as what authority it has. Then, establish norms for how you'll make decisions to avoid some of the inevitable conflicts that groups experience when they must finally make a decision.

Team Authority

Let's be practical. Your team exists because someone with the authority to allow it to exist thinks it's OK for people to use their time in that way. For school-based teams, that person is likely to be a positional leader (principal, department chair, or unit leader) or the school improvement team that's overseeing a process. For other teams, it may be a central office administrator, the superintendent, or even the board.

We've all been in situations where we put a lot of time and effort into making a decision only to hear the positional leader say, "Thanks for your input. I'll take it under advisement." So, before your team spends a lot of time deciding how you'll make decisions within the team, you need to be clear about what decisions the team as a whole is authorized to make. That means working with the authority to be clear about what he or she wants out of the team. For example, are you supposed to do the following?

- Study an issue and come up with options.
- Make a recommendation.
- Make the decision.
- Implement the decision.

You'll also need to know what criteria or limits the authority has placed on the team's outcomes. For example, your team might be tasked with studying the textbook ordering process and devising and implementing a new process—as long as you can complete it by a certain date without new equipment purchases.

If you are not given any decision boundaries or criteria up front have your team write down what authority you think you have and then check with the positional leader.

Four Decision-Making Options

Ideally, group or team members should feel that they are making high-quality decisions and that they have the group's acceptance and support to carry out those decisions. That is the essence of collaborative decision making. We describe four possible decision-making options; which of those options you use will depend on the situation.

1. **Consensus decisions:** All members of the team agree to support the group's decision, even if the selected option is not his or her first preference.

2. **Voting:** Group members vote on various options. The voting takes two forms: *majority vote* and *most votes*. For an option to win, it must receive at least 51 percent of the votes or perhaps a two-thirds majority. The option with the most votes wins, even if it doesn't have a majority.

3. **Consultative decisions:** The team, or one group member, makes the decision in consultation with others.

4. **Command decisions:** A person with positional or delegated authority makes these decisions. Alternatively, the group determines that someone with expert knowledge in a particular area (who need not necessarily be a member of the group) can make the decision.

The first two options—consensus and voting—involve all team members in the decision. The latter two provide alternatives that the team can use either when the whole team is not necessary to make a decision or when an individual has the specific authority or job requirement to make a decision. For example, a school secretary reserves a bus for field trips, so there is no need to call a team meeting to decide which transportation company to use.

Consensus Decisions

When the group's primary concern is that every member is comfortable with the decision, the best decision-making option is consensus. Consensus means that everyone agrees to support the decision, publicly and privately, once the decision is final. It does not mean that decision is everyone's first choice. The key consensus question to answer is, "Can we live with this decision?" However, school teams work in the real world, and sometimes a decision has to be made whether or not the group has reached consensus. Have your group discuss under what circumstances it will be acceptable to use a different decision-making strategy (after a certain amount of time or after a certain number of attempts at reaching consensus, for example). Use caution—make sure that there is a legitimate reason for abandoning the attempt to reach consensus. Don't give up too easily, or you'll erode the group's trust that its input is valued.

Your team will reach consensus only when everyone involved in making the decision is satisfied that his or her concerns have been heard and considered. That's why three elements usually precede consensus decisions: (1) extensive dialogue in which people get to voice their opinions, (2) a thorough investigation of all aspects of the decision—both positive and negative, and (3) a weighing of all the options—not just a favored few.

It's probably obvious from this description that consensus decisions take more time up front than the other decision-making options. However, this up-front investment has a huge payoff down the road in smoother implementation. The higher the stakes, the more desirable consensus becomes. Use consensus decision making when:

- The team needs full support and commitment from all members to successfully implement the decision

- The decision will affect many people, and many will be responsible for implementation
- The decision affects or may change the core processes of those involved

See pages 122–125 for specific consensus decision-making processes such as fist-to-five, round robin, and consensus building on profound issues. While consensus decision making takes time, it's well worth the effort for the quality of the final decision. These processes can help you manage this type of decision making with clear structure and focus.

Voting

When the group needs a more expedient approach due to time constraints or decides that it is not critical to have everyone totally committed to the decision, it may elect to conduct a vote. The team will have to decide whether to keep going until one option has a clear majority (either 51 percent or two-thirds of the votes) or whether the option with the most votes will win no matter what; for example, if option A receives 40 percent of the votes, option B receives 35 percent, and option C receives 25 percent, then option A wins. Because as many as 49 percent of the team could be on the losing side in a majority vote, you have to be very careful when using this decision-making model.

Voting is appropriate when:

- The stakes are low
- The group is very large
- Time is of the essence
- Commitment to the decision is less important than getting on with the task

If your team has a lot of options from which to choose for making a final decision, use the decision matrix (page 119) to help you narrow down the list to the best alternatives. The decision matrix is a quick, visual way to organize a voting process and has the added value of bringing criteria into the decision-making mix so that decisions can be weighed against multiple factors.

Tips for Enhancing the Consensus Process

- Don't try to force compromises.
- Don't avoid tough discussions, or you'll never reach a point where everyone feels his or her concerns have been heard and dealt with.
- Be careful not to rush to a decision; people need time to weigh alternatives before they can put their full support behind one option.
- Seek ways to combine and recombine various positions.
- Don't vote for the final decision; consensus means everyone agrees to support the final choice.
- Do whatever you can to equalize participation, especially if there are individuals who have positions of authority over others in the group.
- When you think you're close to consensus, have someone write a clear statement of the impending decision. Then ask group members if they understand and support that statement, and make any agreed-on changes.

Consultative Decisions

Consultative decisions allow for broader input. One individual or a smaller subgroup of the team makes the decision after seeking advice, input, or expertise from others or conducting research. Consultative decisions work best under the following circumstances.

- The group trusts an individual or subset of the team to make reasonable decisions and accepts the fact that the group as a whole is not the final decision maker.

- The group understands that outside input—seeking advice from an expert or consulting available research—will enhance both the decision and the commitment to implement it. The group recognizes that one individual cannot know all facets of the decision or its potential impact.

- The decision is likely to have vastly different consequences for different people, and the decision maker should consult all groups before making a decision. For example, if having secretaries order cleaning supplies would make life easier for custodians but add to the secretaries' workload, consult with both groups to make sure you understand their needs and the consequences of the team's decision.

- The decision is an interim or prerequisite step for other decisions that the team will make as a whole.

Consulting with others helps decision makers make better decisions because they are informed by others' expertise and knowledge. However, while this method takes less time than consensus and voting, it should not become a permanent shortcut for these more collaborative decision methods since it doesn't take full advantage of the team's wisdom.

Command Decisions

The last decision-making option is *command decisions*. One individual who has official authority, knowledge, power, or status makes the decision. If that person is someone who is not on the team (the principal or school board leader, for instance) and overrules the team's decisions, then for all intents and purposes, the team doesn't actually have decision-making authority and is simply making a recommendation to that person. This can cause problems when the team *thought* it had authority, only to find out when it came time for implementation the person with positional power stopped it. This can happen because decision authority hasn't been clearly specified in advance of the team's work, which is why it's so important to have these conversations early on in the team's process. Another way that command decisions can happen is when the team defers to a member's expertise for particular decisions. For example: "Functionally, all of our software options seem like they will work. Since Dave knows more about software compatibility than anyone on the team, let's let him make this decision, then we can build from there."

Sometimes you may not have a choice about when to use a command decision, such as when your principal, superintendent, or school board is simply asking your team for recommendations. Within the team, however, you can use command decisions in the following circumstances.

- It's the law. For example, when a number of students show up at school without proof of residence, the registration team decides to ask the school social worker to assist the students in getting adequate proof before enrolling them.

- There is little room for movement, leeway, or options requiring quick action to avoid potential negative consequences of not acting immediately. For example, the team discovers that the school auditorium has been double booked for a band concert and a community event, so it decides to move the band concert to a different location.

- The decision is objective, is consistent with an already defined plan of action, and follows the strategic direction of the organization. For example, the school district has a set schedule for administering standardized tests, and the team makes the command decision to offer test-taking

---

Inform Your Team of Consultative and Command Decisions

Usually only one person (who may or may not be on the team) or a small subset of the team makes consultative or command decisions. Although team members will have no say in such decisions, they still need to know the outcome. Provide them with a description of the decision, plus a brief summary of why that particular option was chosen.

tips and strategies as an optional elective to students.

- The team agrees to allow one individual to make decisions, and the leader is willing to accept full responsibility for the result. For example, a teacher on the team has background knowledge and experience working with Spanish-speaking families and is asked to put together an orientation program for families new to the school.

When it comes to decision making, the important thing is not to use the same method for every situation but to decide ahead of time which of the four methods is most appropriate for a given situation. Teams that are intentional about deciding how to decide are well equipped to navigate the tricky waters of decision making.

Conflict Management

High-performing teams establish processes and norms around conflict management. They understand that conflict and disagreement are natural and deal with them in productive ways. The emphasis is on resolving issues, not on criticizing personalities. Diverse opinions are a strength of the team. Individual members take responsibility for their own actions and commit to being flexible and sensitive to others' needs when conflicts arise.

Conflict Management Techniques

The following are techniques teams can employ to address conflict in healthy and productive ways.

1. **Taking preventive actions:** To prevent problems from appearing later on, identify group norms and expectations and agree on consequences for violating them.

2. **Defining a process for resolving conflicts:** Agree as a group on what the team will do to address conflicts when they arise. Here is a process the group might use.

   - Set or review ground rules for respectful resolution.

Respectful Conflict Resolution

Once teams learn how to resolve conflicts respectfully, trust increases, making it easier to resolve future conflicts.

Understanding that emotions are a part of conflict resolution is important. Allow people to have their say—they can vent.

Example: "It sounds like you have strong feelings about this. Could you say more about why you feel that way?"

Work to de-escalate the conflict and emotions by listening actively, acknowledging people's feelings, and reframing the conflict around issues rather than personalities.

Continued➔

- Define the issue in terms of the group's task or mission, not based on individual positions or preferred solutions.
- Allow each person to state his or her point of view on the issue and listen actively.
- Brainstorm solutions.
- Select a solution; assess potential consequences.
- Plan for implementation.

3. **Using consensus-building methods:** Throughout the problem-solving process, periodically check for levels of consensus and work to build understanding and support for the group's decisions. If you really get stuck on an issue, try the Consensus Building on Profound Issues process (Chadwick, 2013) on page 124.

4. **Changing the channel of communication:** If your group appears to be stuck in one way of thinking about an issue, switch the modality of its communication. For example, stop a fruitless discussion to allow for five or ten minutes of silent, individual reflection during which people write down their individual thoughts. Follow this silent period with an open brainstorming session to introduce new perspectives.

5. **Using role play:** Each person on the team is forced to take on a role or point of view other than his or her own and discuss the issue from the new point of view.

6. **Facilitating dialogue:** Balance advocacy and inquiry as a way to explore the meaning of an issue without the need to find an immediate solution or answer.

7. **Using direct confrontation and feedback:** When the situation warrants, the group will stop what it is doing and deal directly with the conflict. This requires an enormous level of trust. The group essentially identifies all of its individual

Example: "I'm hearing that you think people aren't contributing equally to the team. Is that right?"

Move into productive resolution of the conflict using an agreed-on process.

Example: "Let's use fist-to-five to see if we can get to agreement on this issue. Is everyone on board with trying that process?"

If the group doesn't already have a ground rule, define one for how to deal with conflict. Following your own ground rules is a good way to build and sustain trust.

Example: "What if we agree to the ground rule that if any one of us senses the team is entering into an area of disagreement or conflict, we stop and go around the group one at a time to hear each person's perspective?"

and collective issues, places them openly on the table, and takes time to respectfully consider each person's perspective and needs related to the issues.

Giving and Receiving Feedback

Teams skilled in conflict management know how to use feedback for learning. Giving effective feedback takes skill and sensitivity. Receiving feedback effectively requires an open, nondefensive posture. Both require trust.

Just mentioning the word *feedback* gives some people so much anxiety that teams are reluctant to give it. Why is giving feedback so threatening? Perhaps it's because in the past we received feedback that was poorly delivered or delivered with negative intentions. Yet, feedback is a necessary component for any kind of learning. So, for a team to reach its highest levels of performance, it must view feedback as a tool for collaborative learning and learn to provide feedback in a way that is constructive and useful.

In the context of communication, feedback is a tool for sharing data. The data are both subjective and objective and pertain to either an individual's or group's patterns of behavior. Feedback by its very nature is a two-way communication process. There is always at least one sender and at least one receiver, both of whom need to be prepared to engage in the exchange of data. An effective feedback process includes four steps: (1) getting ready, (2) knowing the guidelines for effective feedback, (3) preparing yourself for the session, and (4) conducting the session.

Step One: Getting Ready

Getting ready is as much a part of giving feedback as the actual data sharing that follows. Preparing for the feedback session involves identifying the behavior and reasons for it and assessing the impact of the behavior on the group or individuals.

- **Identify the behavior:** The first step is to be clear about the specific behavior that will be the subject of the feedback message. It is a behavior, not an attitude. The behavior must be something that the provider of the feedback has witnessed and can describe, not something that is based on hearsay.

- **Consider the reasons for the behavior:** Think about possible reasons why the team or team member is exhibiting the behavior. Is this a habit or a behavior about which the individual or group is unaware? Is the behavior a manifestation of individual or group frustration with a task? Is the behavior a substitute for a skill that is lacking? Is the behavior due to an individual's personal circumstances at the time? Is it intended to get the attention of the group or the team leader for some reason?

- **Assess the impact of the behavior:** How severe or chronic is the behavior? If it's a one-time occurrence, ignoring it might be the best strategy. If it's a pattern of ongoing behavior, then feedback is an appropriate option for helping the person or the group become aware of it and the impact it is having on the team. If the group is engaging in disruptive behavior that is getting in the way of its productivity, the healthiest approach can be to pause and discuss what is going on, rather than trying to ignore the problem. For example, if meetings always begin late, pausing to discuss whether starting and ending on time is important to people can lead to a healthy conversation about the impact that starting late has on those who are always there on time. If an individual is chronically disruptive, however, take time to privately give feedback to the individual (see step two for guidelines on effective feedback).

Step Two: Knowing the Guidelines for Effective Feedback

Once you've determined the feedback to give to someone or a group about an identified behavior, you need to ensure the session goes as intended. The intention is to resolve the issue so that constructive action to address the behavior occurs. To reach a desirable conclusion, consider the following elements.

- **Environment:** A general rule of thumb is that you provide positive feedback publicly and negative feedback privately. So, if the feedback is about a behavior that needs to change, make sure you have a neutral, quiet place where you can talk without interruptions.

- **Timing:** You should provide feedback as soon after you observe the behavior as possible but not at the moment, especially if it is during a team meeting. If either the provider of the feedback or the individual or group receiving it is under emotional duress, allow time for people to gather their thoughts and calm their emotions before initiating the feedback.

- **Receiver readiness:** Emotional readiness is an important prerequisite for someone being able to hear and accept feedback. Observe and listen for cues that can give you a sense of the individual's emotional state. Get permission. Ask if you can share some observations with him or her. Be sure that the behavior is something that the individual can control. Is this going to be new news, or has this person likely heard this before?

- **Message:** The message takes into account the needs of both the sender and the receiver of the feedback. It is specific and descriptive with regard to the actual behavior, its frequency, and when it occurred or is occurring. It is not evaluative. The message is a statement of the facts (data) and the perceived or known impact the behavior is having on others. Be careful to choose words that are neutral and void of judgment. The physical posture of the giver is also an important aspect of the message. This is not a power play; this is a collegial sharing of important information that is intended to make everyone on the team accountable for the team's success.

- **Reflection:** Provide permission and time for the receiver to reflect on what he or she heard. Encourage questions and provide clarification where needed, but be sure to give space for processing the information.

- **Action:** Engage the receiver in planning actions that will help him or her and others eradicate the behavior. This is especially important if it is a habit about which the receiver was unaware. Simple, noninvasive cues might be all that it takes to reduce or eliminate the behavior.

Step Three: Preparing Yourself for the Session

Feedback sessions can be stressful for everyone involved. If you find that you're anxious about giving the feedback, consider some of the following tips to prepare.

- **Make sure your facts are accurate:** Double-check your facts to make sure you have all your ducks in a row and that they are indisputable.

- **Anticipate resistance:** What reactions are you likely to get? Anticipate the receiver's objections, excuses, and reactions. Plan accordingly.

- **Write it out:** Script what you are going to say and the responses you might need in the face of resistance.

- **Practice:** Practice in front of a mirror or with a trusted friend, or share the feedback with your dog. Dogs are great listeners and never disagree.

Step Four: Conducting the Session

The time has come. You're in a private, neutral place, and you're ready to begin. Take a deep breath and assure yourself that this is what is best for the team and for the individual or group you're about to address. The following is an example of what the session might look like.

- **State the reason for meeting, and get permission to proceed:** "Thanks for taking time to meet with me today. I'd like to share some observations I've had that I think you can help me understand and deal with to make our team better. The observations involve you, and I'd like to have your permission to share them with you."

- **Provide the facts:** "I've noted that today was the third time in three meetings that you've come in fifteen minutes late."
- **Share the perceived or known impact:** "When you come in late, it disrupts the whole group, and we sometimes have trouble getting back on track. We're also not hearing your voice when you're not in the room. Because punctuality is one of our agreed-on ground rules, your absence makes the ground rules seem unimportant."
- **Ask for reactions:** "What do you think? I'd like to hear your reactions as well as how you think I might help."
- **Engage in planning:** "What are some specific actions that you or I or the rest of the team can take to help you with this?"

Table 3.4 describes the characteristics and examples of effective feedback.

Table 3.5 (page 82) describes tips for and examples of receiving feedback.

If you don't feel comfortable giving or receiving feedback, you may want to practice using these guidelines with your friends and family first, then try them at work with colleagues with whom you feel safe, and finally, when you've built your confidence, try them in other environments where the stakes feel a bit higher. Giving and receiving effective feedback is a learnable skill, and it is one of the most rewarding since it can so significantly and positively change the dynamics of individual and team interactions.

Use of Data

As educators, we certainly know how important it is not to reduce students to numbers and statistics. Traditionally, we've relied mostly on our intuition and experience to tell us whether we're being effective. But the days are long gone when an educator's best judgment is enough proof that what's been taught has been learned. Effective teams place a high priority on basing decisions on data.

Five Data-Collection Ground Rules

1. Keep it simple. Stay focused.
2. Let the data do the talking.
3. Handle with care—data are not for saying "gotcha."
4. Use the right tool for its intended purpose.
5. Start with a question, theory, hunch, or need to know. Then, collect the data.

Table 3.4: Characteristics and Examples of Effective Feedback

Characteristics of Effective Feedback	Examples
Descriptive Describe the situation or behavior in observable terms.	Instead of saying, "You're very hostile to staff," say, "When you use language like *incompetent* and *insensitive* to describe the staff . . ."
Specific Be as specific as possible. Avoid using terms like *always* or *never*.	Instead of saying, "You are always interrupting me," say, "When you interrupt me as you did just now . . ."
Firsthand Make sure to observe or experience the behavior firsthand and that the feedback is not based on rumors, gossip, or suspicions.	Instead of saying, "Everyone appreciates how you . . ." say, "I noticed in the meeting that you often helped us get back on track . . ."
Nonevaluative Don't use words that are judgmental in nature, such as *unacceptable* or *bad.* Simply inform the individual of the specific behavior you are observing.	Instead of saying, "You talk too much," say, "When others are speaking, you interrupt them."
Timely Provide feedback in private as close in time to the occurrence of the behavior as possible, especially if the feedback is not positive. Do not refer to past occurrences.	Instead of saying, "Two months ago you did the same thing!" say, "I noticed you were late for yesterday's meeting."
Behavioral Stick to specific behaviors that can be observed, repeated, or changed; do not make inferences about someone's appearance, voice, attitudes, mannerisms, or tone. Do comment on what people do or say that affects the group strongly (positive or negative).	Instead of saying, "You don't seem to care about the team!" say, "When you are late for meetings, we have to wait to begin, and I feel my time isn't being valued."
Factual Provide facts whenever possible to substantiate your concern or your delight. Describe specific occurrences that are recent.	Instead of saying, "I think you are trying to change the subject!" say, "When I brought up the issue of scheduling and you began talking about the high school band's performance last night . . ."
Honest Be honest without being brutal.	Instead of saying, "You're a real procrastinator . . ." say, "This is the third time you've come unprepared. Are you overextended or unclear about what to do?"

That doesn't mean that data are the *only* input into a team's decisions. W. Edwards Deming, a renowned statistician and management expert, spent much of his life trying to convince people to use data more often when making decisions. However, even he knew that hard facts and measurable

Table 3.5: Tips and Examples for Receiving Feedback

Tips for Receiving Feedback	Examples
Listen Openly Try to put yourself in others' shoes to understand a different point of view, and just listen. This can be tough if the feedback is negative, but remind yourself that your only obligation is to listen. Be open to the fact that someone else may be interpreting things very differently than you are. It would also provide an opportunity to learn how others are perceiving the situation and give you a chance to help them see it differently.	Instead of saying, "I don't know what you're talking about!" say, "I know giving feedback can be difficult, and I appreciate your willingness to share with me. Tell me what's on your mind."
Take Time to Digest Give yourself time to think about what you are hearing. Your immediate reaction might be unnecessarily defensive. Taking time will allow you to take some of the emotion out of the interaction.	Instead of saying, "There's nothing I can do about this feedback right now—I'm not even sure it's true!" say, "Thanks. You've given me something to think about."
Acknowledge Valid Points Whenever you agree, say so and acknowledge that you are aware of this behavior.	Instead of saying, "I'm not the only one who talks a lot in meetings!" say, "I know I talk too much sometimes. I appreciate you helping me get better at listening."
Accept Compliments Thank the person for compliments—no need to argue whether you agree since it's obviously a perception that the person giving the feedback believes to be true.	Instead of saying, "It was nothing" say, "Thank you."
Paraphrase What You Heard Summarize what the person said.	Instead of saying, "I am offended that you're calling me disrespectful!" say, "You're saying you think it's disrespectful of me to keep my cell phone turned on during meetings. Is that right?"
Show That You Understand Provide an example or application of what you are hearing to illustrate that you not only heard but also understood.	Instead of saying, "I'm not interested in being a meeting facilitator" say, "I am interested in participating in the meeting; however, I would be most comfortable participating as a timekeeper or scribe."
Ask for Clarification Whenever you don't clearly understand what someone means, ask for clarification or an example.	Instead of saying, "I am offended that you think I'm irresponsible!" say, "I'm not sure what you mean by saying I 'take my responsibilities too lightly.' Could you give me an example?"
Request Feedback The best defense is a good offense. If feedback truly is for learning, show that you're interested in learning and improving by inviting feedback from others on a regular basis.	Instead of saying, "I will just do the best I can next time, how's that?" say, "I'm not very confident in my role as meeting facilitator. How do you think I did today? Do you have any suggestions for what I could try next time?"

figures show only part of the picture. He cautioned us not to rely too heavily on "visible figures, with little or no consideration of figures that are unknown and unknowable" (1982, p. 121). His timeless message was, yes, we should collect data, but we shouldn't throw our judgment, intuition, and experience out the door (Deming, 1982, 1993).

The key is to think of data as a learning tool. We use data to test theories or ideas. Trying to understand theory without knowledge of its application is meaningless; to apply models and strategies void of a well-thought-out theory is equally meaningless. Cumulative and continuous learning occurs when theory contributes to application, and application either substantiates or modifies the theory (Deming, 1982, 1983).

The Data-Logic Chain

The data-logic chain graphically depicts this continuous learning process. A pursuit into learning begins with a need to know something, a theory, a hunch, or a question that has come to us through some natural flow of *logic*. Then, we test that theory by looking at data from the real world (by making observations, gathering information, measuring, or testing some aspect of our theory). What we learn from the data leads to new ideas and a new set of questions, for which we need to gather more data, and so on.

In our RTI example of the data-logic chain in figure 3.3 (page 84), a school intervention team is charged with assisting Tier 3 students—those most in need of intensive support. The team begins with a question, What are the specific learning needs of each student in need of intensive support (in reading, writing, mathematics, and English language)? Team members then look at test scores and other assessment data to identify the specific learning needs for individual students. These data lead them to ask about the causes of each student's struggles—are there chronic and excessive absences, severe behavior or motivational concerns, or combinations of these factors? The team then determines the most appropriate interventions to address each student's needs (based on data-informed theories about what works). Teachers frequently monitor each student's progress to see

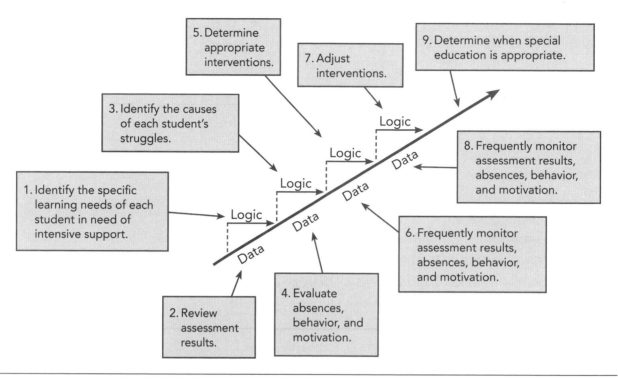

Figure 3.3: RTI example of the data-logic chain.

if interventions are achieving desired outcomes. If the interventions aren't working, the team revises them. The team determines when special education is appropriate.

Chapter 7 describes a variety of tools and methods that school teams can use to gather and interpret data. The first thing to know about data tools is that they are like any other kind of tool—each has its own special purpose. You'll almost never need all the tools at once. The key is to know which tool to use for which purpose.

Cohesiveness

Group cohesiveness happens when team members have a strong sense of belonging to the group and a commitment to its actions. The climate during meetings is comfortable and informal. People share the risks and benefits of their collaborative efforts, trusting their team colleagues to treat them with respect (and vice versa). Like trust, group cohesiveness doesn't appear overnight. It is something the group must work to attain. It is also difficult to measure or observe—but groups know when they have it or do not have it. *Group cohesiveness* is characterized by mutuality, shared vision, common purpose, and interdependence of members.

Techniques for Building Team Cohesiveness

Cohesiveness naturally arises when a team works together to effectively solve problems and implement improvements. Techniques for building cohesiveness include spending time in meetings getting to know each other; spending time talking about the team's mission, vision, values, and goals; celebrating small successes and progress; and developing a team identity. Table 3.6 (page 86) describes these techniques.

Continuously Improving Your Team's Work

High-performing teams regularly improve themselves and all aspects of their work. As we noted in the introduction, high-performing teams implement, evaluate, and improve meetings, communication, and decision-making and problem-solving processes using the PDSA cycle: they plan, do, study, and act (see figure I.1, page 4). When things go wrong, the group tries to understand the problem at its deepest level, focusing on systemic causes and solutions instead of quick fixes. As a result, the team's effectiveness grows exponentially the longer the team is intact. Here are some questions that can help you improve how your team is working.

- Is what we're doing the best use of our time right now?
- How will doing this help us? How will it help our students?
- Do we know if what we're doing is having the impact we want?
- Might there be a better and more efficient way to do what we're doing?
- Who else would love to have the chance to do this and would be delighted to help us get it done?
- Are we working together to learn and improve?
- Do we implement what we learn?

Table 3.6: Techniques and Examples for Building Team Cohesiveness

Techniques	Examples
Spend time in meetings getting to know each other personally. This need not be anything too elaborate. Use simple warm-ups, ice breakers, or check-ins where people share something personal about themselves.	Have a brief warm-up where people share where they were born, something about their family, or a favorite hobby.
Spend time talking about the team's mission, vision, values, and goals. This helps team members develop a sense of shared purpose and see that they are helping their school or district achieve its vision.	At the team's first meeting, ask members to describe how the team's mission does or does not support the school's vision. If you find significant discrepancies, take that information to your positional leaders for discussion. Perhaps the team's mission should be focused on a higher school priority.
Celebrate small successes and progress. It's easy for team members to get discouraged when working on a long or complex project. Celebrating progress can provide a needed boost in morale.	Have a pizza lunch to celebrate completion of a plan.
Develop a team identity by creating a team name, logo, mascot, or saying. Be sure the team name reflects its unique mission or personality.	One team that worked on enrollment called themselves the High Rollers. Teams with a strong identity often use a team name on their meeting agenda and notes and in conversations (for example, "I have a meeting with the High Rollers over lunch today").

The PDSA learning cycle is at the heart of learning how to become an effective team. When teams apply PDSA thinking to everything they do, they automatically build in opportunities to learn. As a result, they become high performing and able to take on whatever challenges come their way.

Final Check: Teamwork Basics

Effective collaboration is both skillful and purposeful. As teams develop and learn together, they become more productive in their collaborative efforts, saving valuable time and generating enthusiasm in the process. Teams that consciously and continuously address the people, tasks, and process issues associated with their collaborative work experience better results because they have accomplished their mission together—and they have enjoyed doing so. Here is a checklist to use with your team.

- ☐ We are familiar with the predictable stages of group development.
- ☐ We use a variety of ways to share information about our work.
- ☐ We intentionally apply different discussion skills as appropriate.
- ☐ We engage in dialogue to better understand each other's views.
- ☐ We have defined our decision-making strategies and options.
- ☐ We manage conflict.
- ☐ We use data-logic thinking in our problem solving.
- ☐ We invest time in getting to know each other.
- ☐ We celebrate small successes and progress.

PART TWO

Using Tools and Processes for Effective Teamwork

CHAPTER 4

Tools for Productive Meetings

Meetings represent a significant investment of time and energy for any organization. Hundreds of thousands of hours are spent in meetings each year. That investment can be magnified many times in schools with a team-based structure as the predominant model for collaboration, professional learning, instructional improvement, and decision making. Because time is such a precious resource for educators, wasting it in ill-planned or poorly run meetings is simply not an option. Meeting solely to impart information from one source to another diminishes the inherent value of bringing people together and wastes an opportunity for collaboration. There are endless ways to share information without convening a meeting to do so.

Meetings are important venues for collaboration. In fact, most of a team's collaborative work time will be spent in face-to-face meetings. The value of collaborative meetings emerges from the synergy created when people come together to pursue a common goal or address a common concern. Collaboration builds understanding, heightens commitment, and generates new ideas and knowledge.

Unfortunately, too many meetings are not designed to enhance collaboration. Like any good lesson, collaborative meetings require forethought and planning. Yet, we rarely take the planning time required for meetings to go well. All too frequently, people come to meetings not knowing what to expect, who will be there, why the meeting is being held, what their particular role is, or how long they are being asked to commit. Meetings that have not been carefully organized or communicated typically accomplish half of what might have been accomplished if they had been planned, resulting in a waste of valuable time.

Who Plans the Meeting?

Typically, the team leader is responsible for making sure that planning for a meeting occurs. If the team leader is also the meeting leader, he or she may do the planning alone (or in consultation with others). If a team rotates its meeting leader role, the team leader should work with that person to do the planning.

Sometimes It's OK Not to Meet

After defining the purpose and objectives for a meeting, the planners sometimes realize that a meeting is not the most appropriate way to accomplish those objectives. For example, if the primary purpose of the meeting is to share information, there are many ways to accomplish this without bringing people together all in one place. If, however, there is a need to have discussion or seek input on a particular item, then perhaps a meeting is warranted. Early planning should help determine if and when a meeting should take place.

Tools and Methods for Managing Tangents

Occasionally, a group finds itself straying off the agenda into completely different topics. This happens for a variety of reasons and may even be productive at times, but it's something that the group should monitor and manage. Here are some strategies for handling tangents.

- **Parking lot or issue bin:** Post a flipchart on the wall at the beginning of every meeting and label it the *parking lot* or *issue bin*. When the group

Continued➔

This chapter provides meeting leaders, facilitators, and participants with tips for determining the best meeting format to use, tools and templates for designing highly effective meeting agendas, and role definitions that will ensure full engagement and understanding of individual responsibilities to achieve well-run meetings.

Elements of Meeting Design

Few of us have been taught how to design, run, or even participate in an effective meeting. Choosing the most appropriate format for the meeting is the first step. There are multiple options for meeting design, but all of them share a few basic elements that the team must consider. Each element is important, and all of them are interrelated to some extent. The basic elements of meeting design are the following.

- **Purpose:** Why is the meeting being held? What results or outcomes do we need to accomplish?
- **Participants:** Who are the essential people to include in order to accomplish the desired results? How will the participants be meaningfully engaged in pursuit of the desired outcomes?
- **Time:** How much time do we need to accomplish the stated outcomes? How much time is available?
- **Methods and tools:** What are the best strategies to use to complete the tasks or achieve the desired results? Which tools are most appropriate for facilitating collaboration focused on the team's common goal?

Purpose

The number-one rule in selecting your meeting format is to determine the purpose of the meeting. If you cannot state the purpose for holding the meeting in a concise and compelling manner, consider an alternative method for communication or decision making. Knowing why the meeting is being held is critical to selecting the appropriate participants, time, and methods and tools needed to achieve the desired outcomes.

Participants

The meeting participants should be individuals who will have a stake in the meeting's outcomes. They will have important ideas to share and contributions to make. They are the people who will most likely be responsible for carrying out the actions or decisions that come out of the meeting process. The complexity of the change the team is considering and the extent to which the participants will be held accountable for the results will help determine who to include.

Time

Meetings vary dramatically in the amount of time teams need to accomplish a given outcome. The two biggest variables affecting the length of a meeting are the magnitude of the change the team is considering and the number of participants involved. Even small, relatively amicable groups will require additional time to understand, process, and ultimately support a significant change. As the size of the group increases, a proportionate increase in the time is needed to build the same level of commitment that a smaller group could achieve.

Methods and Tools

Meetings that incorporate the skillful use of collaborative processes like jigsaw readings, think-pair-share, brainstorming, and the affinity process and tools like decision matrices, flowcharts, and cause-and-effect diagrams are almost always more productive than those that rely solely on one familiar method of meeting—conversation. Collaborative processes engage people in building the logic foundation for the change, provide a forum for sharing ideas and concerns, and equalize the contributions of the individuals involved. The meeting's purpose, levels of participation, and available time will all contribute to the selection of the most appropriate methods and tools for the job. (See chapter 5, page 111, for information about group process and planning tools.)

begins to go off on a tangent, note the issue on the chart paper. Then, get back on track. At the end of the meeting, revisit the page and discuss how to handle the issues listed. There may be some tangents that deserve time and attention on the next meeting agenda.

- **Tangent cop:** If you don't have a facilitator, appoint an individual at the start of each meeting who can help the group be aware when it is going off task. That individual has the authority to call the group back to task.

- **Egg timer:** If the group determines that it is necessary to clarify or explore an issue that is not on the agenda, agree on how much time to devote to the discussion. Use an egg timer or timekeeper to inform the group when the agreed-on time has elapsed. If the issue isn't resolved, the group must decide whether to change the agenda to allow for more discussion (at the expense of other agenda items) or to table the discussion for the time being.

Types of Meetings

Table 4.1 provides an overview of three common meeting formats: (1) turbo meetings, (2) decision-making forums, and (3) dialogue sessions.

Table 4.1: Turbo Meetings, Decision-Making Forums, and Dialogue Sessions

Meeting Elements	Turbo Meetings	Decision-Making Forums	Dialogue Sessions
Purpose	Quickly obtain input on a single topic.	Analyze and resolve a problem or address and plan for a new situation.	Explore meaning and create understanding.
Participants	Anyone with knowledge of or concern about the topic or focus of the meeting	Individuals whom the situation or problem specifically affects or whose work has generated the data	Individuals involved in a significant change or responsible for a broad-based improvement strategy
Time	Limited time—thirty minutes or less	Adequate time—thirty to sixty minutes per meeting (may require several meetings)	Abundant time—blocks of forty-five to ninety minutes
Methods and Tools	Highly structured agenda and use of group process tools to facilitate information gathering such as brainstorming, multivoting, and affinity process	Clearly defined processes focused on a specific problem or data set including a problem-solving process, process-improvement techniques, and data-analysis tools	Neither tight timelines nor specific processes Skillful use of communication techniques such as listening openly, balancing inquiry and advocacy, and actively surfacing assumptions
Desired Outcome	**Action** Next steps, between-meeting work, or an action plan	**Resolution or Plan** A solution to a problem, resolution of an issue, or a plan for addressing the new situation	**Learning** Deep understanding, new perspectives, and new meaning

Turbo Meetings

This meeting format is aptly named *turbo* for its speed and power. Turbo meetings are highly focused on one issue or task, are very structured in terms of time allotments and procedures, and actively engage all of the participants throughout the meeting. Turbo meetings incorporate the use of collaborative processes to keep the team fully engaged, focused, and moving forward. These processes appear in detail in chapter 5 "Group Process and Planning Tools" (page 111). Obviously, not all meetings can or should be turbo. Choose the turbo meeting format when time is limited, input from many stakeholders is desired, and when the outcome will lead to further action or aid in arriving at a next step that will move a group closer to achieving its goal.

Decision-Making Forums

When a school or team needs to solve a problem, resolve an important issue, or create a plan to address a new challenge, it must devote time to fully understanding the problem, issue, or situation from the perspective of all those who are experiencing it. Shared understanding comes through collective inquiry, which is why this format is a good choice when a resolution or solution is needed. In addition to engaging in discussions and analyzing data associated with the problem or situation during this meeting format, the team uses a series of seven steps to move from understanding the problem to identifying and planning the implementation of an agreed-on solution (see chapter 8, page 199). Not all decisions will require a full-blown problem-solving process, but when the decision will have broad-based or systemic impact, taking the time to do it right and engage the appropriate people in the process will facilitate the ultimate success of the plan's implementation.

Dialogue Sessions

Dialogue sessions require more time and skill than typical traditional organizational settings. This format is the best choice when the team faces a complex challenge or when there is notable conflict or resistance associated with a new change initiative. Dialogue sessions provide an opportunity for people to explore their own assumptions and create new perspectives that arise from honest, open exchanges of thought. Though far less structured than either decision-making forums or turbo meetings, dialogue sessions require a skilled facilitator and participant willingness to be completely open with participants' beliefs, perspectives, and knowledge. Dialogue is described in greater detail in chapter 5.

The SMART Meeting Process

A SMART meeting process is based on the PDSA cycle and incorporates the SMART criteria: strategic and specific, measurable, attainable, results oriented, and time bound. SMART meetings can be mapped onto the PDSA wheel as a way to ensure that they are productive and continuously improving. Figure 4.1 illustrates the SMART meeting process.

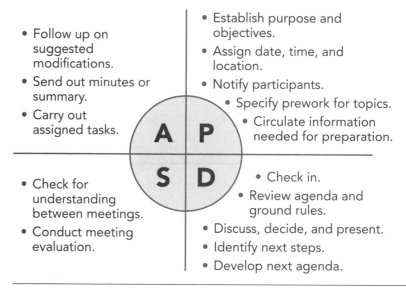

Figure 4.1: SMART meeting process.

The Meeting Plan

Every meeting should have a set of clearly defined steps (plan) that specify the tasks to be completed before, during, and after the meeting (do), including how the meeting will be evaluated (study) and the actions that will be taken (act) to improve the meeting the next time the team gets together. The process begins with the team determining the most appropriate format for the meeting, followed by the development of a plan that incorporates four essential elements: (1) purpose and objectives, (2) logistics, (3) agendas, and (4) communication strategy. The purpose and objectives set the stage for determining the logistics, such as who should attend the meeting, how long the meeting needs to be, the appropriate location for the meeting, and the urgency for scheduling the meeting. The agenda is the meeting map, which specifies the topics that will be addressed, who is responsible for leading each topic, and often, how the team will make decisions or take action on the individual topics. The agenda can also be used as a communication tool to notify participants of their role in the upcoming meeting so they are able to prepare accordingly. It is in this phase of the meeting cycle that any pre-reading or research that will be required is specified and shared.

Purpose and Objectives

Identifying the meeting's specific purpose and objectives (what is this particular meeting about, and what do we need to accomplish?) is the first step in creating the actual meeting plan. This will help the planners decide what the team needs to discuss or decide. Sharing the purpose and objectives with the participants before the meeting helps them know how to plan and prepare to fully participate. Additionally, a detailed plan can help the meeting planners identify whether the whole team needs to be present at the meeting and whether to invite nonmembers.

Logistics

Ongoing teams should standardize the meeting time, date, and location so participants can spend their thinking energy on the content of the group's work and not on the logistics of the next meeting. For example, a school improvement team might decide to meet once a month on the third Tuesday from 3:30–5:00 p.m. in the library. That meeting then becomes a part of each member's normal course of business, and he or she can schedule other activities and committees around it.

For ad hoc or ongoing team meetings, the planners should again think about the purpose and participants of the meeting before selecting the time, date, and location. If the meeting includes parents and community members, it may need to be held outside of normal school hours. The location and meeting environment are especially important if the meeting will require small-group work, audiovisual presentations, flowcharts, other group-process work, or a large number of participants. Let people know the meeting logistics well enough ahead of time so they can plan appropriately (for some participants that might mean months in advance, depending on the nature of their work or family schedules). Before finalizing a date, consider scheduled school and community events and holidays that might coincide with—and therefore compete with—meeting attendance.

Agendas

The meeting agenda is a written plan for how the meeting will happen and what the meeting is expected to accomplish (see figure 4.2). Every meeting, no matter how short or how simple, should have an explicit agenda that communicates the meeting's purpose, topics, time needed, and participants.

Prior to the meeting, participants can use the agenda to plan ahead and come to the meeting prepared. If participants construct the agenda during the meeting, the group can use it to agree on its most important work. Finally, the team uses the agenda throughout the meeting to keep everyone focused, on task, and on time. Refer to the "Meeting Agenda Template" on page 308 of appendix B.

Communication Strategy

An essential element of a meeting plan is how to inform people about the meeting—the purpose and their role. You need to decide how to communicate (email, hardcopy memo, personal communication, and so on), who will communicate, and when to communicate. Email correspondence is often the fastest and easiest way to notify participants. However, if the meeting is to include people from outside the school or district, it is possible that some invitees will not have an email address or that the initiator will not have access to their email addresses. Hardcopy memos can be sent via internal or external mail or sent home with a student. Hardcopy memos take longer, may get lost, and have a cost but are useful in cases where email is not an option. Finally, if it is essential for certain people to attend the meeting, especially if their support for the decisions is critical, we recommend a personal call or visit.

Be thorough in this communication *before* the meeting so that people can come prepared to participate fully. Participants should know what topics will be discussed and whether decisions will be made at the meeting. There should be an agenda, an information packet with key pieces of data or

Constructing an Agenda

To save time, it helps if your team uses a standard agenda format for all meetings. Constructing the agenda simply becomes a process of filling in the appropriate content items. Put the group's most important tasks or items first. Then, if time runs short, the group will have at least accomplished its most important business. Create the agenda for the next meeting at the end of the group's current meeting. This ensures that everyone is involved in setting the agenda and knows what each person's role and responsibilities will be between meetings and at the next meeting.

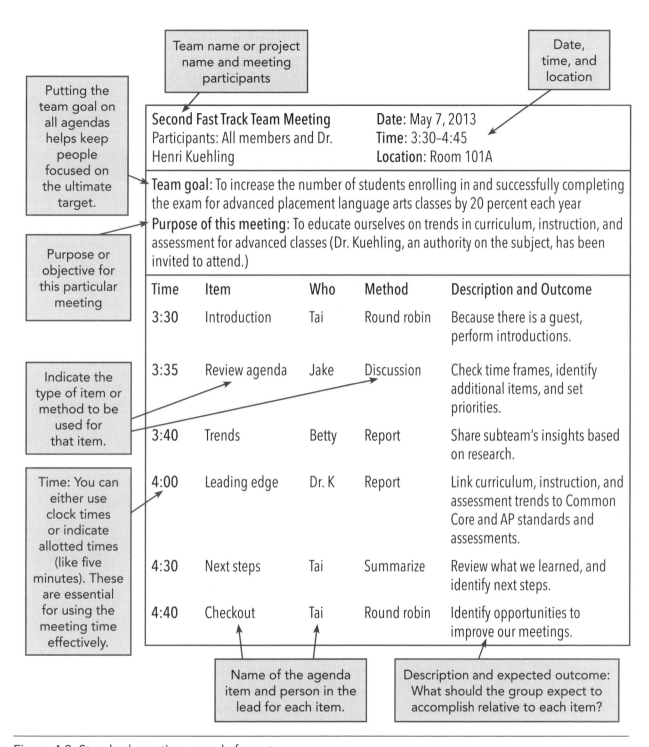

Figure 4.2: Standard meeting agenda format.

background material, and a list of invited participants. If you assign participants specific roles (such as discussion leader or presenter), they deserve a personal call or visit to discuss the nature of the role. This visit should allow them plenty of time to prepare in advance of the meeting.

The Usefulness of Check-Ins

Here are some things you can learn during a check-in.

- "I was up until 3:00 this morning with a sick child." (This person might be impatient, sleepy, or even uninvolved during the meeting.)

- "I have a meeting with a parent right after this meeting and would love it if we could finish just a little early today." (This individual may not be as tolerant of off-task behavior or may be preoccupied with the parent meeting.)

- "I've been looking forward to this meeting, especially the chance to finally decide on the curriculum project participants." (This team member will be disappointed if the agenda item dealing with curriculum is not addressed or decided.)

Simple Rules for Check-Ins

- No discussion, comments, or conversations are allowed during a check-in.

- Keep the check-in short and moving along.

- It is OK for someone to pass rather than make a statement.

The planning phase of the PDSA cycle sets the foundation for an effective meeting. Attending to the four elements (purpose and objectives, logistics, agendas, and communication strategy) in a timely and thorough fashion will bring focus, clarity, and commitment to the next phase of the cycle—actually doing the meeting.

The Meeting Process

Conducting an effective meeting involves following the agenda the planners develop. The designated meeting facilitator guides the team through the meeting, moving through the agenda item by item while also paying attention to pace and participation. The process should lead the team to identify next steps and the agenda for the next meeting. The core of the meeting centers on discussion of agenda content and decisions coming out of the discussion in which all team members have opportunities to contribute. We describe five actions that guide facilitators as they work to ensure that the meetings they lead are effective: (1) check in, (2) review agenda and ground rules, (3) discuss, decide, and present, (4) identify next steps, and (5) develop next agenda.

Check In

The first item on many agendas is a check-in. A check-in signals the official start of the meeting. Each individual makes a brief statement (five to fifteen seconds) about his or her current frame of mind. The check-in helps people settle into the meeting, get focused, discard distractions, and learn about others' situations that may affect behavior during the meeting.

The check-in can have a variety of formats.

- **Round robin:** Move around the table, and allow each person to speak in sequence.
- **Pair and share:** Have people check in with the individual next to them, and then share the other person's check-in.
- **Bean bag:** Have a bean bag or some other small and soft object at the meeting. The person holding the bean bag has the floor, states his or her check-in, and

then passes it on to someone else at the table until each person has had a chance to speak.

- **Speaker picks:** The first person to check in gets to name the next person to speak.

- **Large group:** When the group is quite large, it may take too much time to have everyone check in to the whole group. Instead, have people gather in small groups to check in with each other. Then have one person from each group give a summary or make a statement that reflects the general tenor of the group.

Beginning with a check-in addresses the *people* cornerstone of effective teamwork introduced in chapter 1 (page 19). When individuals feel they are heard and that their personal perspectives and needs are important, they will be far more likely to fully engage in the important work that follows.

Review Agenda and Ground Rules

After the check-in, review the agenda and ground rules. This is especially important if new people are at the meeting.

Reviewing the agenda is another way to achieve focus. It brings everyone's attention to the content of the meeting and provides an opportunity for people to ask for clarification, contribute new items, or discard items that may no longer be necessary. Reviewing the agenda as a whole reminds everyone about the meeting purpose, content, and length. This is important because it helps the group self-regulate. In the process of reviewing the agenda, the group may discover that it has not devoted enough time to a certain item or, conversely, that something has happened since the previous meeting that will make an item less time-consuming (perhaps new information has surfaced or a decision was made).

Reviewing ground rules reminds people of the norms they have agreed to follow. It's not necessary to review them at every meeting, but revisit them periodically, particularly whenever the group senses that it is swaying from its ground rules or if new behaviors emerge as the group develops.

Tips for Effective Agenda Review

During the agenda review, identify a flex item or two on the agenda. A *flex item* is something that the entire group agrees may be eliminated, postponed, or dealt with in a different way if you run out of time at a meeting. Ask individuals to provide additional items if needed or to share information that may change the focus of existing items before the team proceeds further into the agenda. If the time estimates for any item are either not long enough or are unnecessarily generous, this would be the point in the process when adjustments should be made. Finally, check in with individuals who have been assigned or have volunteered for a particular role to make sure each is prepared and clear about what he or she has been asked to do.

Energizing Your Meetings

Each of us comes to the team or group with our own particular needs as a learner and participant. Yet, the vast majority of meeting time is spent in one mode of interaction—discussion. For individuals who are most comfortable expressing themselves or learning from their verbal and auditory channels, this traditional meeting format is just fine. However, that usually doesn't include everyone in the group. Unfortunately, by limiting the interaction to talking, those who learn best through their visual or kinesthetic channels don't fully contribute. The net effect is that we don't gain the full benefit of those people.

Kinesthetic aids help keep participants physically engaged and actively involved in the meeting. These can be actual objects (small, quiet toys or manipulatives) or processes that engage people in physically active ways.

Small objects that people can play with during the meeting can help some people clarify what they are thinking before having to express it verbally. Using the kinesthetic channel helps some people release thoughts from deeper in the subconscious mind, allowing for a more free-flowing expression of ideas. Having something to hold onto or to manipulate during

Continued→

Discuss, Decide, and Present

An underlying goal is to ensure that all members have a chance to participate and contribute. Consequently, the meeting leader needs to ensure that participants engage in discussions that lead to decisions or present information relevant to the content of the agenda. These actions are the meat of the meeting. Devote the majority of the group's time to working on the content and tasks on the agenda. Using different strategies to keep participants engaged and energized is critical to the success of the meeting.

As the team completes each agenda item, have one person summarize key discussion points, decisions, and action items. This summary process helps the group expose discrepancies in how the members interpreted a decision.

Identify Next Steps

One strategy that helps the group feel like it is truly making progress is to have an agenda item devoted to planning the group's next steps. This not only has a positive psychological effect but also keeps the group focused on its future work. Identifying next steps and assignments to be completed between meetings will enhance the group's productivity.

Develop Next Agenda

Developing and recording topics for the *next* meeting's agenda at the end of the current meeting helps the group:

- Feel more ownership in the future agenda
- Know what to expect and better plan for its participation
- See progress

Once the meeting topics have been covered, decisions made and recorded, and action steps identified, the *do* phase of the PDSA cycle is complete but that doesn't mean that the meeting is over. The team conducts the next phase of the PDSA cycle, *study*, before people leave the meeting.

Studying the Meeting Process

Studying the meeting process is an important aspect of building collaborative teamwork and sustaining collegial and cooperative efforts that support teamwork. This process helps leaders gain insight into the strengths and limitations of meetings and determine ways in which the team can strive to improve its performance in meetings. Examining the meeting process can be done informally with a checkout at the end of the meeting or formally through an evaluation.

Checkout

A checkout is conducted just like the check-in, one person at a time, except here the focus is on what just happened in the meeting. A checkout can serve as a meeting evaluation, an opportunity to identify improvements, or a means for individuals to have their final say. It is *not* a time to bring up new items, to challenge decisions, or to rehash meeting topics. The same rules apply as with check-ins.

One useful tool for capturing participants' thoughts and suggestions is to use a T-Chart with one column labeled + (plus) for things that worked well and the other column labeled Δ (delta) for things that need to change in order to improve performance next time. The information can be gathered using round robin, with each person responding in turn or as a quick brainstorming activity.

Evaluation

In addition to checking out, which is an informal evaluation process, groups may want to conduct a formal meeting evaluation. This allows them to track their work progress and their growth as a team. The evaluation can be written or conducted as a structured group process. For example, on a flipchart, draw a line down the middle of the page with a + on the left side and a – (minus) on the right side. Ask each person to identify one strength of the meeting and one thing that could be improved. Record the group's responses on the appropriate side of the line.

Alternatively, you could focus on a few specific issues the group would like to improve. Table 4.2 (page 104) identifies issues that are useful in evaluating meetings.

a meeting can also help keep people from becoming sleepy, especially if the meeting is all talk.

Processes that engage people in a physical activity or some form of creative expression help individuals and groups break out of habitual patterns of thinking. These activities force the mind to consider alternative ways of thinking about a problem or solution. Kinesthetic processes include:

- Drawing a picture of a situation rather than simply talking about it

- Writing down brainstormed ideas before collecting them as a group (brainwriting)

- Role playing a situation or a potential implementation strategy

- Displaying the group's work on chart paper posted around the room and having people walk around the room, writing comments, suggestions, or compliments on sticky notes (walkabouts)

- Constructing artifacts or models

- Writing and presenting a solution via poem, song, or skit

Visit **go.solution-tree.com /schoolimprovement** for more resources about kinesthetic learner techniques for both adults and students.

Examples of Useful Checkouts

- "This was a good meeting. We stayed on time and accomplished everything we set out to do." (Evaluation)

- "I thought we spent way too much time on the bus situation." (Evaluation)

- "I would suggest that the next time we get together, someone be responsible for watching the time, so we don't end up hurried at the end." (Suggested improvement)

- "I just want to say I'm really glad we decided to go with the reading goal." (Individual commitment)

Table 4.2: Topics and Sample Questions for Evaluating Meetings

Meeting Evaluation Topics	Sample Evaluation Questions
Balance of Participation	Did you feel like you had a chance to voice your opinions and to participate? Did the meeting facilitator or others encourage everyone to participate?
Timeliness	Did we start and end on time? Did we manage our time effectively?
Success in Meeting the Objectives	Did we meet our objectives?
Focus	Did we stay on focus? Did we allow too many side discussions?
Adherence to Ground Rules	Which ground rules, if any, do you think were violated?
Clarity of Decisions Made	Do you think we're clear on what decisions were made? Do you think we all share a common understanding of the decisions?
Logistic Concerns	Did the meeting space work well? Were the resources needed for the meeting readily available or easy to access?

A "Meeting Evaluation Form" can be found in appendix B on page 309.

Action Between Meetings

Checking with people between meetings is a good way to keep momentum and to correct miscommunications. The team leader can simply email, call, or stop by to meet with a few team members and ask for their understanding about what took place or was decided during the meeting. This is also a good way to support people in completing their assignments and to communicate the importance of what they are doing.

The action part of the PDSA cycle is absolutely critical to the team's success. If people are well-informed, have been active participants on the team, and are committed to the team's task and purpose, action should not be a problem. However, if people are overcommitted or unclear about the work expected of them, the group can become stuck. Future meetings will be a waste of time if people come unprepared.

Between meetings, help your team with the following actions.

- **Act on ideas for improvement:** Follow through on decisions, modifications, or improvements that the team identified or suggested at the meeting.
- **Carry out assigned tasks:** It is each individual's responsibility to carry out his or her assigned tasks and ask for assistance and clarification if needed. A good team leader will provide gentle reminders and helpful suggestions as a way to support the work of the team.
- **Send out minutes or a summary:** Circulate the meeting record or summary of key points and decisions as soon after the meeting as possible.

The action phase completes the PDSA cycle, which starts up again as the team incorporates its between-meeting work into the planning phase for the next meeting. The cycle continues to inform and improve the ongoing collaborative work of the team.

Meeting Records

Meeting records are essential to effective teams because they document key meeting activities. A meeting record is *not* the same as detailed meeting notes; typically they are brief (one or two pages) summaries of decisions, actions, assignments, and issues.

Use a standardized format to make meeting records easy to complete and read. Consider the following suggestions.

- Put the times, dates, and location of future meetings on the first page for easy access.
- Identify meeting participants and their roles for the upcoming meeting on the first page.

- Keep track of key discussion topics and decisions.
- Keep track of assignments and who is responsible.
- Keep track of side issues that come up during the meeting and address them as necessary.
- Keep the meeting record as a template on your laptop or tablet and fill it in as you go. Then it will be ready to be sent electronically or printed for distribution immediately after the meeting.
- If distributing hard copies, use the same bright-colored paper for the front page every time. That way, it will stand out in a participant's mailbox and people will automatically know that it is the meeting record for that particular team.

Meeting records are best kept in real time as the meeting occurs. Periodically, throughout the meeting, the individual who is keeping the record will want to share what he or she is capturing to make sure it is accurate and complete. This is particularly important when documenting the team's decisions. Meeting records serve as important reminders down the road as busy schedules and distractions interfere with collective memories about what the team decided during the meeting. Look for the "Meeting Record" template in appendix B on page 310.

Managing Team Meetings

Much of a team's collaborative work time will be spent in meetings (though equal emphasis should be placed on what happens *between* meetings). Your meetings will be more effective if you have clearly defined meeting roles; use PDSA (plan, do, study, and act) to plan, conduct, and improve the meetings; and keep useful meeting notes.

Functional Roles for Effective Meetings

Think about meetings you've attended that went well and those that were a waste of time. In all likelihood, a big difference in the effective meetings was that people had specific responsibilities to manage different aspects of the meeting. Although the individual designated to lead the meeting has a prominent role in making the meeting work, all the participants can play a part in helping to facilitate the meeting process. Use the "Meeting Skills Self-Assessment" (page 311) to discover strengths of your team members, and identify skill areas for development.

When meetings are going well, people are engaged in the content—paying attention to the *what* of the meeting. However, every team runs into situations where it helps to have someone paying attention to the *how*: the methods the team is using to conduct the meeting. *Facilitation* is the skill associated with guiding how a team works together.

Even if your team has access to an expert facilitator, every team member can and should develop some skill with basic facilitation. For example, if the team is stuck on a particular discussion point or issue, any team member could suggest that the team take a break or even lead the team through an activity that lets participants address the issue through a different approach. (Use the list of meeting techniques on page 112 that increase cohesiveness to help identify some alternative methods.) This way, team members take on a shared responsibility for making sure the team is using the most effective methods for achieving its goals.

Facilitation also includes paying attention to participation, making sure that all members have a chance to contribute, perhaps by using structured discussion techniques (such as round robin) when appropriate. The more that your team members become familiar with alternative group methods, the more effective you will be.

However, having access to a trained facilitator is sometimes invaluable, such as when dealing with particularly challenging issues or situations. Usually it is easier for a neutral third party to guide discussions and help the group work through strong conflict.

In addition to a facilitator, three other roles—timekeeper, record keeper, and scribe—are instrumental in contributing to the effectiveness of the meeting. Table 4.3 (page 108) describes these four roles.

Managing meetings is not something educators learn in their preservice training and yet it is a critical skill for maximizing collaboration and teamwork. When everyone in the meeting knows what to expect, contributes positively

Coordinating the Functions of Team Leader and Meeting Facilitator

When a team first begins to meet, the team leader often also serves as the meeting facilitator. However, rotating the role of meeting facilitator is a great way to build shared responsibility within the team. These two functions can be separated easily.

1. The meeting facilitator guides the meeting—moving the group through the agenda, making sure the group starts and ends on time, and so on.

2. The team leader guides the team, part of which includes doing the prework needed to make sure meetings will be effective (distributing the agenda and communicating with meeting participants ahead of time to make sure they are prepared).

The meeting facilitator needs to know what is expected from the meeting, so he or she usually works closely with the team leader to develop the agenda.

Table 4.3: Facilitator, Timekeeper, Record Keeper, and Scribe Roles

Role	Definition	Actions
Facilitator	The facilitator's job is to guide the group through the agenda. This role focuses on managing the meeting process and ensuring that the meeting participants are doing the talking and making the decisions. The designated meeting leader has responsibility for facilitating the meeting. However, the team can hire a trained facilitator.	The facilitator ensures that the team implements the actions in the *do* part of the PDSA cycle. In addition to routine matters such as starting the meeting on time, guiding the check-in, introducing each item on the agenda, and closing the meeting, the facilitator has special responsibility for: • Helping guide the discussion by asking participants to contribute • Leading group activities associated with any agenda item (for example, brainstorming and multivoting) • Involving the group in summarizing decisions, actions, and questions about each agenda item so that the group can move to the next item
Time-keeper	The timekeeper's job is to help the team make deliberate decisions about how it spends its limited meeting time. This role ensures effective management of the team's time and prevents the team from this kind of situation: "Our time is up, and we still have three issues to discuss!"	The timekeeper alerts the group when it's getting close to the time limits set for each agenda item and asks the group to decide whether to continue discussion or move on. For example, "We have another five minutes for this discussion, but it doesn't look like we are close to making a decision. Should we continue the discussion now and move another agenda item to the next meeting, or defer this discussion to later?" In this case, if the team is not in immediate agreement about how to respond, the timekeeper turns the decision over to the facilitator to provide a process for the team to decide.
Record Keeper	The record keeper maintains a record of key decisions made, issues left unresolved, and a summary of discussions on each agenda item.	The record keeper uses a standard, concise format the team developed. The format includes who was in attendance and their roles, the content of discussions and decisions for each agenda item, the items the scribe recorded during the meeting, and the assignments to be completed between meetings and who is responsible for each. A sample meeting record format is in appendix B (page 310). The record keeper reviews the decisions made and the assignment list with the team at the end of the meeting. The record keeper is responsible for sending the document out to the team members as soon as possible following the meeting.
Scribe	The scribe keeps a visual representation of the discussion in front of the group during the meeting.	The scribe records brainstorming or other verbal contributions, including the responses to the meeting evaluation process at the end of the meeting, on a flipchart or whiteboard.

throughout the meeting, participates fully by taking on meeting roles, and commits to taking responsibility for coming to the meeting with assignments completed, the experience can be both productive and enjoyable.

Final Check: Tools for Productive Meetings

Running an effective meeting begins well before the meeting starts and continues after the meeting has ended. Managing the time, skills, and talents of all those who are participating in the meeting is a skill set that can be learned and improved with practice. The following checklist will help new and seasoned meeting leaders be increasingly successful in running great meetings.

- ☐ The team has selected the most appropriate meeting format for achieving its goals.
- ☐ The team carefully plans and adheres to meeting agendas on a consistent basis.
- ☐ All participants fully engage in the meeting.
- ☐ All meeting participants contribute to improving the meeting process on a continuous basis.
- ☐ The facilitator leads a process for the team to define and commit to functional roles.
- ☐ The facilitator leads a process for rotating the roles on a regular basis.
- ☐ The scribe records brainstorming or other verbal contributions on a flipchart or whiteboard.
- ☐ The record keeper documents important meeting discussions and decisions and distributes the record after each meeting.

CHAPTER 5

Group Process and Planning Tools

SMART teams are skilled in an array of tools and methods that allow them to work effectively and work together effectively. Indeed, their ability to incorporate collaborative tools into their work leads to more efficient use of time and high-quality work that is completed within time limits. Teams can easily incorporate the three cornerstones of productive collaboration when everyone on the team is familiar with the appropriate methods and tools. When using such methods and tools frequently, teams gain confidence in their ability to tackle even the most difficult and complex tasks.

This chapter addresses three different types of process and planning tools that are useful in a wide range of situations.

1. **Group process tools:** These tools help enrich team members' understanding of a problem, their creative thinking about problems and solutions, and their ability to address issues at deep levels.

2. **Process-mapping tools:** These tools help groups understand and improve work processes and systems.

3. **Planning tools:** These tools help teams imagine, from start to finish, the tasks they will need to accomplish in order to complete projects and initiatives.

What these tools have in common is their ability to help teams bring *structure* to their work—to the interactions within the team and cohesiveness within the project as a whole.

> Until you are willing to be confused about what you already know, what you know will never become wider, bigger or deeper.
>
> —Milton Erickson

Group Process Tools

Group process is a term that refers to the methods and approaches a team uses to accomplish its work. We discuss six group tools in this section: (1) dialogue, (2) brainstorming, (3) affinity diagrams, (4) multivoting, (5) decision matrices, and (6) consensus decision making.

With the exception of dialogue, each of these tools relies on the use of visual organization tools such as sticky notes, flipcharts, and whiteboards. When people can collectively *see* what they are creating together, their ability to think and learn together is enhanced, and time flows more productively.

As a whole, group process tools help team members organize their thinking, discuss difficult topics, better understand problems at their deepest level, and think creatively about how to solve problems.

Dialogue

Dialogue is a true conversation in which talking and listening by all parties create a flow of meaning among, between, and through a group. Out of dialogue emerges a new and shared understanding. Dialogue is a tool for collective exploration of meaning—not a search for the right, wrong, or best solution. The process adds structure to a team's discussion that can lead to a deeper or broader understanding of an issue. Table 5.1 describes essential features of dialogue.

Advocacy means seeking to make our thinking and reasoning visible to others as we test our assumptions and conclusions. On the other hand, inquiry means asking others to make their thinking visible as we compare our assumptions to theirs. Table 5.2 (page 114) defines advocacy and inquiry elements of dialogue-based conversations.

Brainstorming

Brainstorming is a group activity to stimulate creativity and bring out diverse perspectives in a short period of time. It is an excellent way to equalize participation and build collective motivation. Brainstorming is especially useful for gathering a large quantity of ideas to add value to the team's work. The activity encourages people to think out of

Tips for Successful Dialogue

- Be as personal as possible. Speak from your personal point of view.

- Replace seeking resolution with living in and working through the question.

- Allow each person the time and space to reflect, to speak with silence.

- Suspend your assumptions and allow others to question them.

- Perceive disagreement as an opportunity to learn and as a sign that this is a place to dig deeper.

- Remain self-aware so that you can consciously use your feelings and perceptions as a resource.

- Respect different points of view as every bit as valid as your own.

Table 5.1: Dialogue Features and Practices

Features	Practices
Applications	• Help a team get unstuck from a complex problem and resolve conflicts. • Help generate a broad range of ideas when creating values-based visions or setting core values or guiding principles for a school. • Develop results-oriented goals. • Discuss with colleagues the quality of student work and inquire into the meaning of student results. • Develop innovative programs.
Skills	• Understand the difference between advocacy and inquiry. • Understand that advocacy and inquiry are complementary skills. • Use both advocacy and inquiry during discussions of difficult or complex issues.

the box. To ensure that brainstorming sessions are productive, the team needs to follow established guidelines, pose a question to the group, and record all ideas generated in full view of the group. Table 5.3 (page 115) describes applications, guidelines, and procedures for brainstorming sessions.

Affinity Diagrams

An affinity diagram is a tool for organizing brainstormed lists into like categories—things that have an affinity for each other. This tool is useful when you want to involve an entire group in organizing and consolidating many ideas. In this context, developing an affinity diagram serves to:

- Help articulate elements of a vision
- Organize ideas for problem solving
- Group ideas into categories before multivoting
- Organize statements from interviews or focus groups

Tips for Successful Brainstorming Sessions

- Brainstorming works best with relatively small groups. If you have a large group (more than ten to twelve people), break into smaller groups of no more than five or six people.

- Give the group a clear objective or focus question; otherwise, you may end up with answers that are too diverse to be useful.

Table 5.2: Advocacy and Inquiry Elements of Dialogue-Based Conversations

Advocacy	Inquiry
Make your thinking and reasoning visible. <ul><li>State your assumptions: "Here's what I think, and here's how I got there . . ."</li><li>Describe your reasoning: "I came to this conclusion because . . ."</li><li>Distinguish data from interpretation: "These are the data I have as objectively as I can state them. Now here is what I think the data mean."</li><li>Explain the context: "What I propose will affect several groups, and here is how . . ."</li><li>Give examples: "To get a clear picture, imagine that you are in School X . . ."</li></ul>	**Ask others to make their thinking visible.** <ul><li>Gently walk others down the ladder of inference: "What leads you to that conclusion? What data do you have for that?"</li><li>Use unaggressive language and an approachable voice: "Can you help me understand your thinking here?"</li><li>Draw out their reasoning: "What is the significance of that? How does this relate to your other concerns? Where does your reasoning go next?"</li><li>Explain your reasons for inquiring: "I'm asking about your assumptions here because . . ."</li><li>Invite introspection: "What questions do you have about your thinking?"</li></ul>
Test your assumptions and conclusions. <ul><li>Encourage others to explore your model, assumptions, and data: "What do you think about what I just said? Do you see any flaws in my reasoning? What can you add?"</li><li>Reveal where you are least clear: "Here's one area you might help me think through . . ."</li><li>Stay open, and encourage others to provide different views: "Do you see it differently?"</li><li>Search for distortions, deletions, and generalizations: "In what I've presented, do you believe I might have overgeneralized, left out data, or reported data incorrectly?"</li></ul>	**Compare your assumptions to theirs.** <ul><li>Investigate other assumptions: "Would we be willing to each list our assumptions, compare them, and explore if there might be other assumptions surrounding this issue?"</li><li>Check your understanding of what they have said by paraphrasing and probing: "Am I correct that you are saying . . . ?"</li><li>Test what they say by asking for broader contexts or examples: "How would your proposal affect . . . Is this similar to . . . Can you describe a typical example?"</li><li>Reveal your listening processes: "I have been listening for themes. So far I've heard two. Are there others?"</li></ul>

Source: Adapted from Garmston & Wellman, 1999, pp. 46–49.

Table 5.3: Brainstorming Applications, Guidelines, and Procedures

Features	Practices
Applications	Teams can use brainstorming: • As a first step in developing a shared vision as people post their individual ideas, and the group discusses them as a whole • To create a list of solutions when problem solving • To identify steps when mapping a process
Guidelines	In a brainstorming session: • There's no such thing as a bad idea • Quantity of ideas is more important than quality • There is no evaluation or criticism of ideas • Thinking out of the box (freewheeling) is encouraged • Everyone has an opportunity to participate • Building off the ideas of others is encouraged
Procedures	Procedures for successful brainstorming are the following. • **Silent thinking time:** Allow a minute for silent reflection before brainstorming begins. • **Sticky notes:** Each participant records ideas on sticky notes (one idea per note) instead of having a scribe write them on a flipchart or whiteboard. Having ideas written on sticky notes makes sorting and organizing easier and also ensures anonymity. • **Popcorn:** Individuals call out their ideas in any order. A scribe records the ideas on a flipchart or whiteboard. • **Round robin:** Individuals say ideas in turn, one at a time, around the group, until all ideas are out and recorded. • **Brainwriting:** Individuals write one idea on a sheet of paper and then put the paper in the middle of the table and take someone else's paper; they continue to add ideas and build off of what's already written.

Tips for Creating Successful Affinity Diagrams

- Work in small groups (five or six people).

- The facilitator may need to give a few gentle reminders to remain silent. (Not being able to talk during the categorization step may frustrate some people.)

- The emergence of a group-defined organizational structure is what makes this process powerful. Random placement of the notes on the chart paper followed by the team working together to group ideas by categories as they emerge prevents people from assuming they already know the answers.

- Reassure participants that this is an opportunity for people who are not as comfortable talking to really participate on an equal basis with those who are more verbally confident.

The affinity process has six steps, which teams can modify to suit their purpose.

1. Use brainstorming to generate a list of ideas. Have people write ideas on sticky notes. The ideas should be concise and written clearly but large enough so that someone standing several feet away can read the ideas.

2. After brainstorming, have people post their notes *randomly* on a large sheet of paper.

3. Instruct people to start sorting the notes into groups or categories. This is a silent activity, so there shouldn't be any talking during the categorization process. Anyone can move a note into any category. Teams can move notes from category to category—it's OK to move them around several times until a category that makes sense to the whole group emerges. Place orphans (single notes unlike any others) off to the side.

4. Once there appears to be general agreement among the participants about the categories, allow members to start talking.

5. Finalize the categories—discussion may change some of the initial groupings.

6. As a group, write a succinct, concrete phrase that captures the theme or central idea for each cluster of ideas. Write this theme on a header card (a larger sticky note you place immediately above the cluster).

Teams can use affinity diagrams to analyze any language data, such as interview or focus group notes. In those cases, teams select the statements for the affinity exercise from the notes or transcripts, not from a brainstorm. To do this well, first identify the key questions you want answered. Then have team members go through the notes or transcripts and highlight any statements they think relate to the key question. Transcribe these statements onto sticky notes and begin the affinity process.

The affinity diagram example (figure 5.1) shows how a brainstormed list of ideas generated by a complex question, "What do we need to address in our SMART implementation plan?" is easier to digest when the ideas are grouped into like categories.

The affinity diagram process is a simple, efficient way to group lots of ideas. Next steps could include (depending on

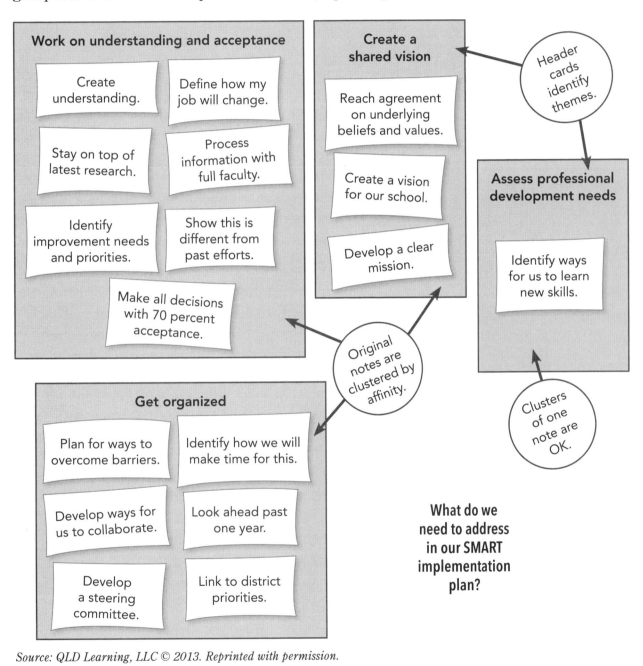

Source: QLD Learning, LLC © 2013. Reprinted with permission.

Figure 5.1: Affinity diagram example.

the situation) prioritizing the categories by importance, creating an action plan, or digging into root causes of problems.

Multivoting

Multivoting is a method for narrowing down and prioritizing lists of ideas when there are too many ideas to decide which ones to focus on. It's a useful method that enables teams to:

- Prioritize which gaps are most important to focus on when identifying strategic priorities

- Determine which goals are most worthy of pursuit

- Decide which strategies are most worth investing in

Multivoting starts with brainstorming or some other method of generating a list of ideas or options for a particular issue. Scribing for the group, a team member records the ideas on a flipchart or whiteboard in full view of the group. You will need a collection of colored sticky dots for team members to use to indicate their votes. The following six steps organize the voting process.

1. Determine how many votes each group member will receive. Divide the number of items by three and round up to the nearest whole number. That is how many votes to give each person. For example, if there are twenty-nine items on your list, each member gets ten votes.

2. Distribute colored sticky dots (one color) to the group. Each person should get as many dots as there are votes.

3. Have people place their dots next to the ideas they favor most. Votes can be distributed one per idea or, if the group agrees, can be loaded up (that is, any individual can place two or more of their dots on one item).

4. After teammates have distributed their dots, refine your list by eliminating any items that received no votes at all or only a few votes.

5. If the refined list still has too many items for the group to reasonably handle or address, repeat the process. Count the number of items on the reduced

list and divide by three. That's how many votes that people will have in the next round. Distribute colored sticky dots (a different color) and have people revote.

6. Continue multivoting until the final priorities reach a manageable number.

Instead of using colored sticky dots, you can record ideas on a flipchart and number them. Individuals vote by writing down the numbers of the ideas they prefer on index cards or separate sheets of paper.

Multivoting is an easy and visual way to make decisions quickly as a group, while honoring each individual member's opinions and ideas. Multivoting should always be accompanied by discussion to ensure that everyone is on board with the final decision.

Decision Matrices

A decision matrix is a table in which teams score alternative decision options against criteria. It's a useful tool that enables you to move from a list of options to a final decision, to simultaneously assess multiple options against multiple criteria, and to compare options in a relatively objective and unemotional way.

Developing a decision matrix follows a multivoting activity to identify the top five to ten ideas from a brainstormed list. These ideas are recorded on the left side of a flipchart page that contains a matrix next to the list of ideas. The following steps guide the team in building the matrix.

1. Identify criteria important to the group (numbers of students served, cost, ease of implementation, effectiveness, time allotted, importance to the mission, and so on).

2. Score each idea against each of the criteria (if you have five ideas and four criteria, you will be coming up with twenty scores). Use a scale of 0 to 5 where 0 means that a particular criterion is not met at all and 5 means it is fully met.

Tips

- Let people know that they can cast all their sticky dot votes on one idea; they don't have to distribute votes across all ideas.

- Discourage *split votes* (tearing the dots in half) or *vote selling* (giving others your sticky dots).

- If there are more than twelve to fifteen items to vote on, consider dividing the list and voting on items from each list separately.

- Create a one-page chart to show the vote totals. Have one member of the team add up all the votes for each item and post it on the chart.

- Leave time for a full discussion after the vote so that everyone who voted understands and can support the final vote totals, even if members didn't get their first choices.

- If there are clearly big differences between high and low votes (one or two items get a majority of votes, while a clear minority prefers a different couple of items), consider voting again after a discussion.

Tips for Creating a Decision Matrix

- Agree ahead of time on what the scale (ratings) means so that there is consistency in scoring the ideas. Some scoring options include:

  - 1-2-3 scores to indicate strength of their correlation to the various ideas being considered

  - Rank order from most to least; in figure 5.2, the four goals would have been rank ordered for each criteria—for the criteria "staff support," the goal "improve reading" would have received a 4, with the other goals scoring 3, 2, and 1.

- It's easier to work vertically through the table (by criteria) than horizontally (by option). That is, start with one criterion and score all options against that criterion. Then move on to the next criterion and again work through all options (as opposed to picking one option and scoring it against all the criteria, then moving to the next option, and so on).

3. Total the score for each idea by adding the scores for each criterion. Those with the highest scores best meet your stated criteria.

4. If some criteria are much more important than others, you may want to weight the criteria. This adds extra complexity to the process, so use weighting judiciously. To start, assign each criterion a value from, say, 1 to 5, where 5 is very important (for example, if cost is most important, it gets a weight factor of 5; perhaps simplicity is less important and gets a factor of 2). Then multiply each score against the weight for that criterion. Add up the weighted ratings for one idea to get a total weighted score for that idea.

5. Discuss the highest-ranking items and choose among them or modify them in ways that may capture the best of several items.

Figure 5.2 is an example of a decision matrix. You can find a reproducible template for the decision matrix in appendix B on page 313. It illustrates how teams can use the matrix to evaluate potential solutions as well as consider alternative data-gathering strategies. In this matrix, team members scored an item a 1 if they felt the criterion was weak for that goal, a 2 if it was moderately strong, and a 3 if it was strong. For example, the criterion "great impact on student learning" was only rated strong for the goal "improve reading"; for all other goals, it was rated weak.

Decision matrices are a relatively quick and easy way to assess the strength of each option based on the criteria that are relevant to the options. As with all decision-making tools, it's important to allow time for group discussion after the vote to ensure that everyone is on board with the final decision.

Consensus Decision Making

Consensus exists when everyone on the team feels that he or she can support the decision, even if it is not his or her preferred option. It is not a majority vote. In this process, it is important that everyone in a group supports a decision, both publicly and privately. Teams can use consensus decision

Goals	Criteria			Total Score (Add each row of scores.)
	Staff Support	Community Support	Great Impact on Student Learning	
Improve safety.	1	2	1	4
Involve families more.	1	1	1	3
Improve reading.	3	3	3	9
Integrate technology.	1	2	1	4

Source: QLD Learning, LLC © 2013. Reprinted with permission.

Figure 5.2: Decision matrix example.

making in a number of situations including choosing the final option or solution to implement, agreeing on ground rules and team roles, and determining implementation strategies.

The procedure for consensus decision making is a reiterative process that begins with making sure that everyone is clear about the decision to make and that everyone agrees on the most important aspects of the decision and set criteria. For example, the opening statement might be: "We are here to decide which curriculum proposal we will support." The next statement clarifies the parameters of the decision: "The option has to be realistically accomplished in six months and reach a minimum of 50 percent of the student body." Throughout the discussion, participants have opportunities to review their progress toward consensus.

These five steps illustrate the consensus decision-making process.

1. Using dialogue skills, the team discusses and weighs the potential consequences of each option, both positive and negative. Team members discuss

Tips for Successful Consensus Decision Making

- If your team is unfamiliar with consensus, make sure everyone knows what *consensus* means and agrees that it is the best method to use.

- Make sure everyone is aware of the timeline for making a decision. Discuss what to do if time runs out and the team has not reached consensus.

- People tend to take the word *consensus* very seriously. They have high expectations for what it means in terms of broad participation in reaching the decision and listening to all viewpoints. Since *consensus* is not the same as a *majority vote*, don't call a decision *consensus* if you really mean you just want a majority of support from the group. People will be upset if they believe the group is going to work toward consensus but then find out that a majority vote decides the final option. (This is why it is important for a group to discuss how it will make a decision before it makes one.)

Continued➔

the extent of the impact of the consequences on individuals and on the district, school, department, or grade level.

2. The designated meeting leader or facilitator does a quick check to see if the group is near consensus. Quick checks help a group evaluate its progress toward consensus. They can also prevent needless discussion by demonstrating when a team has reached consensus and can therefore move on.

3. If there is no single option that gets broad-level support, the group continues the discussion, dialogue, and exploration of options. This process continues until the group believes it has reached consensus. Periodic quick checks throughout these ongoing discussions enable the group to stay focused and advance toward a final decision.

4. When you are fairly sure the team has reached consensus, have a team member write down a statement he or she believes captures the group's decision.

5. In a final consensus check, the group reviews the decision and indicates its support by responding to this question: Do you feel you can support this decision both inside and outside the group? At this point, the meeting leader has a choice of activities in which group members can indicate their level of commitment to the decision.

Figure 5.3 describes *fist-to-five*, a strategy a team leader can use to check the team members' level of commitment to the decision.

Figure 5.4 describes *round robin*, another activity teams can use to determine the level of commitment to the decision.

The consensus process is beneficial when it's important that every member of the team is comfortable with the decision. This is particularly true when a decision will impact many people and carries a degree of risk. Consensus decision making requires an investment of time and effort, and a

Fist-to-five is a quick strategy teams can use to check agreement with a proposed solution or concept. After you have restated or written down the pending decision, ask group members to indicate their level of support by the number of fingers that correspond to their position. If anyone holds up a fist, or only one or two fingers, the group has not reached consensus. You will need more discussion or dialogue. If you get all three, four, or five fingers showing, you can declare consensus.

- **Five fingers:** I'm all for the idea. I can be a leader for this decision.
- **Four fingers:** I'm for the idea. You can count on me to provide support.
- **Three fingers:** I'm not sure, but I am willing to trust the group's opinion.
- **Two fingers:** I'm not sure. But I trust the group's opinion and will not sabotage the decision.
- **One finger:** I can't support it at this time. I need more information.
- **Zero fingers (fist):** No. We need to find an alternative.

Figure 5.3: Fist-to-five strategy for consensus decision making.

Round robin is an alternative activity that groups can use to reach consensus. There is no discussion during this process. The purpose is to make sure that each person gets a chance to state an opinion and reasons with everyone else listening.

The steps in this activity are the following.

1. Go around the group one by one.
2. Each person states his or her vote. Do not allow any explanation at this point. This is a quick-moving check-in during which people say things like "Option A," "Yes," or "I don't know enough to decide."
3. After the group completes the first round, it does a second round during which people give one or two reasons behind their thinking. Again, this is a quick check, so it's important to keep things moving.
4. The meeting leader or other team member summarizes the results. For example, "We agree that the two options based on current curriculum are best but aren't close yet in choosing between those two."
5. The round robin process continues until the group achieves consensus.

Figure 5.4: Round robin for consensus decision making.

- Develop and use a process for arriving at alternative options for the group to explore.
- Use a variety of techniques such as brainstorming, affinity work, and discussions.
- Allocate time for gathering or finding relevant data and research whenever possible.
- After the team reaches a decision, check to make sure that people believe that the integrity of the process that was agreed on was maintained. Use the outcome of this discussion for future improvements in the group's consensus process.

Example of Consensus Building on Profound Issues

Staff in a large high school are upset about the changes a new principal insists are necessary, including a review of all current curriculum to see how it aligns (or doesn't) with core academic standards. Staff members aren't opposing the work outright, but they are venting their feelings to each other outside of meetings and in the parking lot. In meetings, they cross their arms and rarely speak up; they refuse to volunteer for work. The principal asks a neutral facilitator to guide the group through the consensus-building process.

After reviewing the purpose and guidelines, the facilitator divides the 120 staff members into groups of five. In several rounds of conversation, they read through index cards that pose the consensus-building questions. The principal and other administrators are separated and randomly distributed into the small groups, so their voices are also heard. The facilitator stays out of the process, walking around the room, listening. When all the groups are done, they report their ideas for solutions (step five in the process), which are captured on flipcharts.

Continued➜

willingness to listen to many perspectives, but the final result is almost always better than at the beginning of the process because everyone has had an opportunity to reflect deeply on the issue at hand.

If people have been unable to resolve an issue, or there's a history of not talking about what's really going on, you may want to consider a more powerful form of decision-making consensus. Bob Chadwick (2013) developed a process for consensus building on profound issues. It is a way to get people talking about the things that matter to them in real and honest dialogue. It is also a method for uncovering basic beliefs, sharing feelings (as important as thoughts), and working through conflict. Figure 5.5 describes the process for consensus building on profound issues. Note that this process is almost entirely verbal—there are no flipcharts, sticky notes, pens, or markers involved. The purpose of the process is to get people speaking directly to each other in an open, heartfelt, honest way. The facilitator's role is simply to guide the process and not to intervene in any way.

Guidelines

- Establish verbal territory (speak in turn for as long as each person needs).
- Listen with respect (make eye contact, do not interrupt, and remember what the speaker says).
- Use your whole brain to listen and problem solve (the thinking and the feeling brain).

Time

- Four to sixteen hours

Process

1. To set up, sit in chairs facing each other in a circle; no tables or paper and pencils as these can act as distractions or even as barriers between people.
2. Establish grounding. ("Get your voice in the room.")
   - Introduce yourself and your relationship to the issue or problem. For example, my name is Jan, and I am not directly involved in the conflict we're having in our school, but I do hear about it from time to time in the faculty lounge.
   - What are your expectations for the session?
   - How do you feel about being here?

3. Frame the issue; develop details of the issue or problem.

- What is the issue from your point of view? How do you feel about it?

4. Engage in possibility thinking.

- What are the worst possible outcomes of not resolving the issue or problem?
- What are the best possible outcomes of resolving the issue or problem?

5. Generate solutions.

- What new beliefs or behaviors will foster the best outcomes?
- What new strategies or actions within your circle of control or influence will foster the best outcomes?

6. Talk about issues and solutions (steps three to five) one by one in the circle, speaking in turn and balancing participation. If a woman spoke the first time, start next time with a man. If you went around the group clockwise the first time, go around the group counterclockwise the next time. Continue the discussion until areas of consensus start to naturally arise.

7. Use a closing.

- How did you feel about the session?
- What did you learn that would help us resolve the issue or problem?

To conclude the session, all 120 staff members sit in a large circle and one by one share how they feel about the process and what they have learned. A small group of teachers and administrators then volunteer to lead the core curriculum review process with the built-in accountability that they will continually check back with the larger group to make sure the work is achieving the best possible outcomes using the strategies people have identified during the consensus-building activity.

Source: Adapted from Chadwick, 2013. Used with permission from personal communication with A. Rodgers-Rhyme, 2001.

Figure 5.5: Process for consensus building on profound issues.

Group process tools, like the affinity diagram, multivoting, decision matrices, and consensus, can help groups work together much more productively and even increase their level of fun! While it sometimes may seem to slow down a group's work, a good process tool can address many overwhelming problems and issues—if not easily at least with rationality and a degree of ease. You'll discover that the end results are almost always better when using the process tool.

Process-Mapping Tools

Process-mapping tools help teams see processes and systems—the way activities flow in sequence and the way

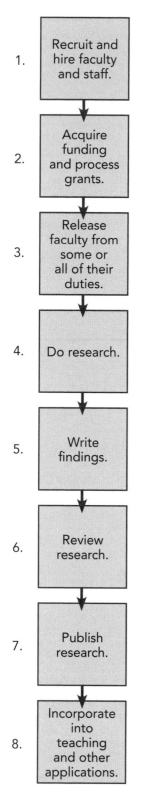

1. Recruit and hire faculty and staff.

2. Acquire funding and process grants.

3. Release faculty from some or all of their duties.

4. Do research.

5. Write findings.

6. Review research.

7. Publish research.

8. Incorporate into teaching and other applications.

Source: QLD Learning, LLC © 2013. Reprinted with permission.

Figure 5.6: Sample basic flowchart for grant-funded research.

roles and responsibilities interact. Flowcharts are the tool of choice here. Because they are created through a collaborative process using highly visual techniques, all team members have a chance to contribute their ideas. Process-mapping tools have many applications, including:

- Describing how processes currently work
- Describing how an improved process will work
- Clarifying roles and responsibilities
- Planning a project

We describe four main types of flowcharts to use with process mapping: (1) basic, (2) top down, (3) deployment, and (4) detailed.

Basic Flowchart

A basic flowchart is a visual high-level picture of how work or activities generally flow in sequence in a process or system. (See figure 5.6.) Teams can use it for an aerial picture of a system or process—one without a lot of detail. This type of flowchart is useful when planning major steps in a process or activity, conducting a functional analysis of a grade-level team or department, solving problems, and creating a plan or developing a new process.

Developing a basic flowchart is a straightforward process with three steps.

1. Decide where the process or system begins and ends.

2. Brainstorm the major steps that occur between the beginning and ending.

3. Sort the steps in chronological order, and number them in sequence.

Flowcharts are a great tool for capturing the steps in a process. When each member of a team can contribute to the flowchart, it can also be educational for everyone. When we take the time to create flowcharts, we are making work processes visible for all, which aids communication and creates a basis for further improvement.

Top-Down Flowchart

A top-down flowchart is a diagram that depicts the major flow (steps) of a process along the top, with detail added vertically below each major step. It is a practical tool when you want to quickly see the major steps of a process along with some detail or when you want to organize work around major parts of a process.

This type of flowchart is helpful when orienting someone new to the school or district to the flow of work or information. Furthermore, the flowchart can support the functional analysis (see page 219) of a grade-level team or department, school, or district to illustrate the flow of work in a core process. A core process is one that is central to the mission of the group or organization, and it is often one that is repeated throughout a year or annually. Examples of core processes include:

- Adopting curriculum
- Registering students
- Orienting new staff
- Hiring new personnel
- Administering standardized tests

The procedure for developing a top-down flowchart parallels that of the basic flowchart. In the top-down flowchart, you identify substeps for each major step in the basic flowchart. The group needs to agree on the level of detail that will be useful for the purpose of the flowchart.

Figure 5.7 (page 128) illustrates a sample top-down flowchart for the special education referral process. In this example, the process begins when a classroom teacher refers a student for special education. All of the subsequent steps are taken by the special education team (though this is implicit, since this type of flowchart only defines steps, not roles), from preparing to assess the student, to assessing, then diagnosing, and finally making a recommendation.

You can also use a top-down flowchart to summarize a much more complex flowchart. Use a shadowed box to depict any step for which you have more detail, such as for step 2.1 in figure 5.7. (Some computer graphics software lets you click on the shadowed boxes to get more detail.) Here,

Tips for Developing Basic Flowcharts

- Agree about the level of detail (altitude) early on that you want to show at this stage.
- To ensure that you focus on the most important steps, try limiting the number of steps in the process to no more than ten.
- Use sticky notes to post the steps in order of time.
- Include verbs in the steps rather than just activities or topics. For example, write *acquire funding* instead of simply writing *funds*.

Tips for Creating a Top-Down Flowchart

- Number the steps using an outline form (1.0 is the first major step, 1.1 is the first substep, 1.2 the second substep, and so on). This number helps the team be specific when referring to the current process or proposed changes; for example, "What if we changed step 3.4?"
- This tool does not show time, decisions, or people responsible for the various steps. Use one of the other flowcharts if you need to show that information.

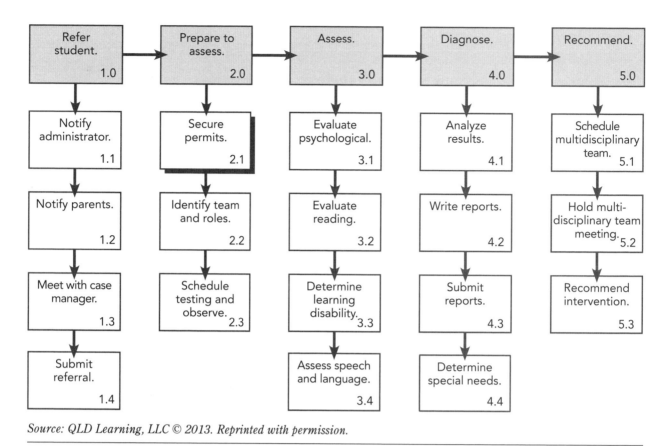

Source: QLD Learning, LLC © 2013. Reprinted with permission.

Figure 5.7: Sample top-down flowchart of special education referral process.

> If you can't describe what you are doing as a process, you don't know what you're doing.
>
> —W. Edwards Deming

too, the numbering comes in handy, because you label the more detailed charts by the outline number. You could, for example, create a separate top-down flowchart for securing permits in the special education referral process. You could identify this new flowchart as the flowchart for step 2.1 (secure permits) of the special education referral process.

Deployment Flowchart

A deployment flowchart depicts each role for the steps in a process. It's useful for visually showing the responsible individuals or groups for each aspect of the work. Teams can use this practical tool to identify areas of duplication and rework, plan a new process, and assist in delegating and assigning tasks.

The process for developing the deployment flowchart includes the following steps.

1. Identify the main functions, groups, or individuals who work on a process. Write these on large cards

or sticky notes, and place them across the top of a flipchart page.

2. Decide the boundaries of the process. Where does it start? Where does it end?

3. Brainstorm all the steps in the process (at first, you don't have to pay attention to order). Write these steps on sticky notes.

4. Place the steps in order on the chart, beginning with the first step and moving down the flowchart in order of time. Place each step under the person and function with the *primary responsibility* for performing that step. If other functions, groups, or individuals play a role in a step (such as by providing information), use an oval symbol under those columns for that step. Connect the ovals to the primary step with a straight line.

5. Draw arrows connecting the primary flow of the work between the groups represented on the chart.

Figure 5.8 (page 130) illustrates a deployment flowchart for staff development. In this flowchart, three functions are involved: a director, staff development specialists, and a program assistant. The staff development specialists first conduct a needs assessment with the teachers and then develop a program based on the teachers' needs, which is scheduled by the program assistant. After the program is scheduled, the director gets involved and communicates the program offering to all teachers; the specialists then develop a program evaluation tool, and the assistant registers participants.

Figure 5.9 (page 131) shows an alternative format for a deployment flowchart. In this format, the team records the areas of staff responsibility (for example, program development or communications) on the left side of the diagram. In this case, use a symbol (usually a rectangle) in the appropriate column showing who does which steps. Other symbols, such as the oval, can depict people who assist with the step but are not responsible for carrying out the work. We find it useful to use different colored sticky notes for steps that don't add value to the overall process. For example, if the

Tips for Creating Deployment Flowcharts

- When mapping a current process, a deployment flowchart can become very messy. By writing the steps on sticky notes, you can easily move them around as you clarify the sequence of work. Take your time, and be patient.

- Use different symbols and shapes to indicate different types of involvement.

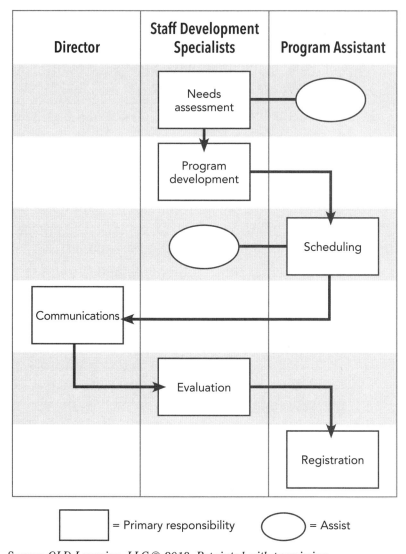

Figure 5.8: Sample deployment flowchart for staff development.

staff development specialists have to seek approval from the director after conducting a needs assessment and before developing the program, the additional inspection step may not add value to the overall process. It would be cause for asking "Why do we need this step?" and "What value-added step could we insert earlier in the process so that this review step would be unnecessary?"

Deployment flowcharts are a useful way of capturing not only the sequence of steps in a process but also who is responsible and who is assisting at each step. You can also add a *time* column on one side of the chart to show the estimated amount of time each step or series of steps should

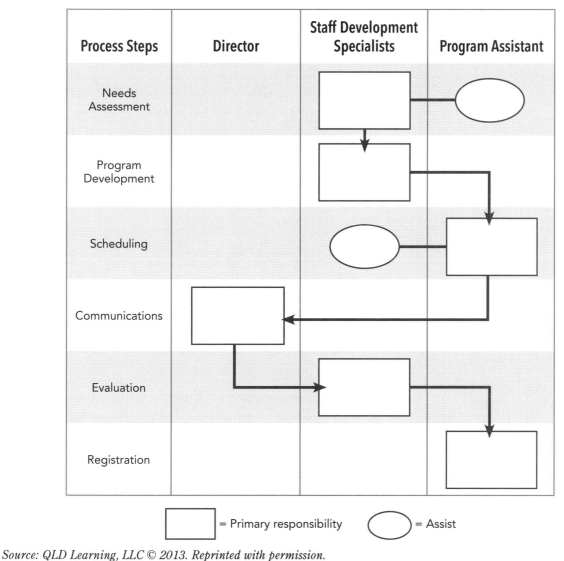

= Primary responsibility   = Assist

Source: QLD Learning, LLC © 2013. Reprinted with permission.

Figure 5.9: Alternative format for deployment flowchart for staff development.

take. Deployment flowcharts are great tools for training new employees, as well as a way to identify hand-offs between people, which can improve communication.

Detailed Flowchart

As the name suggests, a detailed flowchart shows all the steps in the process and identifies key decisions. This comprehensive flowchart is especially useful to illustrate where duplication or rework occurs in the process, map an ideal situation, map a revised situation after the team has made its final recommendations, and serve as a training and orientation tool.

Tips for Creating Detailed Flowcharts

- To avoid confusion later on, it's best if a flowchart reads in the same way that text flows on a page: left to right and top to bottom. That means if there are too many steps to fit in one row, the next sequence of action should start at the left-most position in the second row (don't switch directions and have steps flow right to left in the second row).

- One challenge in using this flowchart is knowing the right altitude or perspective (level of detail) to use when identifying the steps. If it is too general, it won't tell the team much; if it is too specific, it can be unnecessarily time consuming. Which end of the continuum the team elects will depend on the purpose for doing the flowchart and on the individual's familiarity with the details of the work.

- Use a large space to construct a detailed flowchart—all the details will undoubtedly take up a lot of room. There may be steps that don't go anywhere (just trail off); some steps may go around and around in an endless cycle. You want to have enough room to capture every variation.

The procedure for developing a detailed flowchart parallels some of the steps in basic and top-down flowcharts. The process includes the following steps.

1. Decide as a group where the process begins (first step) and where it ends (last step).
   a. What are the inputs to this process? What happens before the process begins?
   b. What are the outputs from this process? What does this process produce?

2. Record the first and last step on sticky notes and post them on a flipchart or large sheet of paper with enough space in between to fill in the remaining steps.

3. Brainstorm other steps you want to include in the diagram. Write these steps on sticky notes and place them on a second sheet of paper.

4. Have a designated facilitator read the notes aloud, with the group telling him or her where to place each note on the main page.

5. When you have finalized the arrangement, draw arrows showing the sequence of action.
   a. Use basic flowchart symbols to indicate different types of actions. For example, rectangles or squares indicate an action.
   b. Use a diamond for decisions and a starburst for delays.

Figure 5.10 shows a sample detailed flowchart for purchasing new instructional resources in a school or district.

You may have different purposes for using detailed flowcharts. If your purpose is to document the existing process, with all its flaws and problems, have team members brainstorm the steps involved in doing this process *today*, including all the steps of rework (when things aren't done right the first time) and duplication. Don't worry about who does each process step or how much time each takes. Arrange the sticky notes in sequence and draw arrows to connect one

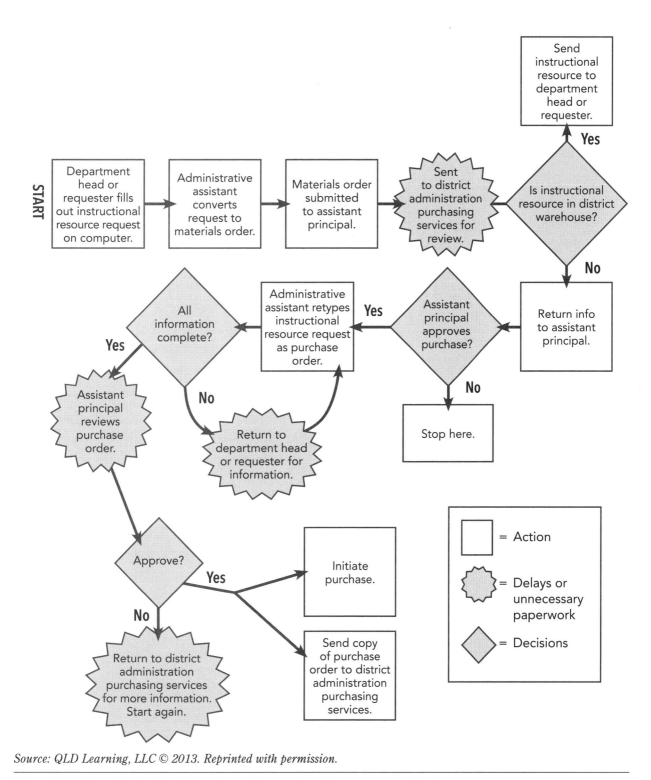

Figure 5.10: Sample detailed flowchart of instructional resources purchasing process.

step to the next. On the other hand, if the purpose is to show how a new process *should* look, include only those steps that will add value. Arrange steps in sequence and draw connection arrows.

Planning Tools

PDSA (see page 4) is the ultimate planning tool. SMART teams apply PDSA to their plans to answer the following questions. What did we plan? How did it work out in practice? What worked well? What didn't work, and why? What did we learn so that we can plan more effectively in the future? Visualizing plans becomes an important part of that learning process.

Planning tools assist teams in mapping out future work. Paying attention to how plans will work out in practice is an important part of team learning and helps future activities go more smoothly.

Flowcharts are the simplest planning tools to map basic steps in a project or process. Additionally, teams can use three other tools to add other dimensions to their planning.

1. **Tree diagrams** help you *imagine*—think ahead to what a plan needs to look like, beginning with the end in mind and working backward from the end of the project or activity. Teams can use tree diagrams to think through the hierarchy from goals to strategies to tactics.

2. **Responsibility matrices** help take the guesswork out of processes, identifying who will do what and in what sequence.

3. **Gantt charts** can help teams add the details of time and sequence and get a visual picture of how the work can or could overlap to be done most efficiently.

Tree Diagrams

A tree diagram is a tool that helps make goals SMART—strategic and specific, measurable, attainable, results oriented, and time bound. Teams use it to identify essential elements of a project, like aligning efforts toward a specific goal. Schools and districts find this tool useful when planning SMART goals across the system or at the classroom and student levels. Notably, developing a tree diagram provides insight when thinking through action plans.

The first step in developing a tree diagram involves determining an area to focus on for improvement. This focus area should be based on a careful analysis of relevant achievement, demographic, or climate data. Consider not only this year's data but also data over time. See appendix A for examples of tree diagrams for the following school-based goals: climate, elementary reading, middle school analytical thinking, and high school writing (pages 284–287).

With the focus determined, you are now ready to follow four steps in the procedure for developing the tree diagram.

1. **Identify a results goal:** Write a results goal in the left-hand box of the tree diagram. When writing a SMART goal at the school level, consider the most important measures you analyze each year. Chances are these measures are state or national achievement tests or key climate measures such as parent, staff, or student satisfaction surveys.

2. **Identify goal indicators:** In the first set of boxes to the right of the goal, identify the indicators that you and the students need to focus on to achieve the SMART goal. Indicators are the standards, benchmarks, objectives, or skill sets that you would look for as evidence of progress on the SMART goal. Ideally, indicators are derived from a careful analysis of test and other assessment data. At the school level, teams should derive them from student data over time; at the classroom level, teachers will want to look at this year's students. Indicators are the key gap areas that are most in need of improvement. Consider using Pareto thinking (pages 9–10) to narrow your list down to the vital few indicators.

3. **Identify measures:** For each indicator, identify measures you'll use to assess progress on that indicator. Faculty members should agree on the measures to use. These measures should include summative (end of year) and formative (ongoing or periodic) tools, as well as standardized and district-, school-, or classroom-developed tools. Other sources of measurement information are unit tests, portfolios, performance assessments, surveys, and observational tools.

   To make the use of measures manageable, consider using components of tests that focus only on the indicators you identified as you monitor student progress during the year.

   When designing new measures, take validity and reliability issues into account as well as alignment of the measure with the goal.

4. **Identify targets:** Identify targets for each measure that are attainable within a given time frame and given your resources and knowledge. These should also be based on a careful analysis of existing data, both snapshot and over time.

   Careful consideration of targets is important to success and to teachers' and students' motivation to work toward the target. For example, a target of 100 percent of students being proficient on a certain measure when only 25 percent are currently proficient may demoralize people before they start.

   Teachers who will be working on the targets should select them; however, the amount of stretch people are willing to commit to should be balanced against the need to achieve school and state expectations. Most importantly, if the target selected is a stretch, resources (time, professional development, and so on) must be made available to support achievement of that target.

   Teams need to carefully consider criteria for accomplishing or making progress on the targets.

Is a target defining a certain percent or number of students achieving a specific level or is it identifying the desired growth rate for students? Teams should consider both level and rate.

Targets are what teams will monitor throughout the year to evaluate progress on the overall SMART goal.

A simple example of how to construct a tree diagram, showing a personal improvement goal, appears in figure 5.11. The diagram illustrates the goal and indicators, measures, and targets for the goal. In appendix A, pages 284–287, you will find four examples of school SMART goal trees.

What If We Fail to Meet Our Targets?

Failure to meet a target should not be a cause for punishment or blame. Rather, it is an opportunity for shared dialogue among the faculty pursuing that target. Why didn't we achieve this target? What theories do we have about why we didn't achieve the target? What could we do differently to achieve it in the future?

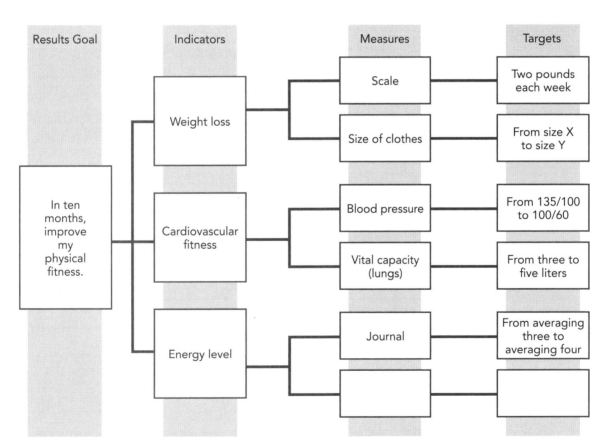

Source: SMART Learning Systems, LLC © 2013. Used with permission.

Figure 5.11: Personal SMART goal tree.

Tips for Creating Tree Diagrams

- Enlarge the tree diagram and post it on a wall so that everyone can construct the plan together.

- Don't worry that every single box must be filled in for the tool to be done correctly; it is simply a way to organize ideas. Conversely, if there are more ideas than there is space on the diagram, feel free to add more space to the diagram.

SMART goal trees help teams visualize their improvement goals using a simple, structured process that creates shared ownership for the final product. Once completed, the targets can be used to monitor progress. When students begin using SMART goal trees as part of a goal-setting and monitoring process, they realize that with effort they can learn and succeed in school. For more information about how and when to use SMART goal trees with students, see *The Power of SMART Goals* (O'Neill & Conzemius, 2006, pp. 130–133) and *More Than a SMART Goal* (Conzemius & Morganti-Fisher, 2012, pp. 66–76).

Your team may be interested in setting goals and targets based on zones of proficiency. If so, consider dividing students' results into zones and then setting targets based on moving students to higher zones. For example, the blue zone would be *proficient*, green would be *above proficient*, yellow *below proficient*, and red *far below proficient*. The example in table 5.4 shows cut scores for the green, blue, yellow, and red zones for four different types of measures. See *The Power of SMART Goals* (O'Neill & Conzemius, 2006) for more on using zones with goal setting and monitoring.

Table 5.4: Cut Scores for Zones of Proficiency for Four Types of Measures

	ACT Composite	Percent Meets or Exceeds	Percent Correct	Rubric (6 points)
Green Zone	25+	90–100	85–100	5–6
Blue Zone	20–25	77–89	70–84	4
Yellow Zone	17–19	61–76	51–69	3
Red Zone	< 17	< 61	< 51	1–2

Responsibility Matrices

A responsibility matrix identifies individuals or groups who have specific responsibilities related to core processes in the school (such as purchasing, enrollment and registration, or scheduling). This planning tool is helpful when you want to clarify roles and responsibilities for carrying out tasks and functions in a department, division, or other type of organizational unit. Developing a responsibility matrix involves four roles for individuals involved in the process.

1. **Decision maker** is the person who makes the decisions about operating or changing the entire process. The decision maker determines priorities and the scope of responsibilities for the process owner. (Sometimes they are the same person.)

2. **Process owner** is the person responsible for doing the task on a regular basis. The process owner answers questions about what to do regarding a specific process or task.

3. **Backup** is the person who operates the process when the process owner is away.

4. **Involved stakeholders** are the people who give input to the process, use the service or products, or are affected by the process and its results. These are the people who should be involved if the process is changed.

Creating a responsibility matrix is a straightforward task that involves identifying the core processes for the department and naming individuals for each of the roles. Figure 5.12 (page 140) is an example of a responsibility matrix for faculty and staff support processes.

Responsibility matrices help identify the key people for core processes so that the decision maker is clear and those most involved in the process can be responsible for making sure it flows smoothly. If problems or questions arise, the responsibility matrix clearly identifies who needs to be involved to resolve them. A reproducible responsibility matrix template can be found on page 314 in appendix B.

Gantt Charts

Gantt charts are scheduling tools for action planning that depict relative timing of process steps. Teams use this planning tool to judge the timing of action steps or the scheduling of steps needed to carry out an action plan. For example, you can use it after you've identified action steps in a top-down flowchart.

Core Process	Decision Maker	Process Owner	Back-Up	Involved Stakeholders
Word processing and computer documentation support	Nick P.	Nick P.	Katie W.	Carl D. and Computer Committee
Coordinate committee meetings (memos, materials, and schedules)	Keisha S.	Phil H.		Giselle S.
Process grant applications	Faculty and Keisha S.	Phil H.		Giselle S.
Coordinate faculty leave	Faculty and Keisha S.	Nick P. Phil H.	Marko A. Carl D. Julie C.	Phil H. Susan B. Giselle S.

Source: QLD Learning, LLC © 2013. Reprinted with permission.

Figure 5.12: Responsibility matrix for faculty and staff support processes.

Teams identify the steps either through a brainstorming session or in a top-down flowchart. Developing the Gantt chart involves the following steps.

1. List the steps or tasks in the action plan.

2. Record the appropriate time intervals (days, weeks, or months) to implement the plan.

3. Estimate how long each step or group of steps will take.

4. Determine starting dates for each step (paying attention to what needs to be completed before you start any given step).

5. Review the chart to identify potential conflicts in timing, resource needs, and so on, and adjust the schedules as needed.

Figure 5.13 is an example of a Gantt chart for a school's curriculum improvement project over a period of eight weeks.

Although you can create the simplest form of a Gantt chart easily by hand, it makes it harder to see timing relationships between steps. For example, does one step have to finish

Tasks	Week							
	May 7	May 14	May 21	May 28	June 4	June 11	June 18	June 25
Conduct primary English language arts assessment.	▓							
Conduct primary mathematics assessment.		▓						
Analyze results.			▓	▓				
Data retreat: set goals.						▓		
Create staff development plans.						▓	▓	

Figure 5.13: Sample Gantt chart.

before another can be completed? Or are the two steps independent—their timing not dependent on each other?

Final Check: Group Process and Planning Tools

Group process and planning tools can help make your team's work easier. Each tool has its own unique purpose, from solving problems at deep levels to generating ideas, making decisions, and planning how to achieve goals. By using the right tool at the right time, you can see dramatic improvement in your team's functioning. Use the following checklist to evaluate your group process and planning tools.

My team uses the following group process tools to make our internal work more productive.

- ☐ Dialogue
- ☐ Brainstorming
- ☐ Affinity diagrams
- ☐ Multivoting
- ☐ Decision matrices
- ☐ Consensus decision making

My team creates visual pictures of processes and plans using the appropriate tools.

- ☐ Flowcharts
  - ☐ Basic
  - ☐ Top down
  - ☐ Deployment
  - ☐ Detailed
- ☐ Tree diagrams
- ☐ Responsibility matrices
- ☐ Gantt charts

CHAPTER 6

Tools for Understanding Perceptions and Opinions

For many of us, our perceptions are our reality, linked to our beliefs, behaviors, and attitudes. Perceptions strongly shape how we interpret information and how we act on that information. Thus, understanding perceptions is key to identifying areas of satisfaction and opportunities for improvement. Teams can use the data tools in this chapter to better understand how staff, parents, students, and community members perceive their schools and what they are feeling and thinking about their schools. There are three techniques to use to gather perceptual data: (1) interviews, (2) focus groups, and (3) surveys. If teams can convert the information they gather from these tools into numbers, they can use quantitative tools (such as bar charts and pie charts) to display results. We'll show examples later in this chapter and provide more in-depth instructions for using quantitative tools.

Collecting and Analyzing Perceptual Data

Perceptual data reveal information about individuals' attitudes, behaviors, and beliefs. While it's important to understand how to interpret and use quantitative data, like assessment results, attendance and dropout rates, special education utilization, and other key measures, strategies for collecting and analyzing perceptual data can inform you about why you are seeing certain patterns in other data, and what to do about it. Five concepts are building blocks to help you gather useful and valid perceptual data.

1. **Sampling:** Gathering data from a selected portion of the total pool of candidates

2. **Stratification:** Gathering data from various subgroups

3. **Disaggregation:** Separating results from various subgroups so that they will be easy to compare

4. **Questioning:** Developing easily understood questions that will be easy to analyze

5. **Quantifying:** Using scales to quantify the extent to which people agree with certain statements

Sampling

When you need to collect perceptual data, the pool of candidates (population) from which you could collect data is often much larger than can be handled—unless you have unlimited resources and time. Experience shows that in most cases you can make reliable inferences about a population by sampling a subset of that population—as long as you think carefully about how to select the sampled subset. Figure 6.1 shows three sample populations and the subset or sample of one of those populations.

Sampling strategies can vary from the very simple (talk to one English language arts teacher in each high school) to very complex (interview five representatives from four different types of schools, two representatives of all key business sectors, and so on). The sampling strategy you use depends on your purpose in collecting data, the stakes in the outcome (that is, the risk associated with being wrong), and how sure you want to be that the results reflect the population as a whole.

To generalize your findings beyond a particular group, your sampling technique must be random and scientifically valid. A truly random and scientifically valid technique ensures that each member of a targeted population has an equal opportunity to be selected for sampling. This requires that you have a systematic way to draw names so that no one name has any better chance than any other of getting into the sample. For example, if you are interested in families'

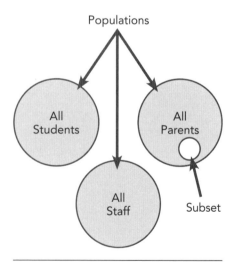

Figure 6.1: Example of sampling in a population.

perceptions, but you are picking only the first fifty names of students from an alphabetically organized school directory, you would end up sampling only those families with names from the beginning of the alphabet, and you would oversample those families that had multiple students enrolled in your school. Especially in a high-stakes situation, such as developing a funding referendum or redefining a districtwide curriculum, you will want to be very systematic in your sampling scheme and in interpreting the results. This approach will require use of a sampling technique involving random number tables. These tables, created to select random samples, have been used in statistics for years and are much more effective than selecting samples based on dice, cards, and so on. Help from a statistician or sampling expert is invaluable in high-stakes cases, but if your situation is less complex, using a random number table to develop your sample is relatively easy to do. Computers generate most random number tables these days, but we have included one in appendix B (page 300) as well.

Alternatively, if your team is developing an agenda for an upcoming school career day, and you don't have time to talk to all staff, speak with a few selected stakeholders.

Stratification

Stratification is the process of setting up the subgroups you're interested in finding out more about before you gather data from them. For example, if you're doing an overall climate survey involving staff, students, parents, and other community members, you may want to design different questions for each group. These different subsets possess or represent significantly different types of knowledge.

Typical subgroups include the following.

- Students in certain grades, parents of those students, and staff for those grades
- Teachers of particular disciplines (for example, fine arts), classroom teachers, and paraprofessionals
- Outside stakeholders, such as business and religious community leaders

Sampling Tips

- Be wary of *sampling frame bias* in which the subset you sample comes from a source that is different in some significant aspect from the larger population you're trying to find out about. The list you use to draw a sample from (also called a *frame*) will make a big difference in the reliability of your results. For example, let's say you're interested in finding out how many low-income families would take advantage of a free early childhood education program. You get a list of families renting apartments in a particular neighborhood, but only some of them have phones, and the list isn't current. If you sample from that list, a number of families that just moved in or who don't have phones won't be represented. You won't be able to say with confidence that your survey results reflect the broader population of low-income families.

- With small samples, it's important to try to get as close to a 100 percent response rate as possible, because results become more and more difficult to generalize from fewer responses.

- Various positions with the school or district such as teachers, administrators, curriculum consultants, and staff

Figure 6.2 illustrates the percentages of distinct groups within a community that responded to a communitywide climate survey about a specific high school. Each subgroup was asked different questions about the school, because each subgroup had a different perspective. In the figure, N represents the number of people who received the survey.

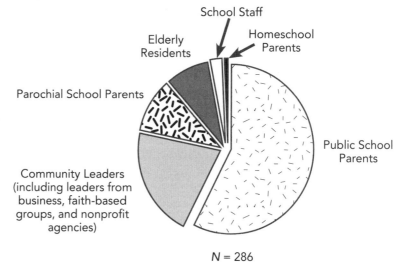

Source: QLD Learning, LLC © 2013. Reprinted with permission.

Figure 6.2: Proportions of community sampled for school climate survey.

As noted previously, you may prefer to sample selected populations. Figure 6.3 illustrates the results of a survey given to parents and teachers. The survey uses stratification to probe different areas of concern for these two subgroups.

Doing surveys well can be a challenge, and because so many decisions are made based on their results, it's often worth getting outside advice on how to set up surveys. This book provides basic guidelines so that you know what to be careful about and can ask good questions of an outside expert. Local community colleges or universities can often provide helpful assistance at no cost, and we encourage you to seek their advice, especially if significant decisions are at stake.

Parent Question
My child is safe at this school.

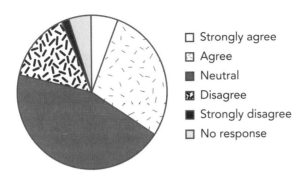

- ☐ Strongly agree
- ▨ Agree
- ■ Neutral
- ▨ Disagree
- ■ Strongly disagree
- ☐ No response

Teacher Question
Teachers are consistent in enforcing the school's code of conduct.

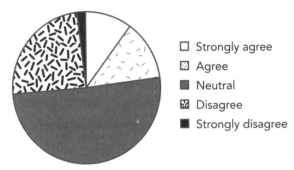

- ☐ Strongly agree
- ▨ Agree
- ■ Neutral
- ▨ Disagree
- ■ Strongly disagree

Source: QLD Learning, LLC © 2013. Reprinted with permission.

Figure 6.3: Results of climate survey given to subgroups—parents and teachers.

Disaggregation

At the analysis stage, you can use *disaggregation* to compare the similarities and differences within the subgroups (for example, by socioeconomic status, race or ethnicity, gender, and so on). One way to disaggregate results is to show separate charts for the various subgroups in your sample. Figure 6.4 (page 148) shows that, overall, Asian parents are far less satisfied with the district performance than Caucasian parents.

Another way to disaggregate results is to compare particular responses side by side, such as responses from Caucasian, African American, Hispanic, and Asian parents. Figure 6.5 (page 149) shows the percentage of parents within each group who gave the most favorable response. In this

get reliable results. Then use the "Random Number Table" in appendix B (page 300) to identify individuals for your sample.

Enter the "Sample Size Chart" using the size of your population (N) to find the recommended sample size (S). If your sample size is three digits (such as 240), you will determine the names from your population list using three-digit values from the "Random Number Table" that are equal to or less than your sample size. For example, if you choose to start at the top of column two, number 167 on your population list will be included in your sample. Moving down the column, 193 on your list will be in the sample, as will 117.

4. Continue until you have a full sample.

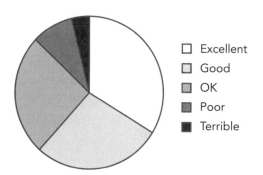

Caucasian Parents
Overall, how well do you think our schools perform in educating your child or children?

☐ Excellent
☐ Good
☐ OK
■ Poor
■ Terrible

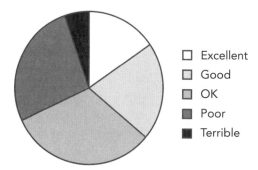

Asian Parents
Overall, how well do you think our schools perform in educating your child or children?

☐ Excellent
☐ Good
☐ OK
■ Poor
■ Terrible

Source: QLD Learning, LLC © 2013. Reprinted with permission.

Figure 6.4: Climate survey showing results from two subgroups within a subgroup—Asian and Caucasian parents.

case, the samples are drawn from separate populations, so it would not be appropriate to use a pie chart to compare them.

Questioning

To gather perceptual data, you need to ask people questions. The types of questions you ask depend somewhat on the format you'll use to ask them. For example, you can ask more complicated questions in face-to-face interviews than you can in a telephone survey.

There are two questioning types you can use: open-ended questions (those with no predetermined answers) and closed-ended questions (those where respondents choose from a list of possible answers). Open-ended questions are more likely to lead to new learning; for example, What

> The real voyage in discovery consists not in seeking new landscapes but in having new eyes.
>
> —Marcel Proust

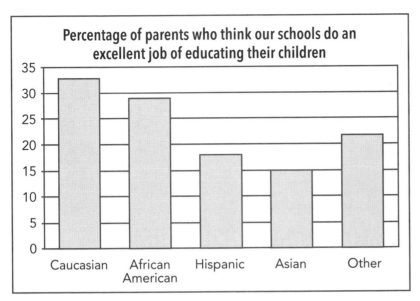

Source: QLD Learning, LLC © 2013. Reprinted with permission.

Figure 6.5: Climate survey results showing most favorable responses among subgroups.

could be done to improve our ninth-grade curriculum? In what ways do you feel our school could better serve the community? However, it is harder to analyze the answers. Closed-ended questions are easier to score but less likely to produce new insights.

Typically, interviews and focus groups utilize open-ended questions, and surveys contain largely closed-ended questions. No matter what type of questions you'll be using, be sure to develop easily understood questions that will also be easy to analyze. Here are some tips.

- Keep questions simple and clear, and include only necessary questions.

- Avoid jargon, bias, and hypothetical questions.

- Ask only questions respondents would know something about—focus on just one thought per question.

- Use rating scales for closed-ended questions, and limit potential responses to just four or five items.

- Include at least one open-ended question at the end even if you're doing a survey that is mostly closed-ended questions. Ask, "Is there anything else you'd like to comment on?"

Quantifying

Scales help quantify the extent to which people agree or disagree with certain statements. Typically, most scales range from three points to six points. Even early elementary students can complete surveys. Teachers can read questions aloud and have students circle the face that describes how they feel. Three types of scales are commonly used in gathering perceptual data—(1) rating, (2) rank order, and (3) gap analysis. Figure 6.6 describes these scales.

Methods for Obtaining Perceptual Data

Interviews, focus groups, and surveys are three methods for obtaining perceptual data. The purpose of conducting interviews and focus groups, in particular, is to learn about the issues around a particular subject. So, one valid data-collecting strategy for interviews and focus groups is to continue gathering data until you stop learning anything new. When you start to think you've heard all this before, it may be time to formally analyze the results and move on. Surveys differ, however. To keep a survey statistically valid, you need to complete your data collection and sampling plans regardless of whether the same themes keep arising.

Figure 6.7 (page 152) defines three topics that can haunt anyone who collects perceptual data: (1) research validity, (2) results validity, and (3) results generalizability.

Interviews

Interviews are one-on-one conversations by phone or in person, using open- or closed-ended questions. With interviews, you can identify and learn about underlying issues and concerns in depth. The understandings you gain from an interview can help to inform the full range of perceptions and serve to clarify questions or needs.

School leaders can find many occasions for using interviews. When designing a new course or program, interview students and parents to get their input about what should be included and how to best engage learning. Teachers can invite students to gather information from each other about

Scales	Examples				
Rating Respondents rate the importance of an issue or relevance of an item on a predetermined scale. Aim for three- to six-point scales. Start with a statement, followed by the scale.	Very Satisfied	Satisfied	Neutral	Dissatisfied	Very Dissatisfied
	Excellent	Good	Adequate	Below Adequate	Poor
	Much Better	Better	About the Same	Not as Good	Much Worse
	Strongly Agree	Agree	No Opinion	Disagree	Strongly Disagree
	5	4	3	2	1
	Usually ☺		Sometimes 😐		Hardly Ever ☹

Rank Order
Respondents rank a limited number of options in order of priority or preference. Keep the number small (five or fewer).

How important to you are the following extracurricular programs?

Please rank their importance in order from 1 to 5, with 1 being the most important.

_____ Drama club

_____ Recreational volleyball

_____ School newspaper

_____ Swim club

_____ Computer lab

Gap Analysis
This scale combines ranking with a rating scale to discover both what is important to people and also how well they feel you are doing. This can help you identify the biggest gaps between priorities and performance. (See appendix A, page 281, for an example of a gap analysis survey.)

	Importance	Satisfaction	Gap
Hands-on projects	1 2 3 4 (5)	1 (2) 3 4 5	−3
Friendly teacher	1 2 3 (4) 5	1 2 (3) 4 5	−1
Interesting homework	1 2 (3) 4 5	1 2 (3) 4 5	0

Importance
1 = Not at all important
5 = Extremely important

Satisfaction
1 = Not at all satisfied
5 = Completely satisfied

Source: QLD Learning, LLC © 2013. Reprinted with permission.

Figure 6.6: Scales for gathering perceptual data.

Research Validity

- Are the questions worded properly?
- Do the questions relate to the purpose of the research?

Results Validity

- What types of people participated in the research?
- Do those people represent the diversity of opinions in the community?
- Was there a good response rate?
- Was the analysis done properly?
- Are our interpretations of the results accurate? Objective?

Results Generalizability

Note: This category of questions relates to surveys only. The purpose of interviews and focus groups is to get a deep understanding of the targeted issues, not to generalize from those results to the opinions of those not included in the study.

- Can we generalize from the results?
- Do the results accurately reflect the perceptions of the larger group?
- Was the sampling procedure random?
- To what populations, settings, or variables can the conclusions be generalized?

Figure 6.7: Guiding questions for gathering perceptual data.

what is working and not working well in a particular course to teach them interviewing skills. Interviews can also serve to identify meaningful questions for a broader survey.

Interviews have advantages over other perceptual tools, notably the high response rate, fast turnaround, and the opportunity to explore complex issues, to probe for more information, and to clarify questions and answers. Despite these advantages, interviews can be costly (especially if paying individuals to conduct the interviews), time consuming, and limited in number.

Preparing for and conducting interviews requires some thoughtful planning. Of course, the first step is to address what you want to know as a result of the interviews. With the purpose established, you can develop five to ten open-ended questions. Following these five logistical steps will ensure the interviews provide the information you are seeking.

1. Create a script for the interviewer to follow. This is particularly important if more than one person will be conducting interviews—you want them all to follow the same protocol. Test the questions and script on several representative people before doing the actual interviews.

2. Develop a standard notetaking system for interviewers. Try out your notetaking system to see if it helps you capture what you want to know.

3. Set up a sampling plan to include representatives from each stakeholder group (see page 144).

4. Once you've completed all the interviews, use an affinity diagram (page 113) to organize the results by theme.

5. Share a summary of the results with the people interviewed, and tell them what the next steps will be. This will reinforce that you heard what they had to say and you're taking action. Even if your next action is a survey, you'll be reinforcing the importance of their input.

Depending on the purpose of the interview, you may find it useful to include a closed-ended rating scale question to your open-ended format. For example, you might ask, "On a scale of one to five, with five being strongly agree, do you agree or disagree with the proposal for an open campus at our school?" Then, follow up with this question: "Why do you feel that way?"

To obtain additional information, do in-depth interviews with selected survey participants to clarify and follow up on responses. Be sure to set up the survey ahead of time to let people know you may be following up with selected individuals; allow them an option to pass and protect their anonymity.

Interviews yield rich information that can lead to unexpected solutions. For example, before surveying a group of parents to find out what their needs and concerns are, you might spend some one-on-one time with a few of them to gain insights into their experiences first and discover that some simple communication improvements like adding translations to newsletters could make a significant difference. Interviews are a great way to find out more about an issue or topic area and can give you input for designing a survey that goes out to a larger group of people, if needed, or framing the kinds of questions to ask small groups of people.

Focus Groups

A focus group is a facilitated conversation with a small group of selected individuals, centered on one specific issue or topic using structured, open-ended questions. Focus groups can reveal issues and concerns among stakeholder groups that are not immediately apparent to your team. You may find that having interviewees together in the same room at the same time will spark greater insights and creativity. Focus group sessions are helpful when you need to understand the full range of perceptions of an issue or when you want to compare perceptions between different groups.

Focus groups can provide data that are useful in developing questions for a survey. Another application is to concept test early thinking about new strategic directions, curriculum ideas, programs, and policies. As a stand-alone data-collection method, focus groups can help clarify issues with which your team struggles.

Tips for Successful Interviews

- Interviews yield rich information—they allow you to really understand what's important to people. However, they aren't statistically reliable—results should not be generalized to larger groups.

- If you use interviews as part of a school improvement process, consider inviting members of the school community to conduct the interviews. The process can be a great relationship builder and a real eye-opener for those doing the interviewing.

Tips for Successful Focus Groups

- Allow the participants to explore interesting areas in depth. A focus group is a guided—not rigid—conversation.

- Focus groups, like interviews, yield rich information. Their results, however, aren't representative of the whole. Written surveys, implemented with larger numbers of people, are a method for validating interview and focus group results.

- Be sure to probe for more information. Ask participants to provide examples and stories to illustrate their points.

- Allow some silence in the conversation, especially when soliciting input from quieter participants.

- Consider holding the session off site.

Like interviews, focus groups provide opportunities to explore complex issues, probe for more information, and clarify questions and answers. Similarly, they can generate survey ideas. The group dynamics can trigger new ideas. Nonetheless, focus groups are costly because they require a skilled neutral facilitator who is usually paid. Organizing focus groups can be complex because of planning logistics and recruiting representative participants. Time is also a factor with focus groups—ensuring that all participants are available at the scheduled time as well as taking time to select a facilitator and work through the logistics of the session with that individual.

Selecting the appropriate subgroups whose ideas are of interest to your project is the critical first step in organizing a focus group. To make the choices, you will need to identify your sampling or stratification scheme. If you are using more than one focus group, decide whether to mix people from different subgroups together or hold separate focus groups for each subgroup. In some respects, planning for focus groups parallels that for interviews. Consider these six steps.

1. Develop five to ten open-ended questions and a script for the facilitator. Test the questions and script on a small, representative group. Revise as appropriate.

2. If at all possible, recruit one or two neutral third-party facilitators. One facilitator can take notes and keep track of time while the other moderates the conversation. If this isn't possible, arrange for recording and transcribing the session (ensure confidentiality, however).

3. At the session, seat participants in a circle and perform introductions.

4. Have the facilitator introduce the first question and guide discussion. Some free-form responses are helpful to ease the participants into the discussion. The facilitator is responsible for ensuring that every participant gets a chance to respond and that no one individual dominates the conversation. A skilled

facilitator knows how to direct the conversation to a specific person, one at a time, as a structured way to ensure even participation. For example, "Maria, what do you think about this? Bill, do you agree with Maria's comments, or do you have a different perception?" The facilitator is also sensitive to the time and moves on to each subsequent question as appropriate.

5. After the session, collect the notes or transcribe the tapes and identify key statements from the group. Use an affinity diagram (page 113) to organize results into themes. If you conduct more than one focus group, combine results. If you want, you can code the statements to see if there are differences between the focus groups.

6. Communicate to group members what you found out and what you will do next.

Focus groups, like interviews, can yield rich information—the trick is to ask just a few questions, listen well, and follow up with probing questions to go deeper into topic areas. The advantage of a focus group over an interview is that participants can spark thoughts and ideas with each other. A caution with focus groups is to make sure you facilitate the conversation so that no one person dominates.

Surveys

A survey is a set of questions that asks people about their perceptions or opinions. Teams can conduct surveys via pencil-and-paper questionnaires or online. Surveys are practical tools to use to find out the perceptions of large numbers of people. They are tools you can use to quantify perceptions, issues, or concerns that interviews or focus groups reveal.

School leaders and teachers find surveys useful in a number of situations. For example, classroom teachers can survey their students and parents to gauge their satisfaction with a number of issues important to them—interesting curricula, engaging assignments, teacher availability, classroom climate, communication about student performance, and so on. Teachers and administrators can also solicit feedback about their leadership style via surveys because respondents tend to be more honest if they can be anonymous. See the example of a high school climate survey in appendix A (page 284), which a principal designed to get feedback from students.

In comparison to interviews and focus groups, surveys are less intrusive. They have the advantage of being able to collect information from large samples more efficiently and with less cost. However, surveys have some disadvantages. They are time consuming to design well. The opportunity for follow up by probing and seeking clarification of answers is limited, if not impossible. The response rate may be limited. In that respect, there is the possibility that those who take the time to respond may be biased; for example, highly dissatisfied, desirous of a new program, active in school events, or unfamiliar with the school's history.

Figure 6.8 is an example of a district climate survey form. The survey provides statements descriptive of the district's climate accompanied by a five-point rating scale indicating extent of agreement. The audience for this survey includes school staff, parents, students, and community leaders.

Like any other tool for obtaining perceptual data, surveys require careful and thoughtful planning. Initially, you need to define the population you want to learn about and determine whether to stratify the population into subgroups. An extension of this task is to make a sampling plan to get a randomly selected subset of the population. Here you consider sample sizes and response rates when you make the plan. Also, think about how you will construct the initial sample frame and steer clear of sampling bias. The next four steps address preparing the survey (its questions, format, and accessibility), distributing it, communicating about it, and sharing the results.

1. **Preparing the survey:** Develop fifteen to twenty focused questions and decide how to score the answers—rating scale or ranking scale. Write an introduction explaining the purpose of the survey, giving instructions for completing it, explaining how you'll use the data, and ensuring confidentiality. Write a cover letter to accompany the survey.

District Features	Scoring
1. Parents feel welcome in our school.	1 2 3 4 5
2. All members of the school community share responsibility for student success.	1 2 3 4 5
3. Teachers set high standards for student work.	1 2 3 4 5
4. Principals create and support a climate of high expectations for staff and student learning.	1 2 3 4 5
5. Central office leadership provides service and support to our schools.	1 2 3 4 5
6. We solicit and respect students' opinions.	1 2 3 4 5
7. Staff feel safe to make suggestions for improving our schools.	1 2 3 4 5
8. We recognize and celebrate individual, team, school, and district accomplishments.	1 2 3 4 5

1 = Strongly disagree   3 = Neither agree nor   4 = Agree
2 = Disagree   disagree   5 = Strongly agree

Source: SMART Learning Systems, LLC © 2013. Used with permission.

Figure 6.8: District climate survey form.

Design a simple, easy-to-understand survey that people will find easy to complete and return. Use the following criteria to evaluate your survey.

- Does it include a clear statement of purpose?
- Is it easy to follow?
- Is it visually pleasing?
- Are the questions simply stated?

Pilot both the survey and the cover letter with some representative members of the population. Change anything that may reduce the response rate or create confusion. Pay particular attention to educational jargon and readability level.

2. **Distributing the survey:** If mailing a written survey, include a stamped, self-addressed envelope or make the survey easy to return by other means (fax, with a student if for parents, or at a convenient

Tips for Developing Effective Surveys

- Be clear about the purpose of your survey. Begin with the end in mind, asking, "How will knowing the answers to these questions help us take improvement action?"

- Beware of overinterpreting results. It's important to note the actual numbers of people who answered a question in a particular way because percentages can be misleading if the sample was small. (Fifty percent of respondents sounds like a big number—until you tell people it was two out of the four people in one subset!)

- Consider reviewing surveys from other teachers or other schools doing similar research, and select questions you want to pursue.

- If surveying internally, consider having staff complete the survey during faculty or team meeting time.

- Overcome language barriers in the homes of students by translating surveys into the family's language.

- Perceptions can change over time, so you will want to do regular surveys, using the same instrument each time.

Continued→

drop-off box). If mailing a link to an online survey, make sure there are no barriers like passwords or security checks that would increase the complexity of taking the survey. Online surveys are particularly easy to administer and are economical.

3. **Communicating about the survey:** Do public relations. Prepare the targeted groups or community. Communicate that this is important and clarify time parameters. Consider following up to encourage people to respond. Show appreciation for their willingness to take the survey. In general, a 50 percent response rate from the population at large is considered adequate based on response rates for mail surveys for nonprofit organizations (Hager, Wilson, Pollak, & Rooney, 2003).

4. **Sharing the survey results:** Share results and action plans with the people you surveyed so that they will want to participate next time. You'll be communicating the importance and value of their input.

You may prefer to conduct the survey by phone instead of or in addition to a written questionnaire. Develop a script for the callers to use that includes a standard introduction about the survey and its role and importance to your school or district. Develop data-collection forms that the callers can complete easily while on the phone.

Final Check: Tools for Understanding Perceptions and Opinions

Understanding perceptions and opinions is key to identifying continuous improvement opportunities. Before launching into using a survey, however, consider conducting interviews or focus groups, because each can yield important information, certainly richer than what can be gleaned from a survey. Surveys are useful when you want to verify the extent to which large numbers of people feel a certain way, but proceed carefully in designing the survey and the sample and in interpreting results. Use the following check-list to evaluate your tools for understanding perceptions and opinions.

My team cares what various stakeholders think. As appropriate, we use the following tools to gather and interpret perceptual data.

- ☐ Interviews
- ☐ Focus groups
- ☐ Surveys

We apply the following concepts to help create data-gathering methods and results that are useful for our purposes and that lead to valid results.

- ☐ Sampling
- ☐ Stratification
- ☐ Disaggregation
- ☐ Questioning
- ☐ Rating, rank order, and gap analysis scales

- • Use pie graphs to show percentages of the whole or total responses in each group.
- • Include the total n (number who were sent the survey), along with the response rate, when reporting results.

CHAPTER 7

Data Tools for Understanding More Than Problems

Data collection is important in many stages of problem solving and process improvement. Data help you in many ways: to refine the definition of a problem by quantifying its frequency or impact, to verify which potential causes of a problem are actual causes, or to monitor whether changes you've made to fix a problem have had the desired impact.

In this chapter, we describe two types of data tools that support each of these uses: (1) cause-analysis tools help you define where to collect data to verify potential causes of a problem, and (2) numerical data tools are versatile charts and graphs that let you use numerical (quantitative) data at almost any stage in problem solving or process improvement.

Use these tools judiciously, avoiding both extremes. Some teams seem to get data happy—they can't seem to stop collecting data and end up inundated with much more data than they can possibly analyze. Other teams are so uncomfortable with data that they act almost solely on instinct and gut feelings, rarely using data. Both of these extremes are ill advised. Every team should use data as much as possible to verify (or disprove) what it thinks is happening; however, you don't want to waste time by collecting unnecessary or irrelevant data.

Cause-Analysis Tools

Do you know the secret to finding effective solutions? You have to know specifically what problem it is you're trying to

> The measure of success is not whether you have a tough problem to deal with, but whether it's the same problem you had last year.
>
> —John Foster Dulles

solve—a task that's harder than it sounds! Just think about all the problems in your school that have been solved over and over again. Obviously, the solutions put in place had little effect on the real cause of the problems.

Do you know the secret to finding solutions that address the real causes of a problem? You have to dig deep beneath the surface symptoms of that problem to uncover the root causes. Three cause-analysis tools—(1) five whys analysis, (2) cause-and-effect diagram, and (3) relations diagram—provide that critical link that helps you make sure you've isolated the underlying or root causes of a problem. There are two important notes to consider about these tools.

1. They help you think logically about *potential* causes of a problem; however, you will still need to gather data to verify which are the *real* causes of a problem.

2. Their effectiveness is directly related to the creativity and depth of thinking that go into creating them. That's why these tools are best used with your team as a whole—you want many minds brainstorming ideas so that you have a broad and deep list of potential causes.

Five Whys Analysis

The *five whys analysis* is a method for uncovering the real reasons underlying a problem—a method for getting to the root causes. You will find this tool helpful when you have tried many solutions that have failed or you are stuck in a complex problem or issue. The approach to five whys analysis is straightforward: develop a problem statement, acknowledge the existence of the problem, identify a potential cause, and ask why that cause occurs. This method involves asking a why question, following up the response with an additional why question, and repeating this process five times.

Table 7.1 illustrates the five whys analysis applied in a classroom and at the school level.

Table 7.1: Classroom and School Applications of Five Whys Analysis

Classroom Application	
Why 1: Why didn't you do your homework last night?	**Response:** I didn't know what to do.
Why 2: Why didn't you know what to do?	**Response:** I didn't remember the instructions.
Why 3: Why didn't you remember the instructions?	**Response:** I didn't write them down.
Why 4: Why didn't you write them down?	**Response:** I didn't have my notebook with me.
Why 5: Why didn't you have your notebook?	**Response:** I got to school late and didn't have time to get to my locker.
Action: I will check this student's record to determine if this is a special cause (single or limited number of incidences) or a common cause situation (recurring) with attendance or tardiness. (See page 187 for more on special and common cause variation.)	
School Application	
Why 1: Why do we have so many discipline referrals?	**Response:** A lot of students act inappropriately.
Why 2: Why do they act inappropriately?	**Response:** They don't know the rules.
Why 3: Why don't they know the rules?	**Response:** We haven't explained and enforced them consistently.
Why 4: Why haven't we explained and enforced them consistently?	**Response:** We haven't agreed on a common set of expectations.
Why 5: Why haven't we agreed on common expectations?	**Response:** We haven't spent time together defining our philosophy and expectations.
Action: Let's make the time to define our philosophy and expectations together so we all get on the same page.	

Tips for Effective Five Whys Analysis

- The number 5 is not sacred. The point is to go down several layers, beyond the obvious symptoms of a problem to the underlying deep causes.

- Stop at a layer where you can still take action. It might be that your team can address an underlying cause identified at your fourth why, but not the deeper cause at the fifth level. For example, an underlying case of low reading scores might be poverty, but it's unlikely your group will be able to do anything about that cause. However, you might be able to do something to support early childhood development programs or to obtain tutors for K–2 students.

- Once you feel you've identified the root cause, consider how you might verify (with data) whether that truly is the cause. If data are unavailable, develop pilot (small-scale) solutions that you think will address the problem. If the solution makes a difference, your guess at the underlying cause was probably close to the truth; if not, repeat your analysis to identify other potential causes.

The five whys analysis can help principals, teachers, and students understand a symptom or apparent concern, issue, or problem at a deeper level. This is important because even if the concern is obvious, the most appropriate actions needed to address the concern may not be. By analyzing a

Tips for Creating Cause-and-Effect Diagrams

- Consider using brainstorming and the affinity process to group ideas first, using sticky notes.

- Create the cause-and-effect diagram on a wall or surface large enough for everyone to post their ideas and to conduct the five whys analysis.

- Never use people's names or positions on the diagram.

stream of possible causes, the problem and the solutions are revealed. This, in turn, guides decisions about what data to collect (or not collect) to understand the depth, frequency, or magnitude of the problem.

Cause-and-Effect Diagram

The five whys analysis is an effective starting point for identifying problems and their potential causes. However, teams need a structured tool to help interpret data. Cause-and-effect diagrams provide that structure. These diagrams are invaluable when you have isolated a problem that has no obvious cause, when you are addressing more than one problem, or when a problem has many complex dimensions. Additionally, cause-and-effect diagrams can help expand the team's thinking prior to focusing solutions on a particular cause.

Among the many challenges school leaders and teachers face is determining the root causes of problems. Meeting such challenges is at the heart of school improvement efforts. In designing a school improvement plan, use a cause-and-effect diagram to outline the possible causes of poor student performance. The diagram you develop will help guide and organize the research you do to determine which causes are the biggest contributors to these problems.

Finding the systemic and process issues that are causing the problems to occur is the primary goal of creating cause-and-effect diagrams—not to find a *who*. Even when a *who* may look like a likely culprit (for example, an incompetent teacher), consider how that person might have ended up in that situation (for example, problematic hiring processes, lack of staff development, lack of mentoring or coaching systems, and so on). Of course, teams have to address such matters; however, doing so is likely outside the responsibility and authority of the team charged with researching a particular problem.

Once you have identified a problem and defined a succinct statement for it, you are ready to identify major categories that are potential sources of the problem. You now have another opportunity to use *why* questions one category at a time until the group feels it has exhausted the possibilities. Capture the ideas on a flipchart, whiteboard, or sticky notes (one idea per note). Continue this process until the group has examined all the categories. The diagram will visually illustrate the most intensely involved categories, and people will be able to see that certain potential causes recur throughout. These are areas for further investigation.

These steps serve to guide the group through creating a cause-and-effect diagram.

1. **Format:** Write your problem statement at the head of the diagram. For example, in the cause-and-effect diagram in figure 7.1 (page 166), the problem "Poor performance in reading and writing at our school" is listed on the center right side of the diagram. Create a central line from which you draw major lines (bones) for each of the categories. Draw a line off one major bone and label it with the first level of cause you identified in your analysis. Draw smaller bones from the first cause until all the ideas the group has generated for that potential cause are listed on the diagram. Continue adding causes and causes of those causes on the diagram.

2. **Vocabulary:** Label the major lines using standard terms such as *people*, *processes*, *policies*, *materials*, *equipment*, *procedures*, *facilities*, *technology*, and *training*. You may prefer to develop your own labels based on the unique aspects of the problem. However, a general rule of thumb is to keep the header categories broad and generic. For example, in figure 7.1, the category terms are *resources*, *students and families*, *climate*, and *standards, curriculum, instruction, and assessment*.

3. **Alternative labels:** Instead of using categories, label the major lines with *surface-level* causes. The smaller bones attached to each major bone would then be factors that contribute to that surface-level cause. For example, suppose the problem statement is "Students are failing to learn material for the standardized test." A smaller bone off that cause might be "delays in the purchasing of updated books." The interpretation of this sequence is that delays might cause students to use out-of-date textbooks, which might contribute to them failing

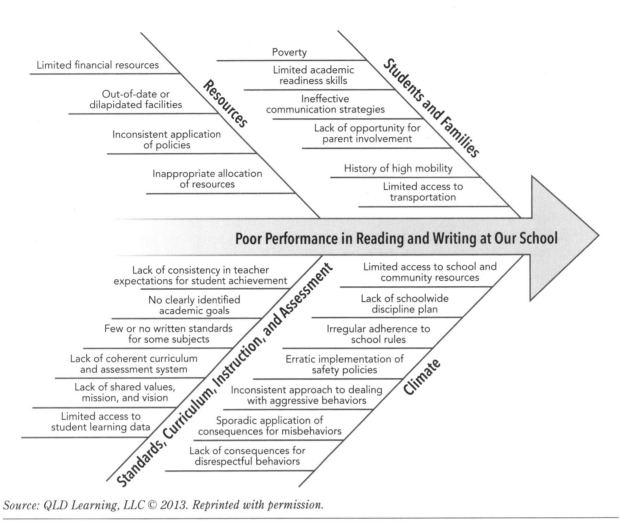

Figure 7.1: Sample cause-and-effect diagram.

to learn material relevant to the requirements of the standardized test.

The cause-and-effect diagram is a tool for the collaborative exploration of possible reasons why the problem being analyzed persists. There are several benefits from using this tool. First, the graphic organizer keeps the team focused on the same aspect of the problem as it delves more deeply into trying to understand the problem. Second, after completing the diagram, the team can step back and look for areas that are particularly dense in terms of the number of possible causes identified. It can also look for recurring or repeated patterns of causation across the various categories. These are two indicators that it may have unearthed a real potential cause. Finally, once it analyzes data from a visual perspective, the team can both identify data it will need to verify and localize the causes of the problem.

Relations Diagram

A relations diagram is a systems thinking tool that helps illustrate the dynamic relationship between significant aspects of complex situations. This tool is useful when you are investigating a problem that is part of a larger system or set of processes that you can't easily analyze using sequential thinking tools like cause-and-effect diagrams.

Figure 7.2 illustrates a relations diagram that examines the links and potential causal relationships of various aspects of school improvement. Some of the relevant categories are *student engagement*, *SMART goals*, *after-school clubs*, *student achievement*, and *staff development*.

Tip for Creating Relations Diagrams

Once you have identified one or two drivers, use the five whys analysis to help you uncover what it is about those issues that causes problems elsewhere. That will help you develop focused solutions that will reduce or eliminate the underlying causes of problems.

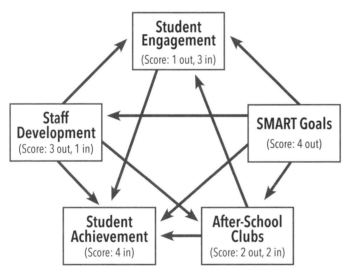

Source: QLD Learning, LLC © 2013. Reprinted with permission.

Figure 7.2: Relations diagram.

The procedure for creating a relations diagram is similar to that of a cause-and-effect diagram. The team brainstorms all the factors contributing to the problem or the main area of concern (in this case, school improvement), records these on sticky notes, and arranges the notes in a large circle on a sheet of paper or whiteboard. When the team has assembled all notes, it discusses whether the individual factors are causing or contributing to the impact of each of the others or whether they are *being caused* by or are *affected* by the others.

The following actions based on the notes determine the format of the relations diagram.

- Each time you decide that the idea or factor on the note you started with contributes to another factor's impact, draw an arrow *from the original note* to the other note.

- Each time you decide on a connection between the original idea or factor with another note, draw an arrow from the second note to the first note.

- Continue working your way around the circle until you have identified the relationships for each note.

- Count the number of arrows going *out* of each factor. The factor with the most number of arrows going out is a *key driver*, and possibly a key cause of or contributor to the other factors. This issue deserves more investigation into its cause and impact.

The relations diagram, also known as an interrelationship diagram, is especially useful in detecting important connections or links inherent within a complex system. By systematically examining both the links and the directionality of causation, users of this tool are able to focus their improvement efforts on the key drivers that will have the greatest impact on the whole system. This tool is also useful as a planning tool during the process of implementing a complex solution, because it highlights the factors that are most critical to the success of the implementation.

Numerical Data Tools

The remaining tools described in this chapter provide different ways to understand and present numerical (quantitative) data. There are two approaches for finding meaning in numbers.

1. **Creating pictures:** For most people, it is extremely difficult to look at a table of numbers and identify patterns or meaning with any accuracy. Charts and graphs are pictures that make it easier to see patterns and trends (or the lack thereof) in a set of numbers.

> We need to measure, not count.
>
> —Peter F. Drucker

2. **Performing calculations:** Statistics are calculations that describe some property of a set of numbers. An average or a median, for example, is a statistic that tells us about the midpoint of the data values. Such calculations also help us easily compare groups.

This section focuses primarily on the first of these strategies—creating pictures of data—because, for many everyday uses, pictures are easier to create and easier to interpret than statistics. Most people have a visceral reaction in response to a data chart—they get a gut feeling about what data are telling them—that simply doesn't happen when they look at a table of numbers or set of statistics.

However, basic statistical calculations help us make sense of large amounts of data. Some of the most powerful tools in this chapter combine pictures and calculations—you get the intuitive learning that comes from looking at a visual display of the data, plus the rigor of the statistical calculations. When you are plotting data over time, for example, you can use statistics to help you plan and, in certain cases, predict how your system will behave in the future. The important thing is to know when it is more appropriate to compare and when it is more appropriate to predict based on the data you have.

The tools in this chapter fall into two categories.

1. **Snapshot tools** give you a picture of what's happening at any given moment in time.

2. **Moving picture tools** let you determine pattern and trends over time.

There is software for displaying both snapshot and trend (moving picture) data, from straightforward spreadsheets to dashboards that summarize data from information systems. (Visit **go.solution-tree.com/schoolimprovement** for examples.) However, we provide specific how-to directions for all the tools in case computers or software are not available.

Snapshot Tools

As their name implies, snapshot tools capture a picture of what's going on at a given point in time. You would use

---

Guidelines for Helping Pictures Tell Their Stories

Use these tips to create useful pictures of data.

- Other people should be able to interpret the graph just by looking at it. All labels and titles should appear on the graph.

- Be careful not to allow overinterpretation. Snapshot graphs do not allow the interpreter to predict what will come next or to know what came before the particular point in time in which the data were collected. Moving picture graphs don't explain why something happened, only when.

- Ask, "What conclusions can we draw from this graph? What other questions do we have?"

Tips for Disaggregating Data

- Make sure the categories being compared are mutually exclusive; that is, they don't duplicate counts and information isn't overlapping.

- Be cautious when drawing conclusions based on differences between groups. Analysis by disaggregation is best done when the measure has been administered in a standardized way and sampling techniques have minimized bias.

- To avoid jumping to conclusions based on demographic characteristics, follow disaggregation analyses with problem solving, using tools and techniques such as five whys analysis, cause-and-effect analysis, and brainstorming.

- If analyzing survey data, be sure to identify demographic variables up front so that you have the information by subgroup when the survey is returned.

- If too few individuals are available to analyze as a subgroup, confidentiality issues can arise.

snapshot tools to understand what is happening in your classroom or school today. Snapshot tools are useful for comparing different groups of data (for example, cohorts of students on the same measure, different classes, or different schools) at one point in time. They should not be used to predict what results will be in the future. We describe five snapshot tools: (1) bar charts, (2) histograms, (3) distribution charts, (4) Pareto diagrams, and (5) scatterplots.

Three of the snapshot tools—bar charts, histograms, and Pareto diagrams—are sometimes all generically referred to as *bar graphs*. They all use bars of varying heights to indicate the frequency or impact of problems. Their visual similarity hides subtle but significant differences. For example, the bars in a bar chart do not touch because each bar represents a different category. The bars in histograms do touch because they represent different segments of a single measure. Pay close attention to the instructions for how to create the various charts, as they detail important differences. As you become more familiar with these charts, you'll learn how to pick out the different features that convey important messages about the data being displayed.

Snapshot tools are useful for displaying disaggregation results. Disaggregation is the process of separating and then analyzing results a different group achieved (see page 147). This process is useful in identifying differences across subgroups of students in terms of their performance, as well as identifying which subgroups if any are responding to certain instructional methods differently than others.

Bar Charts

A bar chart is a snapshot tool that uses bars to represent how often a given problem or outcome (perhaps a test score) occurs during different times, classes, and so on. For example, the bar chart can show group or individual scores on a particular measure. The data should reflect independent, mutually exclusive categories. For example, the bar charts in figure 7.3 show results of eighth-grade mathematics tests disaggregated by race and free or reduced lunch.

Preparing a bar chart involves collecting numerical data on the frequency of problems in various groups or events and

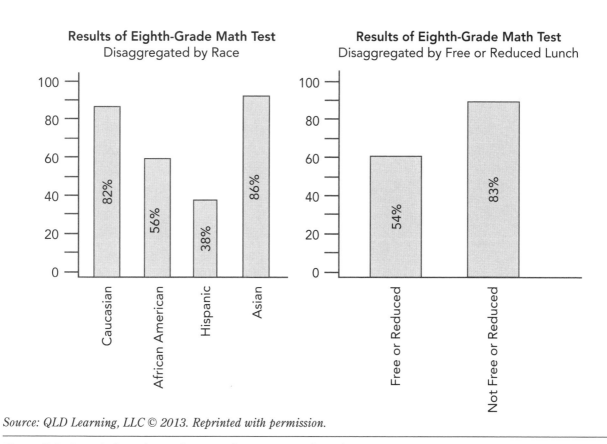

Source: *QLD Learning, LLC © 2013. Reprinted with permission.*

Figure 7.3: Sample bar charts showing disaggregated results.

identifying the highest data value in the collection. If necessary, you can round up to the nearest whole number. On the chart, divide the vertical axis into equal intervals with the highest value reflecting the highest data value recorded. For example, in figure 7.4 (page 172), the highest data value for reading is 90 percent in year 2012. On the horizontal axis, label individual categories; in figure 7.4 these categories are reading, language arts, writing, social studies, and science. Create vertical bars to show how each group or individual performed. Finally, check to make sure that the chart has a title and each axis has a label.

The bar chart in figure 7.4 shows the percent of students scoring proficient or advanced on an eighth-grade test of knowledge and concepts in three time periods—2011, 2012, and 2013.

Tips for Creating Bar Charts

- Make sure the categories being compared don't include duplicate counts or overlapping information.

- A visible space should separate each bar to show they are in fact representing separate pieces of information.

- Bars should be visually the same width so as not to imply differences in volume.

- If you have more than three or four years of data on one measure, a good rule of thumb is to use a line graph that connects the separate bar charts to show the data over time.

Tips for Creating Histograms

- Bars should touch each other because all data points can be found somewhere along the horizontal axis.

- Bars should be the same width visually so as not to imply differences in volume.

- Try to keep the number of class intervals to between five and ten. Too many intervals will create a tight, high pattern, while too few will create a flat picture that doesn't tell you much.

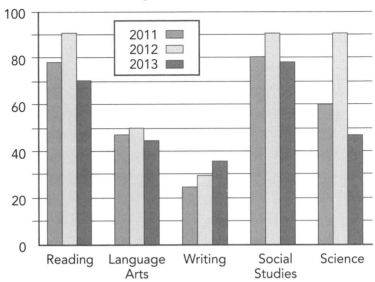

Eighth-Grade Test of Knowledge and Concepts: Percent of Students in Our School Scoring Proficient or Advanced

Source: QLD Learning, LLC © 2013. Reprinted with permission.

Figure 7.4: Sample bar chart.

Bar charts are descriptive and comparative graphic representations that reflect mutually exclusive categories of data generated at a particular point in time. They are easy to develop and analyze. The simplicity of the look, as well as the ease with which conclusions can be drawn, makes them the tool of choice for many. The caveat, however, is that they are limited in terms of the complexity of analysis that can be done. They are also limited by the fact that, because they represent a single moment in time, they are not predictive in nature.

Histograms

Histograms are snapshot charts illustrating the full set of continuous data across an entire spectrum. The charts show how often different values of a given measure occur during the data-collection period. Because the items are all part of a complete set, the snapshot of the items shows the range of variation in the data set. Histograms are useful tools for seeing the distribution of a large set of snapshot data. For example, you may have collected eighteen or more data points over time, plotted them on a run chart (see page 188), and may be interested in seeing the shape of the variation.

Figure 7.5 shows the distribution of grade point averages for tenth graders in a school year. The histogram shows the number of students on the vertical axis and their grade point averages on the horizontal axis.

The starting point for creating a histogram is collecting data on how often different values of a single continuous measure occur. A continuous measure is one where any value within a given range is possible. Examples include test scores, income levels, and student height. From the data set, determine the range—lowest to highest number—of the entire sample. The following five steps describe what to do with the data to place them on the histogram.

1. Decide the number of class intervals you need, making sure the intervals are exactly equal in width. For example, if you have test scores that range in value from fifteen to ninety-five points, you wouldn't learn much by labeling *each* data value along the horizontal axis. Instead, cluster the values into eight class intervals of ten points each (15–24, 25–34, and so on). Make sure your class intervals are mutually exclusive. Every data point should fit into only one class interval.

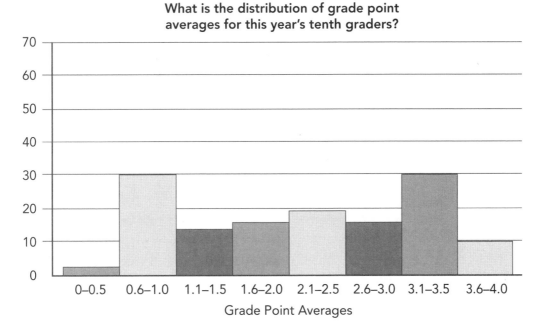

Source: QLD Learning, LLC © 2013. Reprinted with permission.

Figure 7.5: Sample histogram.

2. Count the number of values within each class interval. (This gives you the frequencies of occurrences for each interval.) Label the vertical axis with equal intervals that reach a value as high as or slightly higher than the largest count. For example, if the highest count value is seventeen, you could label seventeen equal intervals of one along the vertical axes (1, 2, 3, . . . 17), nine intervals of two (2, 4, 6, . . . 18), or five intervals of 4 (4, 8, . . . 20).

3. Label the class intervals along the horizontal axis. For example, the horizontal axis in figure 7.5 (page 173) lists grade point averages.

4. For each class interval, create a bar to a height equal to the count of occurrences within that class. In figure 7.5, the bars represent the number of students in each class interval.

5. Title the graph, and label each axis.

The histogram is a unique type of bar chart that reflects a continuum of data points that are displayed in connected bars representing equal ranges or volumes of data. It is useful as a way to compare results that span the entire scope of possible outcomes such as grade point averages or numbers of students within each decile, lexile, or zone of performance.

Distribution Charts

A distribution chart shows each data value as a dot (or other symbol) along an axis. This type of snapshot tool is useful when you are communicating statistics such as averages and standard deviation (which are highly sensitive to extreme data points) and want to show people how the observed data values are distributed. A distribution chart provides a simple descriptive tool that creates a picture of the data.

Figure 7.6 shows the distribution of test scores for twenty subjects.

This simple distribution chart of test scores conveys a lot of information very quickly. The viewer can tell that in this class

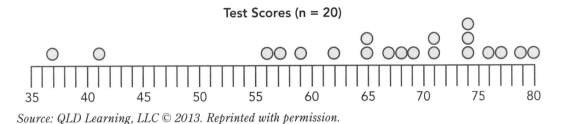

Figure 7.6: Sample distribution chart.

test, scores ranged from 37 to 80, all but two students scored above 55, and the majority of students scored 65 or higher.

Preparing a distribution chart is a simple task. From your data set, label an axis with individual data values. Place a dot (or other symbol) above the axis for each time that value was observed. Decide which statistics to include on the graph: total *n* (number of students), mean (average score), mode (most frequent value), standard deviation (variation from the mean), median (number in the middle of the data), range (difference between the highest and lowest values), and so on. Finally, give the chart a title and label the horizontal axis.

Interpreting Histograms and Distribution Charts

The shape of distribution charts and histograms reveals important information about the set of data values they represent. There is not much interpreting that can happen with a simple distribution chart like that in figure 7.6, because it only has twenty data points. The more data you have, the more likely it is that the data values used to generate a distribution chart or histogram will start to take on a characteristic shape.

The charts in figure 7.7 (page 176) show three typical shapes: *normal distribution*, *bimodal distribution*, and *skewed distribution*. In a normal distribution (also called a *bell curve*), the data are distributed symmetrically around a central peak. Normal curves play an important role in evaluating the results of standardized tests. Bimodal distribution shows two distinct peaks. The interpretation is that there are two distinct processes at work. For instance, if you saw a bimodal distribution in reading scores, one subset of students might be receiving more tutoring or reading practice than another subset of

Tips for Creating Distribution Charts

- Distribution charts differ from the various bar charts because each individual data value has a symbol. (Bar charts, histograms, and Pareto diagrams use bars to show collective information, such as the percentage or counts of data values falling within various intervals.)

- Distribution charts are different from bar charts because the categories are numerical.

- Distribution charts are different from histograms because each number on the horizontal axis is discrete. There are no intervals as there are on the histogram axis.

Normal Distribution

Distribution of Third-Grade Reading Scores for First Elementary School (Current School Year)

$n = 112$ Midrange = 48.5

Mean = 49.8   Median = 50

Range = 37–60   Mode = 50

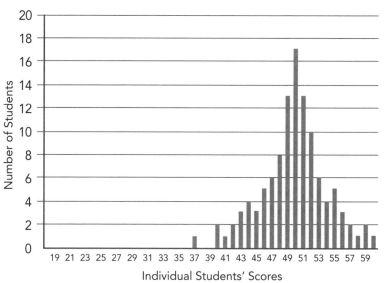

Bimodal Distribution

Distribution of Third-Grade Reading Scores for Second Elementary School (Current School Year)

$n = 112$ Midrange = 46

Mean = 48.5   Median = 52

Range = 19–60   Mode = 42 + 56

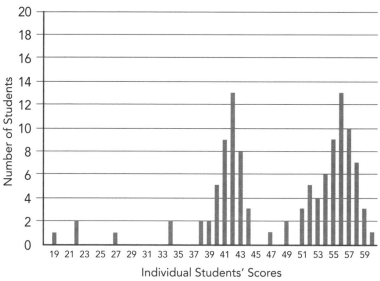

Skewed Distribution

Distribution of Third-Grade Reading Scores for Third Elementary School (Current School Year)

$n = 109$ Midrange = 46

Mean = 52.2   Median = 54

Range = 32–60   Mode = 56

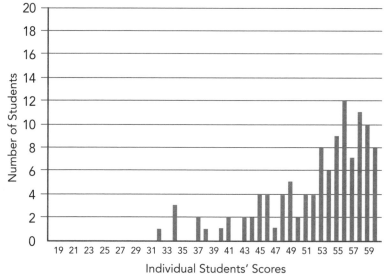

Source: QLD Learning, LLC © 2013. Reprinted with permission.

Figure 7.7: Three types of distribution—normal, bimodal, and skewed.

students. When the distribution trails off much more in one direction than another, the shape is a skewed distribution. Notice the third graph in figure 7.7 is skewed with a tail to the left. The data values cluster toward higher values and trail off toward lower values. When compared to a group with a normal distribution, this group would be said to be higher performing.

In addition to interpreting distributions based on their overall shape, you can also use various numerical values that fall into two types or categories of statistics: (1) measures of central tendency and (2) measures of dispersion.

1. **Measures of central tendency:** Mean, median, mode, and midrange provide single numbers that tell you something about where the data values cluster. In practice, teams use them to represent how a typical student performs (but as you'll see in the following pages, this is not always a valid use for these measures).

2. **Measures of dispersion:** Standard deviation and range are measures of dispersion that indicate the spread of the data.

Understanding the Normal Curve

The normal curve is a bell-shaped graph that shows the symmetrical dispersion of data around a central peak. Figure 7.8 (page 178) illustrates the special properties of the normal curve. The properties of the normal curve are the following.

- It is representative of the general population.
- It is symmetrical. The area to the left of the mean (x) equals the area to the right of the mean.
- The tails never quite touch the baseline, but continue to approach it as the curve moves away from the mean.
- All the measures of central tendency (mode, median, and mean) are the same value.
- The height of the curve at any given point denotes the frequency of scores at that point.

Statistics and Non-Normal Curves

The interpretation of some of the statistics described here (such as standard deviation) is based on having data that are distributed normally (that is, they would form a normal curve when plotted). Obviously, data that form a skewed or bimodal distribution are not normal, and you have to be careful about how you interpret statistics for such data sets.

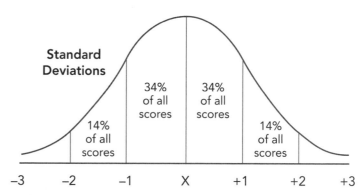

Source: QLD Learning, LLC © 2013. Reprinted with permission.

Figure 7.8: The normal curve.

Norm-referenced data are reported using standard scores such as stanines and positional measures such as quartiles and percentiles. Typically, reports include national, state, and local norms. Figure 7.9 illustrates the application of norm-referenced data for a fourth-grade student at the sixty-fifth percentile.

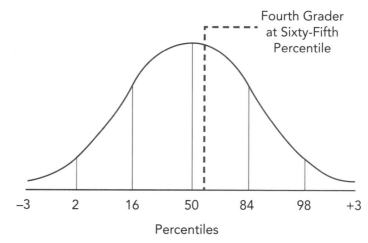

Source: QLD Learning, LLC © 2013. Reprinted with permission.

Figure 7.9: Normal curve with norm-referenced data.

Deciding the Measure of Position for Norm-Referenced Tests

Teams can report results of norm-referenced tests in a variety of ways depending on which measure of position they use as the reference point. Table 7.2 shows some of the common reference points related to norm-referenced tests.

Table 7.2: Measures of Position for Norm-Referenced Tests

Measure of Position	Example
Standard Scores A standard score is simply any raw score that has been redefined in terms of a standard, constant mean and a standard, constant standard deviation.	SAT scores are standard scores with a mean of 500 and a standard deviation of 100. ACT scores have a mean of 20 and a standard deviation of 5.
Stanines A standard score widely used on standardized tests, stanines slice the normal curve into nine categories, with a mean of 5 and a standard deviation of 1.96.	A stanine score of 7, 8, or 9 falls into the top 30 percent of the normal curve, representing above-average performance.
Quartiles Quartiles are numbers that divide the ranked data into quarters; each set of data has three quartiles. The upper limit of the first quartile is the number at which one-fourth of all the scores fall below that value. At the upper limit of the second quartile, half of the data points fall below that number (the value of the second quartile is also the median value). The third quartile is the number for which three-fourths of the population earned a lower score.	Twenty-five percent of the population will fall into each quartile. When reading your local results, you will use the national scores at each quartile to determine the percent of your students in each.
Percentiles Percentiles are numbers that divide a set of ranked data into one hundred parts; each set of data has ninety-nine percentiles. The logic is the same as for quartiles. At the ninetieth percentile, 90 percent of the population earned a lower score.	If a student's score places him or her at the ninety-eighth percentile, he or she scored better than 98 percent of the test takers in the population.

Each of the examples in table 7.3 (page 180) is based on the raw data from test scores for ten sixth graders who took the advanced reading test (listed here in descending order): 98, 93, 87, 85, 85, 75, 71, 69, 68, and 50. Measures of central tendency may be similar for data sets, but the picture of the variation in each data set might be very different. The three distributions shown in figure 7.7 (page 176), for example, all have very similar means, medians, and ranges, but obviously the shapes of the distributions are very different.

Pareto Diagrams

A *Pareto diagram* is a bar-type chart that shows the frequency or impact of different problems or causes in order

Table 7.3: Measures of Central Tendency and Measures of Dispersion

Measures of Central Tendency	
Measure	**Example**
Arithmetic Mean (average, x, $\overline{X}$) The arithmetic mean is the center point of a group of data. The average of all values is calculated by adding up the values of the data points and dividing the sum by the number of occurrences. The average (mean) might be thought of as a group's typical characteristic, assuming there are no points that fall a great distance from the other points (outliers).	Ten sixth graders took an advanced reading test, scoring 98, 93, 87, 85, 85, 75, 71, 69, 68, and 50. Sum of all values = 781 Number of occurrences = 10 Mean score = 78.1
Median The median is the midpoint of the data. Half of the data points fall above the median, half fall below. If the number of data points is uneven, the median is the value of the data that occupies the middle position when the data are ranked in order of size. If there is an even number of data points, the median is the average of the two middle values.	There is an even number of scores, so we add the two middle values, then divide by two. The two middle values are 85 and 75. Median = (85 + 75)/2 = 80
Midrange The midrange is computed by calculating the figure that lies halfway between the highest and lowest extremes.	Highest score = 98 Lowest score = 50 Midrange = (98 + 50)/2 = 74
Mode The mode is the data value that occurs most frequently in the data set.	Because 85 appears twice, it is the mode.
Measures of Dispersion	
Measure	**Example**
Range Range is the simplest measure of dispersion. It is the difference between the highest and lowest data points. It simply tells us the distance between the extremes.	The sixth-grade reading scores range from 50 to 98 (a range of 48 points). If a second set of students took the exam, the range would likely be larger or smaller.
Standard Deviation Standard deviation is a statistical measure of dispersion that helps you judge the spread of the data. The normal curve spans approximately six standard deviations. Closely grouped data will have relatively small standard deviations, and more widely spread-out data will have larger values.	On a test, if the mean is 50, and the standard deviation is 10, a score of 60 falls one standard deviation above the mean.

from the highest to lowest values. A line shows the cumulative impact of subsequent problems as you move from left to right across the chart. Some people find it helpful to think of a Pareto diagram as a hybrid of a bar chart and histogram. It is a bar chart because it compares separate, discrete categories of information. It is like a histogram because the categories represent the sum total of the data.

A Pareto diagram is useful when you need to focus your actions on high-leverage points—the areas that are most likely to yield the greatest results. Similarly, you may find this snapshot tool useful when you want to choose a place to begin problem solving.

Preparations for a Pareto diagram parallel those for other snapshot tools. You use existing data or brainstorm to identify the activities, problems, and issues that you want to compare and rank in order by priority. Determine the unit of measurement you're interested in comparing, such as performance on achievement standards, frequency of occurrence, lost instructional time, or annual cost. If necessary, gather additional data on each problem category either by conducting a new study or by reviewing historical data.

Remember to be wary of historical data. You need to make sure that the definitions used in the past are the same as those you are using now. For example, if you are collecting data on different types of behavioral referrals, you must make sure that they were categorized the same way. Otherwise, the data will be irrelevant to your current situation.

With that content assembled, you are ready to complete the next steps in creating the Pareto diagram.

1. List the categories on the horizontal (*x*) axis and frequencies on the vertical (*y*) axis. List the categories in descending order from left to right on the horizontal axis with bars above each category to indicate frequency. You can combine categories containing the fewest items into an *other* category and place it on the extreme right as the last bar.

2. Compare the relative frequency of each category by adding up all observations and determining what percentage of the whole each item represents.

3. Draw the cumulative percentage line showing the portion of the total for each.

Figure 7.10 is an example of a Pareto diagram showing behavioral referrals. It shows the reasons for and numbers of referrals for 668 subjects.

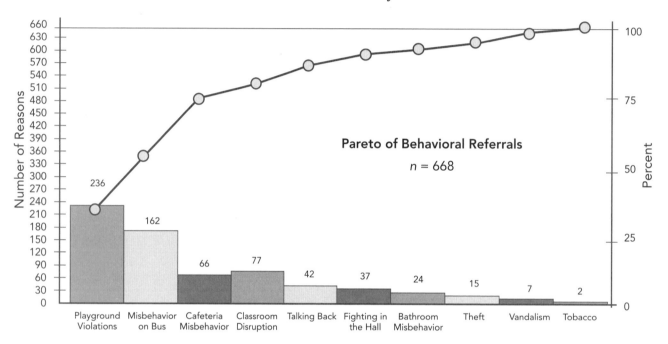

Source: QLD Learning, LLC © 2013. Reprinted with permission.

Figure 7.10: Sample Pareto diagram.

It is possible to use Pareto thinking even if you cannot create a Pareto diagram. In many cases, school teams find it difficult to collect data on the issues of greatest interest to them. Finding a new way to rank problems by importance or impact enables teams to focus on the most important—the vital few. Conducting a Pareto analysis is one way to target problem areas and work toward finding solutions. Figure 7.11 is an example of Pareto analysis of academic areas in which students are struggling the most.

The Pareto analysis is an excellent tool for helping teams focus on areas of concern that, if resolved, could have significant impact on overall performance, whether it relates to student learning, efficient operations, or improved safety. The

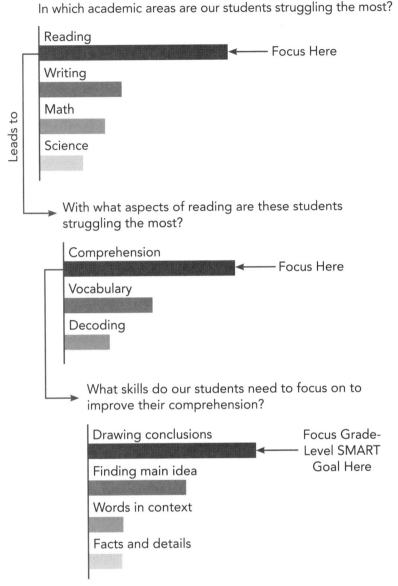

In which academic areas are our students struggling the most?

Reading — Focus Here

Writing

Math

Science

Leads to

With what aspects of reading are these students struggling the most?

Comprehension — Focus Here

Vocabulary

Decoding

What skills do our students need to focus on to improve their comprehension?

Drawing conclusions — Focus Grade-Level SMART Goal Here

Finding main idea

Words in context

Facts and details

By targeting the most problematic area and progressively breaking into smaller elements, teachers can focus instruction where the most significant gains occur.

Source: QLD Learning, LLC © 2013. Reprinted with permission.

Figure 7.11: Sample Pareto analysis.

analysis is both a statistical process as well as a way of thinking. Once understood, this tool will become a natural part of the team's vocabulary and repertoire for improvement.

Scatterplots

A *scatterplot* is a graph that shows the strength of the relationship between two variables. Teams can use it to investigate the relationship between two variables or to determine a cause-and-effect relationship from paired data. Similarly, you can use a scatterplot when you have continuous interval (numerical) data for two different variables, both measured on each item or person.

There are many sources of paired data that can be presented in scatterplots.

- Test scores and attendance
- Class size and student performance
- Dollars invested and student achievement
- Parent involvement and satisfaction with the school
- Class size and reading scores measured for each class
- Behavioral referrals and number of after-school programs offered at each school

The procedure for developing a scatterplot is straightforward once you have identified the paired data you wish to examine. Record the two measures you gather on each item such as for each student, class, or school. For each pair, determine which of the two you think might cause or influence the other. That is the *independent variable*. The other item in the pair is the *dependent variable*.

Formatting the scatterplot includes the following five steps.

1. Construct a graph with an *x*- and *y*-axis. For example, in figure 7.12 (page 185), GPA scores are listed on the *x*-axis and ACT scores on the *y*-axis.

2. Label the *x*-axis with the intervention (independent variable).

3. Label the *y*-axis with the effect (dependent variable) you are measuring.

4. Determine appropriate intervals for each type of data and label the axes accordingly.

5. Plot the paired data points.

To interpret a scatterplot, look for patterns in the scatter of data values. Graphs can have three types of correlations.

1. **Positive correlation:** Two variables both increase or decrease together (for example, as attendance increases, test scores also increase).

2. **Negative correlation:** One variable increases as the other decreases. For example, as the number of students who qualify for free or reduced-price lunch increases, average kindergarten readiness levels decrease.

3. **No correlation:** The variables are not related in any way, producing a graph with data that appear to be randomly scattered throughout. An example is the number of books checked out of the library each week graphed along with the price of candy bars at the local grocery store.

Figure 7.12 is a sample scatterplot showing a positive correlation between grade point average (GPA) and American College Testing (ACT) scores. *GPA* is the independent variable, and *ACT scores* is the dependent variable. (Caution: Even if the plot reveals a relationship pattern, it does not prove that changes in the independent variable cause changes in the dependent variable.)

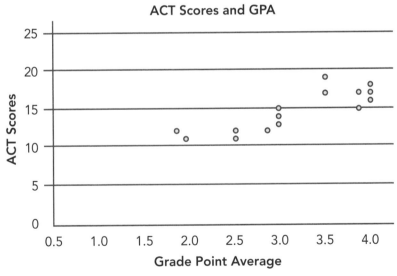

Source: QLD Learning, LLC © 2013. Reprinted with permission.

Figure 7.12: Scatterplot showing a positive correlation between ACT scores and GPA.

Figure 7.13 shows a negative correlation: reading scores decline as class size increases.

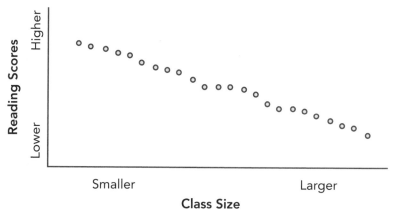

Source: QLD Learning, LLC © 2013. Reprinted with permission.

Figure 7.13: Sample negative correlation.

Interpreting the correlations—positive or negative—on the scatterplots sets the stage for you to dig deeper into the nature or possible reasons for the correlations. For example, in figure 7.12 (page 185), the correlation between GPA and ACT scores is positive; in figure 7.13, the correlation between reading scores and class size is negative. To explore the potential causal relationships, the team could use a cause-and-effect diagram or conduct a five whys analysis. It is important to keep in mind that just because a pattern shows up in the data doesn't mean that one variable causes the other or that there is any causal relationship between those variables and others that may emerge from further analysis. In the case of two variables that appear to have no correlation, further causal analyses would not be useful.

Snapshot tools provide useful pictures of data captured at a particular point in time. They can be analyzed relatively quickly by simply viewing the graphs and drawing some surface-level conclusions about what might have been going on at that moment in time. Alone, however, they have limited or no value when it comes to understanding potential causes or predicting potential futures.

Moving Picture Tools

There are basically two types of moving picture tools: (1) run charts and (2) control charts. Teams can use them to

Correlation Is Not Causation

- Correlation is a measure of the connection or association between two variables. Correlation is a necessary—but not sufficient—condition for establishing a causal relationship between two variables.

- Causality implies correlation; correlation does not imply causality.

- For example, researchers have found that SAT scores have a relationship to students' grade point average their first year of college. This does not mean that good SAT scores cause students to do well in college. But SAT scores and GPA do seem to be related. There may be a third variable that is causing both SAT scores and GPA to be high.

understand patterns in the variation over time. Understanding variation allows us to distinguish between important and unimportant changes in process performance (that is, from the standpoint of improvement).

Variation is how much data values change from one point in time to another. Everything varies: assessment scores, the time it takes to do a task, budget overruns, behavioral referrals, and so on. A key to improving results is to reduce variation in the processes that produce those results and move the average higher. Variation comes in two forms.

1. **Common cause variation** is created by many small factors present in every process or situation. The way the system is designed and managed affects this variation. Examples of common cause variation include teachers who are routinely ill-prepared in their subject areas, students not coming to school ready to learn how to read, or test scores that consistently (and predictably) vary a few points up one year, down another, and so on.

2. **Special cause variation** is created by a specific situation, circumstance, or anomaly. Examples include the average performance on a weekly quiz that drops or peaks dramatically for no apparent reason, or a barrage of behavioral referrals that are issued after a new behavior policy is put in place.

Processes that have only common cause variation are stable or in control because their behavior is relatively predictable. The amount of common cause variation may be more than you'd like, but you can count on a stable process to perform within certain limits, making it relatively easy to predict and plan. Processes that also have special cause variation are out of control because their behavior is unpredictable, making it difficult to plan.

There are different strategies for reducing common cause variation as compared to special cause variation.

- **Common cause strategy:** The only way to reduce common cause variation is to make a fundamental change in the system. You'll need to look at what's

> Experience by itself teaches nothing. You must have a theory and you must take action.
>
> —W. Edwards Deming

"Don't Tinker" Does Not Mean "Don't Innovate"

The key message in working with variation is that you have to understand what factors influence variation in order to make any significant improvement. The lesson is that you shouldn't make random changes in a process hoping for better results. However, that doesn't mean you should stop changing a process entirely. There is still room for innovation and experimentation, as long as you are prepared to monitor the effects of these actions and make sure they have not made the situation worse.

happening at all times in the process, and use problem-solving strategies to identify process changes (see chapter 8).

- **Special cause strategy:** Find out what is different in the process when the problem (or desired result) appears. Eliminate the cause, or replicate it if it is a good special cause (for example, an exceptional teaching practice). Note that simply removing special causes usually does not lead to dramatic improvement—it will only return the system to predictability.

An understanding of variation will fundamentally change how you define problems. For one thing, you'll discover that factors inherent in the system (common causes) cause most variation. The only way to affect that variation is to change the system.

An understanding of variation will also change how you perceive solutions. Once you realize that there needs to be fundamental system changes to produce fundamentally different results, you begin to realize the futility of actions such as raising standards and simply exhorting everyone to work harder. You'll also begin to see that tinkering with a system is more likely to increase variation than reduce it. These types of changes do not fundamentally affect the system and therefore cannot lead to improvement.

Run Chart

A *run chart* is a chart of data with points plotted in time order and tests performed to determine whether the variation is due to special or common causes. This tool is helpful when you want to monitor performance over time or you want to understand the pattern of variation over time. The information on a run chart can help you detect trends, shifts, or cycles and determine the type of improvement strategy to use.

The procedure for developing a run chart starts with collecting data points—at least seven and preferably more—over time. This means taking the same measure at regular intervals such as weekly, monthly, or quarterly. Formatting the run chart includes the following four steps.

Tips for Creating Run Charts

- Because the tests for common and special cause variation require multiple data points to detect trends or patterns, interpreting and acting on results based on just a few data points may be misleading or even harmful. For example, if a school board looks at three years of test scores from different schools in the district and concludes that the principals of the "failing" schools need to be reassigned, the negative consequences for

Continued➔

1. Construct a horizontal (*x*) and vertical (*y*) axis. (For example, figure 7.14 lists the time intervals on the horizontal axis and the number of referrals on the vertical axis.)

2. Label the time intervals along the *x*-axis. Divide the *y*-axis into equal-sized intervals that cover a range slightly larger than the range of actual data values.

3. Plot the data in time order.

4. Determine the median (midpoint). Draw a line at this value on the chart. This becomes the centerline.

Figure 7.14 is a run chart showing behavioral referrals submitted to the office each week.

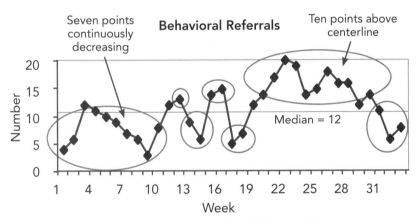

Source: QLD Learning, LLC © 2013. Reprinted with permission.

Figure 7.14: Run chart for behavioral referrals showing special causes.

The data vary unpredictably at certain times (such as smaller circled clusters that appear to randomly go up or down from the center point—no special cause) and somewhat predictably at other times (such as larger circled clusters that show either an upward or downward trend or a consistently high performance above the center point—a possible special cause). By analyzing the clusters of data, the team can go back to see what might have been happening during the weeks where special causes may have been occurring (for instance, the third week through ninth and twentieth through thirtieth). This chart depicts simulated

those who have been building relationships with staff, families, and students around school improvement efforts for the past two years will set the schools back, not improve results.

- Because you need many data points to construct and interpret a run chart, this tool lends itself well to measures that are taken quite often in the cycle of a school or classroom (for example, attendance, classroom quizzes, homework assignments turned in, discipline referrals, and medications). You can also plot less-frequent measures if you have enough data points (for example, average ACT scores, average graduation rates, college or job placement rates, and so on).

- Changing a measure or assessment will usually change the results. A run chart is a useful tool to use to communicate these changes, such as when a state increases the standard that students must achieve to pass proficiency levels on a state test. The run chart will show a special cause drop in the overall context of historical variation.

A Run Chart by Any Other Name

Because run charts depict data in time order, they are often called time plots. The name *run chart* derives from a particular type of test for special causes. (See page 188.)

data. In the real world, you would look at all your data at the first sign of a special cause, and apply your own knowledge to what might be happening.

Guidelines for Special Cause Variation

Statisticians follow a set of standards to identify special cause variations such as those figure 7.15 illustrates. The standards specify the conditions for the runs for the number of data points. A *run* is a group of data points below or above the median. Each time the data cross the median, a new run begins. There can be runs of only one data point if the next data point then crosses the median (see figure 7.15). Use the Runs Table in appendix A (page 283) to help you count runs and take appropriate action.

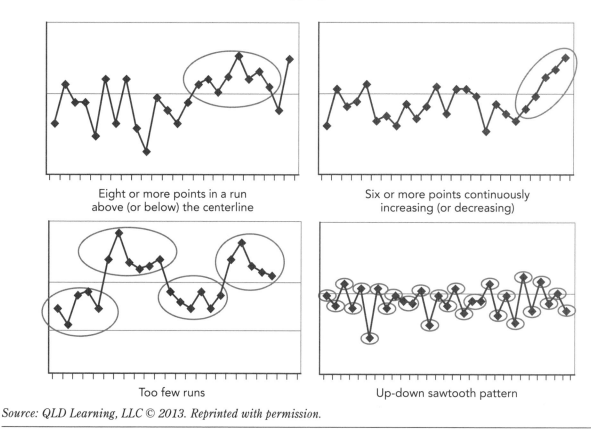

Eight or more points in a run above (or below) the centerline

Six or more points continuously increasing (or decreasing)

Too few runs

Up-down sawtooth pattern

Source: QLD Learning, LLC © 2013. Reprinted with permission.

Figure 7.15: Criteria for special causes.

The standards for special cause variation are:

- Too few or too many runs for the number of data points
- Six or more data points continuously increasing or decreasing
- Eight or more data points all together either above or below the median indicating too few runs
- Fourteen or more data points in an up-down sawtooth pattern

Control Chart

A *control chart* is a type of run chart that also indicates the range of variation built into the system (indicated by control limits added to the chart). Control charts are useful when you want to find out whether a particular data point is truly outside the normal range of variation for the system. Similarly, they are useful for demonstrating that the action you took resulted in not only improved performance but less variability around performance.

School leaders and teachers will be aware of situations in which they can apply this type of data tool. You can plot your school's prior and current test results, behavioral data (for example, attendance or referrals), or classroom assessment results to see if there are significant trends. You can also use the tool to monitor the impact of an instructional strategy, a specific curriculum, or program intervention on student achievement. To do so, you plot results seen before the change and then plot results you obtain after the change. Then, apply all the tests for special causes to see if there is a significant change (up or down) in achievement after the change.

You can use control charts with data that are not time ordered; however, in that case the only special cause test that applies is whether a point is outside the control limits. For example, you could plot the test results from many schools and determine the range of variation to see if any of those schools were outside the limits (truly underachieving or overachieving). Other special cause tests, such as those on pages 192–193, deal with time-ordered data.

Using the Runs Table to Determine Special or Common Cause Variation

First count the runs in your data. A run is a set of data points that are together on one side of the median. Each time the data cross the median, there is a new run. (Note: Because of the way a *run* is defined in this particular test for special cause, it is possible to have a run of just one data point.) Then count the total number of data points that are not on the median.

Next, go to the "Runs Table" in appendix A (page 283), and locate the number of data that are not on the median. To the right of that number, locate the least number of runs expected and the most number of runs expected. If your data set has fewer or more runs than expected, you have a special cause. If not, you are looking at common cause variation.

Tips for Creating Control Charts

- You should have at least eighteen data points before performing the calculations that add control limits to a run chart.

- A standard deviation roughly corresponds to 2.66 points from the mean. The control limit calculations are for a type of control chart called an *individuals chart*, which is the control chart to use when you have relatively slow-cycling data, such as test scores, behavioral referrals, attendance figures, and so on.

Developing a control chart involves the following ten steps.

1. List all the data points in time order.

2. Calculate the *moving range* (R) between each two adjacent numbers. The moving range is the difference between adjacent numbers. (See table 7.4.)

3. Calculate the average of the moving ranges ($\bar{R}$). The average is the sum of all moving ranges divided by the number of moving ranges. For example, in the data set in table 7.4, the average of the moving ranges is 4.3 (13 divided by 3).

4. Calculate the average of the data points ($\bar{X}$). The average is the sum of all the data points divided by the number of data points. In the example above, the average is 10 (40 divided by 4).

5. Calculate the upper control limit.

    $UCL = \bar{X} + 2.66\bar{R}$

    UCL = Average of the data points + (2.66 × average of the data ranges)

    For example:

    $UCL = 10 + (2.66 \times 4.3)$

    $UCL = 21.44$

6. Calculate the lower control limit.

    $LCL = \bar{X} - 2.66\bar{R}$

    LCL = Average of the data points – (2.66 × average of the ranges)

    For example:

    $LCL = 10 - (2.66 \times 4.3)$

    $LCL = -1.44$

7. Plot all the data points in time order.

8. Draw a line on the plot at the mean (average of $\bar{X}$).

9. Draw in the upper and lower control limits.

10. Apply the tests for special causes and interpret the chart. In addition to the tests described for run charts (page 188), look for any points outside the

control limits. Points beyond the limits provide an additional signal of special cause variation.

Table 7.4: Time-Order Data Points

Data Points	Range Between Adjacent Points (= Moving Range)
12	2
10	3
13	8
5	

A worksheet for computing control limits, using the ten steps outlined here, appears in appendix B on page 315.

Figure 7.16 depicts a control chart of student performance results over time. Note how the chart changes after a change in instructional strategy.

Weekly Classroom Assessment

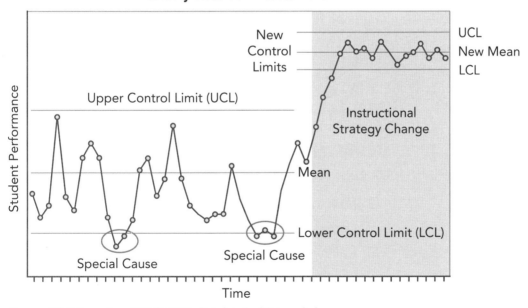

Source: QLD Learning, LLC © 2013. Reprinted with permission.

Figure 7.16: Control chart of demonstrated results of instructional change.

Moving picture tools provide us with many different ways to analyze data over time to determine whether the potential causes of what we are seeing in the data are due to common or special causes. They also have predictive qualities when statistical trends can be documented. These analyses are most appropriate for processes that occur repeatedly over the course of time (hourly, daily, weekly). Enough data are needed to be able to statistically detect patterns, trends, and movement. The more data you have, the more confident you can be that your conclusions will be accurate.

Final Check: Data Tools for Understanding More Than Problems

Instead of feeling drowned in data and starved for information, we can move toward making meaning of data by asking ourselves, "What do we need to know? How can we best find out?" Then, we can select the appropriate data tool for gathering, analyzing, and interpreting the data. With data in hand, we need to once again ask, "What more do we need to know? How can we best find out?" In this way, we become better informed as decision makers, more knowledgeable about our systems and our practices, and better able to make improvements on behalf of our students. Consider the following checklist to determine your use of data tools.

My team probes for the underlying causes of problems through:

- ☐ Five whys analysis
- ☐ Cause-and-effect diagrams
- ☐ Relations diagrams

My team uses a variety of tools for analyzing numerical data, getting both a snapshot of the current situation and a moving picture that shows the history of performance by using:

- ☐ Bar charts
- ☐ Histograms
- ☐ Distribution charts

- ☐ Pareto diagrams
- ☐ Scatterplots
- ☐ Disaggregation
- ☐ Run charts
- ☐ Control charts

My team realizes how important it is to understand *variation* when choosing appropriate reactions to problems in the workplace.

PART THREE

Implementing Effective School Improvement

CHAPTER 8

Systems Thinking for Coherent School Improvement

The farmer in James Bender's epigraph for this chapter illustrates a principle that's known as *systems thinking*, a focus on optimizing performance for the system as a whole, often by working across traditional boundaries. We know from research that higher-quality learning and teaching result when schools operate like a system rather than a heap of pieces (Hargreaves & Fullan, 2012; Hirsh & Hord, 2012). Schools achieve more when teams—not just individuals—are learning together, when the school as a whole is focused on a common mission and vision, and when professional learning is aligned and congruent with that focus. We know that for most schools the ability to be effective is directly related to the larger district's effectiveness and efficiency. In short, we know the power of thinking and acting like a system.

The principles, tools, and methods we describe in this chapter and throughout this book lay the groundwork to help your teams start thinking like a system. A *system* is a collection of parts that interact to function as a whole. One truism concerning a system is that it cannot be divided to get identical separate parts; alternatively, a heap of parts can be so divided. For example, a pile of sand can be divided, and you will have two piles of sand. A horse, however, will not be two separate horses if divided!

Another truism about a system is that each part continually affects the others over time. For example, what happens with your course registration process today could affect a student's learning tomorrow. If a student couldn't get into a course that lays the foundation for getting into advanced

Each year the farmer entered his corn in the state fair, where it won a blue ribbon. One year, a newspaper reporter interviewed him and learned something interesting about how he grew it. The reporter discovered that the farmer shared his seed corn with his neighbors. "How can you afford to share your best seed corn with your neighbors when they are entering corn in competition with yours each year?" the reporter asked. "Why sir," said the farmer, "didn't you know? The wind picks up pollen from the ripening corn and swirls it from field to field. If my neighbors grow inferior corn, cross-pollination will steadily degrade the quality of my corn. If I am to grow good corn, I must help my neighbors grow good corn." He is very much aware of the connectedness of life. His corn cannot improve unless his neighbor's corn also improves. So it is in other dimensions.

—James Bender

placement (AP) classes (which would likely lead to higher SAT and ACT scores), this could, in turn, affect whether a student goes on to college.

To help your teams develop a common understanding of systems and how they function, we recommend Suzanne Bailey's (2000) systems metaphor exercise. This exercise is designed to help teams sort through priorities and decide which programs and activities can cease, which need more focus, and which are simply in a maintenance mode. You can use it as part of an ongoing process of assessing, renewing, and celebrating initiatives. The exercise is based on the metaphor of a gardener and will help participants focus on how programs and activities move through a cycle from buds to blooms to full flower to withering flower to compost (which feeds the next cycle of innovation). Figure 8.1 shows the systems metaphor exercise.

Time required: Four hours

Steps

1. **Identify the functions of your school system:** Have your team brainstorm what functions, programs, ideas, and so on are present in your school system. Include everything from fully functional systems to ideas they have heard from rumors. Categorize these ideas as follows.

   - **Seeds**—Ideas or mandates on the horizon blowing in from the outside that haven't landed yet but are coming

   - **Buds**—New programs just starting this year that need lots of attention, training, focus, and funds

   - **Blooms**—Programs that staff have put in place and adopted but still need attention

   - **Full flower**—Programs in full implementation by almost all staff with results beginning to show; support is still needed for modifications.

   - **Withering flower**—Programs that may no longer serve the school's priority needs but continue simply because they are automatic; they have become second nature to all staff and will continue happening with no special attention or funding; they can fall off the tree to make room for new programs.

   - **Compost pile**—Previous programs no longer being implemented, but they built the skill foundation needed for new ideas; all but forgotten, they nourish the roots of the tree.

- **Garbage can**—Programs that have not produced results or are no longer funded
- **Pests**—Things that eat away at the roots of the tree (for example, distractors and detractors, political infighting, lack of resources, and so on)
- **Energy**—Things that keep the tree energized and growing (resources, trust, communication, skills, capabilities, and so on)

2. **Post the sticky notes on the tree:** Some parts of the tree will be fuller than others; some will be emptier—there will almost always be patterns.

3. **Talk about the patterns:** What causes them? What are our beliefs and values that serve as the roots of the tree?

4. **Clarify the group's vision:** What does the preferred future look like? Record that vision in the skies above the tree.

5. **Determine goals for reaching that vision:** Record these in the trunk of the tree.

6. **Revise the tree:** Go through the sticky notes in the branches and evaluate each one based on the program's ability to help reach the vision and goals. Some programs will need to be cycled off the tree (these are no longer relevant or will not produce results toward the vision), while others will need to be added.

Source: Adapted from Bailey, 2000.

Figure 8.1: Systems metaphor exercise.

Aspects of Systems Thinking

Systems thinking is a way of thinking and talking about the forces and interrelationships that shape the behavior of systems. Systems thinkers look at events and see three aspects operating at the same time: (1) patterns of behavior, (2) systemic structures, and (3) mental models. These aspects of systems thinking are evident to educators involved in advancing school improvement efforts—efforts that will enhance professional learning and student achievement.

Patterns of Behavior

We are all accustomed to perceiving events in isolation. We would not necessarily see a connection between a disruptive third-grade class one day and a rambunctious kindergarten

> Upon this gifted age, in its dark hour, falls from the sky a meteoric shower of facts. . . . They lie unquestioned, uncombined. Wisdom enough to leech us of our ill is daily spun, but there exists no loom to weave it into fabric.
>
> —Edna St. Vincent Millay

class a week later. Each teacher would deal with the problems separately in his or her own classes.

However, a systems thinker would look for trends and patterns across traditional boundaries. For example, a principal who is a systems thinker might ask the following questions: "What is the cause of this behavior in the two classrooms? What do the classrooms have in common? Do other classrooms have this same characteristic? Am I seeing disengaged learning, a lack of consistent behavior expectations, or new teachers struggling for classroom management? Am I seeing this in other parts of our school? What policies, procedures, practices, and processes might be leading to this behavior?"

Doing so can expose deeply rooted problems that can surface in a variety of guises. Being able to see the underlying problem lets a systems thinker identify improvements that have far-reaching impact. Variation tools, such as a run chart and control chart (page 191), are designed to help us see those patterns and trends when our intuition and perceptions cannot. The historygram process (page 234) is another way to identify patterns in human relationships.

Feedback Loops

Another tool for understanding patterns and cycles is a *feedback loop*. Feedback loops drive everything that changes through time. Most people think in linear, nonfeedback terms—they see a problem, decide on an action, expect a result, and think that's the end of the problem. Figure 8.2 illustrates this linear process.

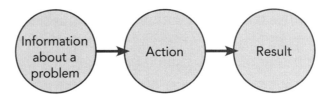

Source: QLD Learning, LLC © 2013. Reprinted with permission.

Figure 8.2: Linear thinking.

On the other hand, a systems thinker understands that in reality an action produces a result that in turn creates future problems and actions—with no beginning or end, only a constant dynamic interaction. Figure 8.3 illustrates this circular, reiterative process of systems thinking.

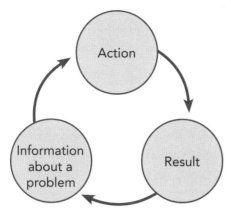

Source: QLD Learning, LLC © 2013. Reprinted with permission.

Figure 8.3: Systems thinking.

Every action and change in the world occurs within a network of feedback loops. Understanding feedback loops is essential to understanding and managing change. Among other things, thinking in terms of feedback loops helps you anticipate unintended consequences to a proposed change. For example, suppose a school considers a simple change in its lunchroom policy. The faculty and staff would have to think carefully to ensure the change wouldn't cause students to opt out of the hot lunch program, because having fewer students participating could lead to budget problems, recess problems, and perhaps even health issues for the students.

To understand feedback systems, consider that every system is made up of two variables—*level* and *rate*.

1. **Level** is how much (accumulation)
2. **Rate** is how fast accumulation occurs (the flow)

In filling a bathtub, the amount of water defines the level, while the flow of the water is the rate that changes the level. A group's degree of frustration is a level that changes in response to the changing surrounding pressures. Consider these situations: a school's budget is a level that changes in response to changing state funding policies; a school's average test scores are at a level that changes with the focus on results-oriented school improvement and professional learning. Schools can develop feedback loops in multiple layers to

Three Principles of Social Systems

A *social system* is any group of people who share common space, whose actions affect and influence each other (even slightly), or who have a shared purpose. For example, a school is a social system, a department team is a social system, and a community is a social system. Three principles of social systems are relevant to the ideas in this chapter.

1. The source of most difficulties is internal to the system—although the tendency is to blame outside forces or *them*.

2. Often people take actions they believe are solving the problem, when in fact the actions themselves are the cause of the problem in the first place.

3. The nature of the dynamic feedback structure of a social system tends to mislead people into taking ineffective, even counterproductive, action.

describe such system interactions and, thereby, enable educators to better understand patterns of behavior across events.

Consider the real-life example of level and rate interactions in a school district, where the district has been underinvesting in staff for years (a rate of investment). Teacher salaries are low; there is little staff development once teachers are on the job; and teachers have been left to their own devices (producing a lower-than-desired level of performance). In short, there has been no system for improving the quality of the teaching and learning process. Over the course of many years, student achievement continues to decline (a low performance level). Over those same years, as parents talk to other parents, families have begun moving out of the district or choosing to send their children elsewhere (an increasing rate of abandonment). The district has lost more than 60 percent of its students over ten years (level). Scores have continued to decline (level). With the loss of students comes the loss of resources, resulting in the district cutting staff development even more (a decreasing rate of investment in professional learning). The district is now officially in a state of crisis (a low level of performance).

In another example, a school team convenes to look at programming options for the following year. As the team explores the possibilities for introducing new strategies such as multiage structures, multiple-grade teams, and reductions in class size, team members' enthusiasm heightens (level) as does their desire to make the changes quickly (rate). What the team forgets is it cannot implement changes of this magnitude (level) swiftly (rate) because so many other parts of the system must also change. The introduction of new structures and smaller class sizes has an impact on scheduling, facilities, philosophies of teaching and learning, communication with parents, and the like. Fortunately in this case, the principal is aware of the entire system and can help the team understand the impact that such changes will have both in the short and long term. The team comes up with a series of strategies for addressing these systemic issues, including working with their colleagues to develop the same level of enthusiasm they have for the change.

The links between level and rate are sometimes obvious, sometimes not. To uncover and understand the level and rate stories in your school or district, consider the following four steps.

1. Gather together a group of people representing different perspectives and describe various stories of crisis and control in your school or district.

2. Sketch out these stories by drawing feedback loops to show cause and effect and reinforcement loops.

3. Conduct a dialogue to talk about how things got to be this way and what is keeping the problem or issue from being resolved. Use relations diagrams (page 167) or cause-and-effect diagrams (page 164) to get at the underlying root causes of the problem.

4. Decide together what action you will take to put in place a long-term, more systemic solution that addresses underlying causes and dynamics.

Consider how a feedback loop or loops are at work, and apply the concepts of level and rate to understand how patterns of behavior affect the performance of a system.

Systemic Structures

A systems thinker also understands how structures in a system relate to a system's performance. Structures include how people work together, policies and procedures, school calendars and schedules, contracts, job descriptions, and how decisions get made, among many others.

For example, in the low-achievement district caught in the negative feedback loop by underinvesting in staff, school day and contract agreements may be contributing to the lack of time for teacher professional learning. Perhaps the district's policy of giving teachers a small amount of dollars to spend on their own professional development each year, with no alignment to improving student achievement, is also contributing to the situation. A systems thinker examines all such possibilities.

When things go wrong—someone makes a mistake or isn't performing well—first ask what system structures might be contributing. For example, in the case of a struggling teacher,

Other Examples of the 85/15 Rule

- A state test assesses student knowledge of earth science, but the curriculum does not include earth science. Subsequently, students do poorly on this section of the state test. Who can make a change in the curriculum? Can the students alone? The teachers alone? Who has responsibility and authority for the 85 percent?

- Students come to school without needed supplies such as paper, pencils, calculators, and so on. Each school has a limited operating budget and cannot request more than its allotted amount. As a result, students either go without needed materials or teachers buy materials with their own money. Who can change the budget priorities?

- In many districts, teachers are regularly surplused, or let go, based on third week counts and individual teacher seniority. If a school needs a reading specialist but that teacher is surplused, the school loses the teacher, with the result that students needing extra assistance receive none. Who has responsibility and authority over changing the labor-management contract or policy?

what is it about our recruitment, selection, hiring, and development policies and processes that might be contributing to his or her difficulties?

Keep in mind that nearly all employees come to work wanting to do a good job, wanting to feel and be competent. Look for barriers in the system that are preventing that from happening (and treat the other folks as special cases to address individually, not with blanket policies).

Blame the System, Not the Person

There is a rule of thumb associated with systems that has a profound impact on how you approach improvement. It's the 85/15 rule.

- Eighty-five percent of the problems in a system are due to inherent problems with that system. Schools can only change them through the intervention of the people who shape the system (principals, superintendents, and so on).
- Only 15 percent of problems are under the control of the individuals working within the system.

What does this mean in practical terms? In a simple example, think about the staff who have to enter registration data into a computer. They can determine when they start and begin their work, but they must use hardware and software purchased under administrative and budget policies set at the school or district level. Similarly, it is the administration that determines whether and how these staff are trained in the software. Staff also have no control over the input for this system: the design of registration forms, who completes the forms, and so on.

Using the 85/15 rule, whenever you encounter a problem, you look for causes within the system before trying to blame an individual. Suppose, for example, that you encounter student registration data that were entered incorrectly into the computer. The first reaction of someone who is not a systems thinker might be to blame the data-entry person for being incompetent. By contrast, a systems thinker would wonder why the person either did not know how to do it correctly or did know but was prevented from doing so. For example, was he or she trained properly? Is the software particularly difficult to use?

The 85/15 rule teaches us that fundamental, systemic improvement requires not only action from the individuals closest to the issues but also support and involvement from the decision makers who designed the system in the first place. A systems thinker understands the futility and danger of blaming individuals for problems when most of the variation in performance is due to the system's design.

Another consequence of the 85/15 rule, and systems thinking in general, is an appreciation for a collaborative approach to improvement—that whatever the broader system does or does not do will uniquely affect each person within a system. Each will have insight into different parts of the puzzle, and you need to bring all the pieces together to see the whole puzzle.

Mental Models

A systems thinker is also aware of mental models: the underlying assumptions that act as filters for all we perceive. These filters can cause problems when we leap to conclusions without data. The systems thinker listens for these mental models in himself or herself and in others, and brings those assumptions to the surface through reflection, inquiry, and dialogue. See the discussion of mental models and an example in chapter 3 (page 65).

Jumping to conclusions based on a particular mental model leads us to put certain fixes in place that aren't fixes at all but simply exacerbate the problem or create new problems. The way out of this trap is to become aware of our mental models and be willing to discuss them as a team before we jump to conclusions individually.

Suboptimization is one aspect of systems thinking that many people have a hard time grasping: you can't optimize the performance of the system as a whole by optimizing the performance of its individual pieces.

Think of it this way. An orchestra plays at its best when each individual section—the strings, horns, woodwinds,

> The discipline of working with mental models starts with turning the mirror inward; learning to unearth our internal pictures of the world, to bring them to the surface and hold them rigorously to scrutiny.
>
> —Peter Senge

percussionists, and so on—adjusts its performance to that of all the other sections. What may work best for the second violinists may make it harder for the violas or cellos to play well. They must listen to one another carefully if they are to come in at the right moment, playing at just the right pace, strength, tone, pitch, and key. The net result is a beautiful, harmonic symphony.

In most schools (and in most businesses), each part focuses on optimizing its own performance. Each classroom, department, or unit dedicates itself to achieving its own aims and purposes regardless of what happens in the other units. Some examples include the following.

- Students are given two hours of homework a night—by *each* academic teacher.
- Schools close the payroll office during the lunch hour to give their staff time off—precisely the time when teachers are free to complete business-related tasks.
- Schools cancel afternoon classes to give the parent-teacher organization (PTO) time and space to prepare for a fundraiser.
- Schools single out individual teachers for teacher of the year—without acknowledging the tremendous support and assistance from colleagues who helped these teachers be so successful.

What's the alternative? We have to accept that some sub-optimization of the parts may be necessary to optimize the whole.

Strategies for Improving Processes and Systems

The key to making improvements is to begin thinking about your school as a dynamic organism comprised of many interrelated processes. A *process* is simply a series of sequential steps leading to an outcome. Every process has inputs, which are transformed through the process steps (that should add value to those inputs) to create a desired output that those who depend on the process use to do their work.

Every person associated with the school and district—students, families, teachers, support staff, administrators, and board and community members—is engaged at one time or another in a process. Consider the following.

- Students who flow through the K–12 system encounter processes during registration and enrollment and when scheduling classes, attending classes, engaging in extracurricular activities, taking tests, eating lunch, getting locker assignments, and graduating.

- Teachers involved in the K–12 system work with processes such as hiring, orientation, professional learning, teaching and assessing, best practices research, curriculum development, and school improvement.

How well these and other processes work has a lot to do with how people perceive the quality of the school and district.

People can effectively change results by working on—and improving—the underlying processes and systems that create them. Improvement is as much a mindset as it is a set of tools or methods. There's a saying in the continuous quality improvement world in regard to Murphy's Law: "When Murphy speaks—listen!" (Box, 1989). Someone truly interested in continuous improvement knows that mistakes and errors are opportunities to learn from a process—to understand what's gone wrong so it can be fixed. For example, if a school district typically has errors in its fall registration process—with the result that students are double-registered, enrolled without their free or reduced lunch support, or not registered at all—that's a perfect opportunity to dig deeper into the causes of these problems and fix them so they won't happen the next time around.

Real teams live in the real world, where things go wrong every day. Yet sometimes all the talk about improvement teams, problem solving, long-term solutions, and even "focusing on the vital few" can give the impression that schools can only improve by involving lots of people in an

> If you keep doing what you've always done, you'll keep getting what you've always got.
>
> —Anonymous

extensive effort. In fact, there are three different levels to fix every problem: (1) solve the immediate problem, (2) improve the process that created the problem, and (3) improve or redesign the system that created the process that led to the problem.

- **Level one:** Solving the immediate problems is a necessity. If you and your team encounter an obvious error or problem, you have to take immediate action to prevent further damage—especially because our work directly impacts students' welfare and because we operate so often in the public eye.
- **Level two:** Improving the process that led to the problem should be the minimal goal of most teams—to improve the process so that the problems or gaps the team identified will not happen again.
- **Level three:** Improving or redesigning the system is the ideal approach because it usually has far-reaching impact. However, such changes also require extensive effort and input, not to mention authority, so they may not be feasible in some cases.

Consider the preceding example about school fall registration problems (page 209) from the perspective of the three levels of fix. In addition to correcting double registrations and registering students as individual situations are discovered, to ensure that no student goes hungry, a level-one fix might be to automatically issue temporary meal tickets to students who encountered registration problems and didn't receive their free or reduced lunch tickets.

In the meantime, an improvement team could step back and ask, "Why are we having these registration problems?" The team could create a flowchart and look for places where responsibilities were unclear or unnecessary steps were included. Its investigation (including the use of data) could lead to permanent improvements in the registration process—a level-two fix.

Ideally, a team with a broader mission could look across several processes—not just registrations—and ask, "Do the problems identified with the registration process occur elsewhere in the organization?" The answer might uncover policies, procedures, and norms causing widespread problems, errors, or inefficiencies. Fixing those underlying problems could lead to improvements across many processes, such as registration, enrollment, scheduling of classes, and assignment of advisors. That would be a true level-three fix.

The remainder of this chapter describes various methods your team can use to identify and make improvements in your school's processes, which will mostly fall within the realm of level-two fixes. However, keep in mind that if you encounter obvious problems, you should also implement level-one fixes so the problems do not continue or worsen. Similarly, keep your eyes open for deeper, system-level improvements (level-three fixes) that can have a broad impact on your school.

A Problem-Solving Process

When a problem has been around for a long time, and previous efforts to resolve it haven't resulted in sustained improvement, it may be worth the time to dig deeply into its causes in order to develop a more systemic long-lasting solution. In these cases, a group of people who understand the problems and the process (because they work with it every day) convenes to address and resolve the problem at a deep level (level-two or level-three fixes).

The challenge of solving problems in groups is that most of the people in the group are there because they already have a solution in mind. They come to the group with preconceived notions about the problem—what it is, how bad it is, and how to fix it. What typically happens is that the group jumps right into arguing about which solution is best before it has taken the time to really define and understand the problem from all the angles. This approach is ripe for conflict and disengagement.

An effective team will talk about the process it intends to use to attack the problem. A methodical, easy-to-understand process unfolds naturally and moves the group through a logical progression of thinking. The process engages all participants and helps the group investigate the full spectrum of

Resist the Solution Temptation!

The more people get involved in discussing likely causes of a problem, the more they start thinking about potential solutions. The purpose of using the seven-step method is to avoid the rush to solutions before you can verify causes with data. You can, however, document solution ideas that team members suggest at this stage, and revisit them in step four.

Tip for Avoiding Problems Disguised as Solutions

Beware of solutions in disguise! Sometimes problems are stated as the opposite of some desired solution. For example, the statement "We don't have enough computers" is a problem statement that poorly disguises the speaker's preferred solution ("Buy more computers!"). If you hear solution-oriented statements, ask the speaker what benefit would come from implementing the (disguised) solution: "How would having more computers help us?" Once you've identified the underlying problems, you may find other solutions that might work just as well, be less expensive, or be better for more people.

Example of Defining a Problem

This is the third year in which more than 60 percent of our sixth graders and 40 percent of our seventh graders have received warning reports for potential failures due to incomplete homework after the first six-week grading period (current state). We want our junior high school students to be able to successfully complete their homework assignments and turn them in on time (desired state).

the problem. The seven-step problem-solving method (see figure 8.4) is just such a process.

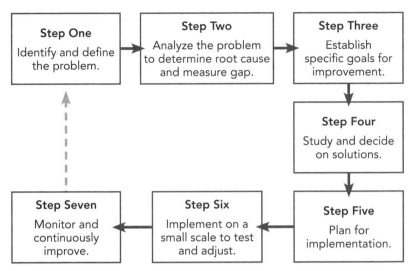

Source: QLD Learning, LLC © 2013. Reprinted with permission.

Figure 8.4: The seven-step problem-solving method.

Note that throughout the following process, teams should collect, analyze, and interpret data to ensure they are solving the right problem with the right solution.

Step One: Identify and Define the Problem

The purpose of step one is to develop a collective understanding of the problem. Problems often manifest themselves in different ways throughout a school. Each person who works in the school may experience the problem in a unique way. When problem solving in groups, it is important for each person to have the opportunity to describe the problem from his or her perspective. This will ensure that the group understands the whole problem, not just one or two pieces of it.

If you are facilitating or leading your team, first have the group members discuss what they think the problem is, where the problem occurs, who sees it as a problem, how often it occurs, and what aspects of quality are in jeopardy as a result of the problem. Use data as much as possible to confirm (or disprove!) what people think is happening. Once you start using data regularly, you'll be surprised at how often everyone's perceptions (including your own) can be inaccurate.

The following guidelines and questions can help define the current state of the situation.

- **State the problem:** What is the problem we're attempting to solve?

- **Collect data:** In what areas does the problem occur most often? For whom is this a problem, and how bad is it? How often or how much does the problem interfere with student learning? What's at stake if we don't solve this problem? What's at stake if we do solve this problem?

- **Understand problem context:** How did we come to have this problem? What is the history? Consider using the historygram process when examining these questions (see chapter 9, page 233).

- **Focus on change:** What do we want to be different after we solve this problem? What is the desired state we would like to achieve?

In addition to listening to each other, the group may want to ask their colleagues in the school or community to verify or extend their thinking about the problem.

The process of identifying and defining a problem can be lengthy and challenging, especially if the group is diverse and each person experiences the problem quite differently. Too often when teams set out to solve a problem, they end up with a superficial approach because the real, whole, and underlying problem is not detected.

Be patient with learning as much about the problem as you can before attempting to define it too narrowly. The time you spend up front in the definition and identification phase could save you huge amounts of time later on in the process.

Once your group has learned about the ways in which the problem manifests itself, write a simple, concise statement that captures the essential elements of the problem being addressed. A problem statement should:

- Be short, objective, and factual rather than imply a solution

Verifying Potential Causes

There are two ways to verify whether potential causes actually contribute to a problem. The first is to gather data that link the presence of the cause with the occurrence of the problem. If it is not easy to gather data on a potential cause, you can also experiment by making changes in a process, procedure, or policy to remove the suspected cause. Be sure to treat the changes as actual experiments—try them on a small scale and define specific procedures for measuring performance before and after you make a change.

Example of Problem Source

The problem statement identifies a problem with middle school students not completing and handing in their homework. The group already knows how many and which students are having the problem but they don't know what is causing the problem or what impact the problem is having on student learning. After conducting a cause-and-effect analysis, the team suspects that the way in which these students organize their materials and the many different ways in which their teachers give homework assignments are two areas that should be studied further.

- Identify key characteristics of the problem—where and when it is observed, the impact it has on student learning, any observable evidence of its existence, and who it is a problem for
- Describe the problem at its deepest level of manifestation

When everyone is clear about what problem the group is solving, you can then begin to analyze why you think the problem is occurring.

Step Two: Analyze the Problem

It is important at this stage that all individuals have the same information concerning the problem and understand it in the same way. Analyzing the problem for root causes and gathering additional data about the problem provide a deeper understanding. Your team should answer four key questions.

1. Why is the problem occurring?
2. Where is the problem occurring?
3. How big is the problem?
4. What are the biggest drivers of the problem?

Why Is the Problem Occurring?

The first level of analysis is to determine why this is a problem and why the problem exists. Use the five whys analysis (page 162) or cause-and-effect diagrams (page 164) to dig deeper and deeper into root causes of the problem. Be careful; these tools identify *potential* root causes. You will need to verify the causes with data or experimentation. You will be using the data-logic chain (see chapter 3, page 83) throughout the problem-solving process as you theorize about what is going on, gather data to verify your theories, and then theorize again about what may be causing the problem, gather data again, and so on.

Where Is the Problem Occurring?

Flowcharting the processes in which the problem is evident will help the group pinpoint where in the system to look for potential solutions. Flowcharts illustrate how work flows over time (see chapter 5, page 126). Regardless of what type of flowchart you choose, the first step is to determine the scope of the process you will be depicting. Where does it start? Where does it end? Once you've determined those boundaries, you can begin to identify the steps and their sequence.

How Big Is the Problem?

The team needs to gather data to show how big the problem is—how often it occurs, what impact it has, and so on. Importantly, the team determines the most important gap or need and then gathers data to measure the extent of the problem in relation to that need. Many of the snapshot data tools (see chapter 7, page 169) can help answer this question.

A subset of this question is whether the frequency or impact of the problem is changing over time. Here, run charts or control charts (see page 191) are essential.

What Are the Biggest Drivers of the Problem?

Sometimes a straightforward cause-and-effect approach cannot address a problem because the potential causes are intricately linked. In such cases, asking about the big drivers can help identify the root causes. A relations diagram (see chapter 7, page 167) is useful for answering this type of question.

Step Three: Establish Specific Goals for Improvement

Problem-solving goals should meet SMART criteria. The team's definition of its goals will relate directly to its purpose and to the problem it is attempting to solve. If the group is working on more than one problem, it will have more than one goal. There may also be multiple goals for one problem, especially if during the analysis step the team unearthed more than one potential root cause or more than one major area of gap or need.

Table 8.1 (page 216) illustrates a sequence that shows how to link problem statements with verified causes and improvement goals.

Example of a Problem Occurrence Solution

The group studying the middle school students with homework problems has several alternatives. It could work with the students to create a detailed flowchart of all the steps in the process from the time assignments are given until the homework is turned in. Or the group could also use a flowchart to show how each teacher assigns homework (and identify ways to standardize the process to make it easier for students to successfully organize and complete their assignments). A third alternative is to create a flowchart that depicts the process students who don't have trouble getting their homework in on time use. Such a chart could show steps that other students could use.

Table 8.1: Linking Problem Statements With Verified Causes

Team Type	Problem	Causes	Improvement Goals
School Climate Team	There is poor attendance at Family Fun Night (only 10 percent of parents attended the past two years).	Fifty percent of parents who did not come report they never heard of the event and do not recall seeing any announcements.	Increase attendance at Family Fun Night by 30 percent over the course of the next two years.
School Climate Team	There are too many behavioral referrals.	Most referrals are related to hallway incidents; an increase happens when hallway supervisors are reassigned.	Reduce the number of behavioral referrals related to hallway incidents by 20 percent each year over the next three years.
School Improvement Team	Less than 25 percent of students in grades 4 and 5 scored at or above proficient in nonfiction writing.	Students found the assignments confusing. Students felt they had little opportunity to practice prerequisite skills.	Fifty percent or more of students will demonstrate proficiency in nonfiction writing per the district writing rubric.
School Improvement Team	Too many students receive failure notices six weeks into the semester.	The biggest problems are in the sixth and seventh grades. Records show many students in those grades have missing or incomplete homework.	Reduce by half the number of sixth- and seventh-grade students who receive failure notices after the first six weeks due to missing or incomplete homework.
Ongoing Department Team	Poor attendance at team meetings. (Average attendance was 50 percent for the past twelve months.)	Policies on attendance are not clear. A shift in classroom schedules interferes with the standard time set for the meeting.	Increase attendance and participation at team meetings to an average of 80 percent for the entire school year.

Step Four: Study and Decide on Solutions

Through problem solving, your team will have begun the process of identifying possible solutions. This is the point where the team pulls together and enhances the ideas that have emerged from its analysis of the problem. First, go back through your meeting records and find the ideas that you've already generated. Then, brainstorm and discuss additional ideas. That way, you can be sure to start with a list that both respects people's original ideas and what the team has learned through its efforts up to this point.

Typically, a team will generate many potential solutions to a problem. Narrowing the ideas down to a manageable few can be a real challenge for some groups because it is the part of the problem-solving process that often has the most emotion attached to it. The challenge is less for teams that have diligently included all members along the way and have done a good job of collecting and analyzing information about the problem. For such teams, deciding on the solution is seen as just another step, not a point of conflict.

One way to narrow the ideas is to look for research to identify promising practices in the area of concern. Another option is to develop a set of criteria relevant to the decision you face. The criteria can derive from the team's responses to these questions.

- Is the solution *doable*? What time, energy, and financial resources are required?

- Is the solution *equitable*? To what extent will a wide variety of students benefit?

- Is the solution *evidence based*? Is there a history of positive results?

The group should decide on the criteria together and then match each idea to each criterion to find the best fit. A decision matrix (page 119) can help you keep track of the criteria your team is using and how each potential solution matches those criteria.

Once your team decides on the solution it will propose for the problem, you need to document both what the solution is and why that option was chosen (that is, how well it fits your criteria).

Step Five: Plan for Implementation

Planning tools and templates can help the team reach conclusions in ways that will ultimately facilitate implementation and garner collective support for the team's

---

Example of Problem Magnitude

A team knows that 60 percent of sixth graders and 40 percent of seventh graders have exhibited the problem of not completing and turning in their homework. The team might also want to know if those percentages change during the year; if there is a correlation between homework assignment completion and test results, the type of assignment, the level of support at home, and so on; or if there are common demographic profiles of students who struggle with homework, such as attendance, enrollment in special services, behavioral factors, after-school employment, and so on.

Approval for Solutions and Plans

Sometimes teams will need to get approval from their positional leader before they begin implementing a chosen solution. Check with your positional leader to determine when he or she wants to see your ideas. Some will want to check the proposed solution before the team develops a plan; others will want to see the plan accompany the proposed solution.

recommendations. Chapter 5 (page 111) describes a variety of tools that can help your team with this step.

Figure 8.5 gives examples of questions your team should ask itself before finalizing its implementation plan.

Implementation Plan Impact

- Who will be affected if this decision is implemented?
- Who will be responsible for seeing that it is implemented?
- Do the people who must implement the change believe change is needed?

Implementation Plan Tasks

- What are the important tasks or actions that must be taken to ensure successful implementation?
- Who should do each task and when?

Implementation Plan Skills

- What skills will these actions require?
- Do the people who will need to implement the decision or solution have those skills?

Implementation Plan Resources

- What resources will be needed to do this well?

Implementation Plan Outcome

- How will we know if we have been successful? How will we measure our progress? When should we measure our progress?

Figure 8.5: Questions to guide the implementation plan.

An implementation plan should address each of the topics in figure 8.5, providing ways to involve and communicate with everyone the change will affect. The plan should also reiterate the team's mission. Clearly stated tasks, doable time frames, reasonable costs, and lots of involvement on the part of those who must ultimately accept and perform the change will all help facilitate effective implementation.

Step Six: Implement on a Small Scale

This step is one that most teams miss. If at all possible, test your solutions and implementation plan on a small scale, and get feedback from those who are implementing it to see if it's manageable and productive. This is the essence of the PDSA cycle (page 96). The plan doesn't have to be implemented for a long time (such as a year-long test) but should be tried for a sufficient period to gather enough data to see whether or not it works. If it does seem to be manageable and working, implement the solution broadly. If it isn't working, find out why and either make adjustments or try a different strategy.

Step Seven: Monitor and Continuously Improve

Continuous improvement is driven by repeated application of the PDSA cycle, each time working with larger scales or longer time periods. Initial improvements are sometimes the result of a halo effect: improvements appear to be working simply because people are paying attention to the problem. Therefore, build in a long-term mechanism for monitoring results to ensure that improvements are both real and sustained. Then, as the solution becomes the new way of operating, it can be incrementally improved again and again.

Functional Analysis Process

Being clear about the aim of a system is key to improving how the system functions overall. A school or district work units, departments, divisions, and other ongoing organizational units can make significant improvements in their performance by first working through a functional analysis.

Maury Cotter, Jessica Simmons, and Kathleen Paris (1997) define an eight-step functional analysis process. Originally developed through a collaborative effort with the Department of History and Office of Quality Improvement at the University of Wisconsin–Madison, the process is applicable to any analysis of system functions.

The steps in the process are the following.

- **Step one:** Clarify mission, values, and recipients of our service (or *customers*).
- **Step two:** Create a system flowchart.
- **Step three:** Identify core processes.
- **Step four:** Identify responsibilities for core processes.
- **Step five:** Learn recipient needs.
- **Step six:** Prioritize and flowchart processes.

What Is a Small-Scale Test?

A small-scale test should have one or more of the following characteristics.

- **Short time frame:** We'll try it out for two weeks (or four months, as appropriate).
- **Geographical limits:** We'll try it out at Ozawa Elementary before taking it to other elementary schools.
- **Just a few people:** We'll work with three of the ten art teachers.
- **Cost:** The test will cost no more than 25 percent of the total budget.

A small-scale test could also include observing how well solutions similar to yours have worked in other settings. For example, if you are experimenting with student self-assessments or a new technology, find other schools that have used procedures or equipment close to those your team wants to use and arrange an onsite visit.

A system is a network of interdependent components that work together to accomplish the aim of the system.

—W. Edwards Deming

Customers in Education

Education is a human system, not a manufacturing system. However, the concept of a *customer* does seem relevant if you do the following.

- View educational systems as providing services to students and families (the ultimate aim being to educate students well).

- Believe that in these times of school choice, students and parents are evaluating and choosing schools based on the quality they provide—much as consumers choose between products.

- See that there are many internal processes in educational systems, and each of these processes has customers, the people who depend on the quality of what that process produces in order to do their work well—such as hiring expert teachers and administrators to benefit the school community.

Many people in education are uncomfortable with the term *customers*. If that's the case, look for alternative terms that convey the same intent as customer, such as *recipient, client, beneficiary,* or *user*.

- **Step seven:** Make improvements to processes.
- **Step eight:** Check results, and hold gains.

You will want to have all the members of the work unit or department work through this process together so that all will share a common vision of the purpose of what they do, how they do it, and how they personally fit into the bigger picture.

Step One: Clarify Mission, Values, and Recipients of Our Service

Members should brainstorm their answers to each of the following questions on sticky notes and group them using the affinity diagram process (see chapter 5, page 117). Use the multivoting process (see chapter 5, page 118) as needed to narrow down the list. Be sure to talk about each piece in enough depth that there is shared understanding and consensus. Key questions for your team to consider are: What is our purpose or mission? Why do we exist?

In responding to these questions, you are defining a particular purpose, or set of purposes, the department or work unit fulfills in the larger organization. This needs to be articulated clearly and succinctly. Chapter 9 (page 245) provides insights into developing a mission for the organization.

In working through step one, the team focuses on questions about the recipients of the services the organization provides: Who receives the services we provide and products we create? For whom are we doing this work?

In the process of answering these questions, the group will probably find that there are primary and secondary customers (or recipients). *Primary customers* are those without whom the department or work unit would not exist. They really need you, and you need them! *Secondary customers* are those people you serve—who count on you to get their work done—but their work is happening on behalf of your primary customers as well.

Our beliefs drive our values—we value what we believe in. What are our values? This question gets to the heart of how we want others to perceive us: What do we believe about the work we do? How should we conduct ourselves? How should we treat each other and those we serve? Lastly, even more importantly, how do we practice those beliefs now, and what more do we need to do to actually live those beliefs? The answer might be a statement of core values or a list of guiding principles—or both.

At the conclusion of discussions in step one, the team should have a shared perspective of how its work supports the broader purpose of the school district and how it wants to operate as a department or work unit and should have a prioritized list of customers.

Step Two: Create a System Flowchart

This step focuses on clarifying, at a high level, how your work unit or department provides its main services or products. The key is to agree not to go into too much detail—yet. Have members talk about the core processes they use to carry out the mission (you may want to break into smaller groups around these functions). Using sticky notes to chart the core process, decide on the first step (first major activity) and the last step, then fill in the intermediate steps. Use the top-level flowcharts to talk about how the core processes connect or interact with one another. The example in figure 8.6 (page 222) shows, at a high level, how research, education, and support processes coordinate to serve an organization's customers.

Constructing the flowchart provides insights into this question, What do we do to carry out our purpose or mission? The answer to this question involves identifying the major activities you engage in to serve your customers and describing how these activities relate to each other. These responses will provide a clear picture of what the school, department, or unit does to accomplish its mission.

Step Three: Identify Core Processes

The purpose of this step is to be very specific about the tasks and activities each individual staff member engages in on a day-to-day basis. The analysis here provides answers to the question, What are the primary staff functions? The guiding framework all along continues to be the organization's mission and those it serves.

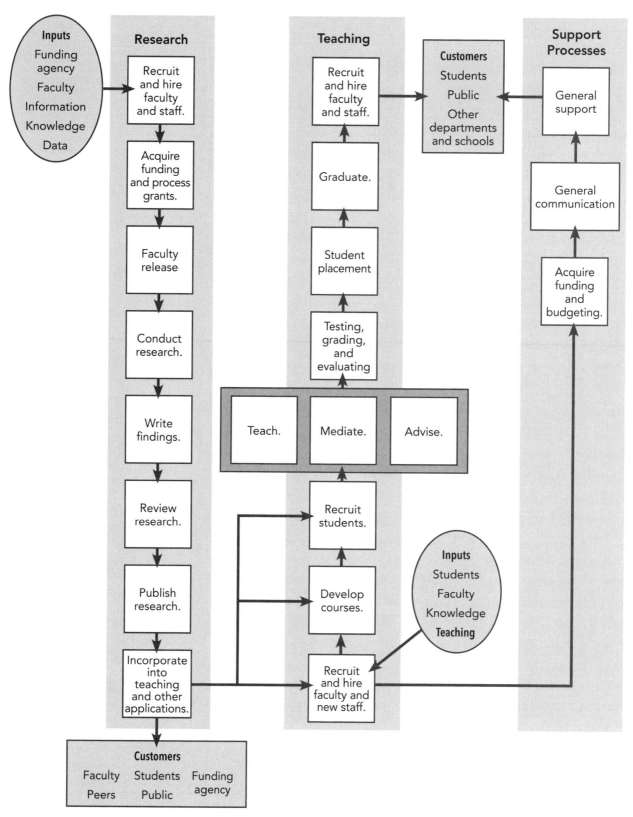

Figure 8.6: Sample top-level flowchart.

Each staff member should brainstorm his or her tasks and activities on sticky notes, and then sort these under the system flow steps. You may want to use color coding or another system to identify different participants. By sorting tasks and processes under system flow steps, you will get a clear picture of how every member's job activities support the mission across the many processes.

Step Four: Identify Responsibilities for Core Processes

This step helps you begin to identify specific responsibilities for managing the core processes, essentially building into your school, department, or unit a mechanism for ongoing, continuous improvement. The guiding questions for this step are: Who is responsible for the primary functions? Who are the decision makers, process managers, backups, and others involved?

Use a responsibility matrix (see chapter 5, page 138) to answer these questions and share it with everyone so that people can go to the right person with their questions. This task enables the team to identify gaps in and overlaps of roles, responsibilities, and functions and clarifies the decision-making structure.

Step Five: Learn Recipient Needs

This step helps you understand how to add more value to your work unit or department. By talking with customers, either directly through interviews or indirectly through written surveys, you will get a rich amount of information about what to improve about your area. You might even discover that certain activities you thought were essential to delivering your service are not really necessary, thereby freeing up resources to focus on higher-priority activities.

Answers to these questions enable you to find out what customers of these core processes want and need: What are you getting that you need? What are you getting that you don't need? What do you wish you were getting?

Watch Out for Complexity

Complexity is a general term for unnecessary work—anything that makes a process more complicated without adding value to the service or product it produces. Complexity comes about when people continue trying to fix problems in a process without a systematic plan for doing so. They may try to solve one piece of the process or rearrange or add a step, not realizing the solution negatively impacts every other part of the process. As problems accumulate, they add more and more steps to compensate or work around them. Each of these extra steps adds another opportunity for mistakes and errors and adds to the overall time the process takes. The amount of time fixing and reworking buries the real work—where value is really added to the process. The solution is to step back and engage in a level-two fix to change the process in fundamental ways that eliminate the need for the complexity.

Step Six: Prioritize and Flowchart Processes

In this step, you review the tools you have used to investigate the system's organization and functions. From these tools, you can respond to these questions: Which processes are most important to our clients? How do these work now, step by step? For more on flowcharting processes, refer to the detailed flowchart description and example in chapter 5 (pages 131–134).

Step Seven: Make Improvements to Processes

The key task in this step is to eliminate rework, duplication, and nonessential steps. The team focuses on this question: What changes do we need to make?

Step Eight: Check Results, and Hold Gains

This step enables you to check how the improved processes are working. If the processes are functioning appropriately, teams can standardize them to hold the gains. Identify how teams can continue with improvements.

A Process for Solving Complex Problems

Sometimes groups get stuck in problems that seem so complex and overwhelming that it's difficult to see through to a level-three fix that will truly resolve difficulties. Here's a four-step process for breaking through the gridlock of a complex problem.

Step One: Identify the Original Problem Symptom

Hold a forum or series of focus groups or interviews to get more data from a large group of stakeholders. You might ask these questions: "How are you experiencing the problem now? How does it impact your work? How does it impact students and families? How does it impact others? What is your desired state?"

In this step, it's easy to fall into the trap of focusing on a single event. Be sure to avoid doing so. Looking back over time will provide perspective that enables the team to identify a class of symptoms that have been recurring. Use the historygram process (see chapter 9, page 233) to identify key events in the progress of the problem, with general time frames of when each event occurred. Looking at the events over time can expose patterns and trends, leading to greater understanding.

Another important question in this step is, Whose interests do we serve by the way things are? This question is very difficult for people to answer when their interests are the ones being served! It might be useful to invite friendly observers who are knowledgeable about the system and problem to give their objective feedback.

Prioritizing your need to know is a critical task in this step. It's important to not overload yourself with irrelevant data. What information do we have or need to have that has importance to the problem? What do we need to know? How can we find this out?

Keep your priorities in focus by always asking, "How will knowing this help us solve the problem? What will we do with the information we get?"

Step Two: Map Out All the Quick Fixes

Quick fixes are level-one actions taken during previous efforts to solve the identified problem. Use feedback loops (page 202) to map out all the previous fixes that have been attempted. You are looking for the balancing loops that preserve the problems by keeping them in control. (Perhaps if the problems were out of control, there would be more impetus for finding permanent solutions.)

Step Three: Identify the Impact

Look for ways that past solutions affected the organization —especially unanticipated effects that locked people into patterned responses. In the example of registration problems that resulted in eligible students not being identified for free or reduced lunch, the level-one fix was to provide lunch tickets to those students. The unanticipated consequence was

---

An Example of Breaking Through

A registration and enrollment team realizes students are getting lost in the system. The team holistically discovers that a multitude of miniprocesses have sprung up at each school to address the very diverse registration needs of different student populations (for example, English learners, special needs, or homeless). Additionally, the fact that there is no electronic data entry at the school sites where students are registering further complicates the process, causing the whole system to operate manually and slowly and with errors and duplication. After looking carefully at all the fixes that had been put in place (flow-charting myriad ways students register), the group decides that a central registration site is the best solution. It surmises that the resulting standardization would make all the processes run more smoothly, and the one-stop-shop location would make it easier on families. The team pilots the system in one section of its district, gathering feedback from the families and other stakeholders and monitoring cycle time and errors before implementing the fix.

that student demand for lunch exceeded what the food service team had prepared. Examine the side effects of quick or level-one fixes from the perspective of all the players in the system.

Step Four: Identify Fundamental Solutions

By now, you have defined the problem clearly, carefully, and fully, and it's time to decide whether you have enough information to identify and select potential solutions or to go deeper into root-cause analysis (pages 162–168). If you decide you know enough to develop solutions, be sure the selected options address the problem from everyone's perspective.

Even when confronting a complex problem, a step-by-step approach that is based on a clear understanding of the problem and the historical fixes and their effects can lead to clarity about fundamental causes and appropriate solutions.

Final Check: Systems Thinking for Coherent School Improvement

The systems metaphor that appears at the beginning of this chapter is a team exercise that promotes understanding of how an organization is truly a system with many interdependent parts. To assess whether they are designing and using truly robust—significant and sustainable—strategies that will result in an improving and coherent system, teams can use the following checklist.

We are thinking like a system when:

- ☐ Our school looks for patterns and underlying trends, not just isolated events
- ☐ We know what effects our process and system have on other parts of the system and how changes outside our process and system affect it
- ☐ We are presented with problems, and we look at the process rather than blaming the person

> Assume that any significant innovation, if it is to result in change, requires individual implementers to work out their meaning.
>
> —Michael Fullan

- ☐ We are working to align our processes to optimize the system as a whole

We have a strategy for continuous improvement that:

- ☐ Reflects the appropriate level of fix
- ☐ Incorporates a conscious approach to problem solving
- ☐ Links directly to goals focused on student and adult learning
- ☐ Is based on research and best practice
- ☐ Provides tools to help us identify the vital few activities most likely to have the greatest impact on teaching and learning

CHAPTER 9

A Schoolwide Improvement Process

In many school districts, the principal is responsible for ensuring that his or her school develops and submits a school improvement plan to the central office for approval. More often than not, the principal ends up filling in the blanks of a district template, turns it in, and checks it off his or her growing and unwieldy to-do list, which is why, once turned over for approval, so many school improvement plans end up in a pile or a file, never to be seen again.

Having a plan and working the plan are not one in the same. When a leader develops plans in isolation, those who must carry them out seldom embrace them. A schoolwide improvement process puts planning and implementation into the hands, minds, and hearts of the people who are ultimately responsible for achieving the goals and improving results—the teachers. Additionally, a robust schoolwide process provides a vehicle for collaborative learning and continuous improvement of both the process and the results, neither of which is possible when only the principal is responsible for the plan.

This chapter provides the cultural context, structures, tools, and timelines for leading and implementing the SMART school improvement process. Based on the five core questions for SMART schools (see page 235), this process aligns school-based improvement with the district's strategic priorities and the goals and plans of professional learning teams. The process incorporates the use of common curricular standards, effective instructional practices, and assessments for learning and informs response to intervention decisions on a continuous basis. The SMART school improvement process addresses all seven of

Learning Forward's (2011) standards for professional learning because it is a job-embedded, data-driven process that engages all members of the professional learning community in making better decisions on behalf of student learning. Professional learning that increases educator effectiveness and results for all students (Learning Forward, 2012):

- Occurs within learning communities committed to continuous improvement, collective responsibility, and goal alignment

- Requires skillful leaders who develop capacity, advocate, and create support systems for professional learning

- Requires prioritizing, monitoring, and coordinating resources for educator learning

- Uses a variety of sources and types of student, educator, and system data to plan, assess, and evaluate professional learning

- Integrates theories, research, and models of human learning to achieve its intended outcomes

- Applies research on change and sustains support for implementation of professional learning for long-term change

- Aligns its outcomes with educator performance and student curriculum standards

In short, the SMART school improvement process connects the dots of reform by incorporating the best-known practices in curriculum, instruction, assessment, and professional learning. Aimed specifically at improving student learning outcomes, the process provides important links between theory and practice, as well as between practice and results.

Guidelines for Your SMART Leadership Team

The SMART school improvement process represents a significant undertaking and as such warrants careful planning, oversight, and leadership. A SMART leadership team comprised of dedicated teacher leaders and the principal leads and oversees the process.

To select your school's SMART leadership team, use the following guidelines.

- If your school has an existing teacher leadership council, advisory team, or school improvement team, select one of these (or a combination) as an appropriate group to engage as leaders of the improvement process.
- Team membership should be representative of the school population of teachers and academic support personnel and must include the principal.
- Team members should have the time and authority to make decisions about the school's goals and agenda for change.
- Team members should be willing to participate as leaders of the process and willing to act in a leadership role with their peers.
- The team should be a respected body within the school and its members viewed as leaders.
- Team membership should be voluntary or through peer selection. Mandatory membership is not the best approach for this work.

The role of the SMART leadership team is to lead the school through the SMART school improvement process and to guide and monitor the implementation of schoolwide strategies for improvement of student learning. The team has the responsibility to ensure implementation, model skills, coordinate the improvement process, monitor the improvement process, and build leadership capacity.

1. **Ensure implementation:** The SMART leadership team is *not* required to be the "implementer" of the

process. That is the shared responsibility of the entire staff. Instead, this team will take the lead in making sure that the process is implemented in a way that addresses the unique needs and culture of the school. The implementation will look a little different at each of the schools, but the basic tools, structures, language, and activities will be consistent across the district.

2. **Model skills:** It is not necessary that members of the team know anything about the SMART school improvement process at the outset. They can learn the process, tools, and skills for leadership and team performance as they go through the process. Additionally, team members will learn and model skills in the areas of facilitation, data analysis, and goal setting.

3. **Coordinate the improvement process:** This improvement process has five meetings or phases of implementation. In order to conduct the various activities associated with each, the team will need to address time and space issues for professional learning, both schoolwide and at the grade or department levels. For new instructional practices, this team may need to assist in finding and scheduling appropriate professional development resources and strategies.

4. **Monitor the improvement process:** A certain amount of monitoring will be necessary to ensure that the process is done with integrity (for example, to see that some level of standard practice is taking place). This includes but is not limited to regular team meetings at the grade and department level to monitor student progress, the use of SMART goals to focus team and schoolwide improvement efforts, the use of data to inform professional learning and improvement, and research associated with any new practice that is being implemented. Though this leadership team has the responsibility to oversee these activities, the supervisory responsibility remains with the principal.

5. **Build leadership capacity:** This entire process is predicated on the belief that no one individual or even one team can or should be responsible for improving student learning. Every person has both the right and responsibility to be a learner and a leader on behalf of student learning. A unique role of this leadership team is helping to build leadership capacity throughout the organization. That means inviting people into the work of leadership by modeling, engaging in, and facilitating important team dialogues around student achievement.

Teams of any kind—SMART or otherwise—operate within the context of the school environment. Their chances of success are directly related to how much work the school has put into creating an environment that encourages a focus on priorities, supports the use of data for reflecting on past and current practices, and promotes collaboration among the teachers, staff, students, parents, and community.

Historygram Process to Prepare Your School for Change

Improvement requires change. So before beginning any schoolwide effort, the SMART leadership team will need to prepare the school for change. The first step might be to acknowledge that there will be resistance to change. There may be good reason for the resistance. Depending on how the school introduces change (sent from up high versus created on site), it could appear to be yet another fad or political demand that people view as an unnecessary distraction. It is important to put the change into a context that is meaningful —a context that acknowledges and honors past contributions and successes.

The historygram process is a way to build a bridge between the past and the future, a way to honor the past while moving forward. It allows those who have been around the longest to talk about past parades they joined or led. The school community as a whole takes time to reflect together in an effort to understand the patterns, cycles, and trends of their

> When you start on your journey to Ithaca,
>
> then pray that the road is long,
>
> full of adventure, full of knowledge.
>
> —Constantine P. Cavafy

collective history. Figure 9.1 describes the historygram process.

Materials

- Markers, tape, or self-stick chart paper
- Large pieces of shelf or butcher paper, tagboard, or foam core
- Magazines (optional)
- Scissors (optional)
- Large (5 × 7) index cards

Directions

- Bring together a diverse group representing many parts of the school community. Include people who have been around a long time as well as those who have just joined the school, just moved to the community, and so on.
- Group people according to when they came into the school or district.
- Have each group develop storyboards showing the following information from its school era.
    - Major initiatives and their goals
    - Major crises or turning points
    - Symbols, ceremonies, and traditions
    - Events in the world
    - Events in the community
    - A name or title for the era
    - Values that we want to take into the future
- Have each group share its story.
- Capture the values separately on a collective poster for teams to develop into a vision of the school's future at a later time.
- Have the group as a whole summarize the learning by identifying themes, patterns, and cycles that have made up the school's history, and identify patterns they want to continue or stop.

Figure 9.1: Historygram process.

This process gives the entire school community an opportunity to view the number and types of changes that have occurred and gives people a chance to take the best parts of the past with them as they move into a new, uncertain future. In doing so, people feel honored and can view the tremendous accomplishments they have been a part of achieving throughout their time in the organization. People literally see their contributions and their successes. But they also see that they have experienced a lot of change, reinforcing the value of resiliency and continuous improvement.

Core Questions for SMART Schools

Any number of improvement approaches and models are available to support schoolwide improvement. Each tends to have the same essential elements: the use of data, collaboration in teams, a results orientation, and a process for learning and ongoing improvement.

The SMART school improvement process engages the full faculty in conversations and activities designed to bring coherence and shared accountability for the success of the school. Teachers, aides, support staff, and administrators collectively move through a series of five core questions. For some of the activities, you can also involve parents and community members. Who to involve at each phase is a decision the SMART leadership team makes. (See chapter 2 for information about how teams function.)

The SMART school improvement process is organized around five core questions: (1) Where do we want to be? (2) Where are we now? (3) How will we get there? (4) What are we learning? and (5) Where should we focus next?

Core Question One: Where Do We Want to Be?

The answer to this question defines the kind of school that captures the passion and commitment that drew educators to the profession in the first place. Ideally, this question will evoke a sense of meaning, community, and trust not only for the staff but also for the parents who send their children to this school each day, the community members who support this school with resources, and the students who would choose this school over any other if given the option. This question begs further reflection about what we value, what

---

School Improvement Is Not a Dirty Word

For many schools, the term *school improvement* is pejorative—it means the state or district has identified the school as underperforming and therefore in need of improvement. Although low-performing schools have the most to gain from adoption of a formal school improvement process, schools that may be performing adequately or even well are missing a wonderful opportunity for re-energizing and renewal when they ignore school improvement. In this book, *school improvement* refers to processes for building strong, vibrant professional learning communities— SMART schools—that are committed to continuous, never-ending improvement because it's the best way *to do school*. It's always the best way, not just when we're in trouble, not just when we have new staff coming on board, not just when we have a new strategic plan, but now, always, and long into the foreseeable future.

we stand for, and where we want to go—together—as we learn and improve over time. This first core question sets the tone and the foundation for how schools will behave, the priorities that teams will select, and the direction that teams will pursue well into the future.

There are three elements to answering this question.

1. **Core values:** What we care about most deeply when it comes to our work, our relationships, and our results

2. **Vision:** What we aspire to achieve and to become

3. **Mission:** What we exist to do—our purpose

Core Values

Core values are deeply held commitments that drive the conduct of the people within the school. When we live and work according to our core values, they become the driving force behind our actions. Anyone visiting your school will see them at work; they are anchored in behaviors and observable to even an untrained eye.

Core values are not always readily apparent. By their very nature, they are deeply embedded in the value systems of the people who must define and live by them. That is why it is important to dedicate time for individual reflection in preparation for bringing people together in a collaborative process. Once people have had time to think about their own personal values, the collaboration with others builds shared understanding and commitment to the organizational values that will shape and define the school's culture.

An activity for examining core values allows individuals and the group to examine the core values that will serve as building blocks for their preferred future. People pick among four values they have identified as deeply important to them. In the end, they can keep them all, but the journey is what causes the highest priorities to emerge. The procedure for examining core values follows.

1. Working in small groups of six to eight people, have each individual fold a blank sheet of paper into quadrants, creasing the edges firmly so that

the sheet can later be torn into four equal sections, and then unfold the paper. (You may want to demonstrate what it should look like as groups fold and unfold the sheet.)

2. Ask everyone to reflect quietly on the things he or she values most in life. These should be things that get at the heart of who participants are as people and what drives them to live their lives the way they do. These are bedrock convictions, not just nice things to have. Then, ask them to write a word or short phrase that describes their four most deeply held values, one per section on the now-unfolded paper. (Hint: If people are struggling to come up with what these might be, suggest that they think about the Golden Rule. How do you want to be treated? What do you believe about how others should be treated? What's most important to you in your everyday work or family life?)

3. Once everyone has completed the four sections, have them tear the paper into the four pieces and hold them like they would a hand of cards, words toward themselves.

4. The facilitator then takes the entire group on a journey of priorities.

   "As you set out to explore life's opportunities, values in hand, you make your way through busy streets and noisy crowds, looking for symbols of your preferred future. You spot an intriguing image ahead. Moving quickly toward the image, past the protection of a tall building, a gust of wind blows one of the values out of your hand. Gone! Which three are left? (Have participants discard one of their values by laying it words down in front of them.)

   "Still excited about the possibilities, you carry on toward the image. As you make your way, you can feel the tension lessening, and you begin to see a broader view of what the future could be. There are many ways to turn, but you commit to one path. To do so, you must relinquish one more of your values. This time, however, you know that your value will not be lost in the wind but will go to help those on the road not taken. (Have participants discard one more of their values by laying it down on top of the first one, words down.)

"The final leg of the journey is filled with anticipation. You are nearing your destination—the goal is in sight. Along the way, others are supporting you, assisting you to close the final gap. As a statement of your appreciation, you share one of your values with them, keeping one last value to yourself." (Once again, have participants discard one more value by laying it down on top of the other two.)

5. As a table team, have one person scribe as each person shares the final value that he or she kept. If more than one person kept the same value, the scribe should tally how many times that particular value was kept. Once teams have tallied all final values, collect the rest of the values in reverse order using the same collection-and-tally process.

6. Which values were consistently among the top one or two? Which values appeared at every level? The scribe should make a list of the top four to six that the group could agree represent the value priorities of the table. Those are then compared with all other table groups' lists.

7. The final step is to reorganize the whole group into four to six small groups, each with the responsibility to write a statement for one of the values along with a description of what it would look like if that value were being lived on a regular basis in your school.

Core value statements take on many different forms and formats. The content should be unique to the organization, reflecting the words, beliefs, and convictions of those who contribute to their creation.

Figure 9.2 is an example of core value statements from the Whitewater Unified School District's Strategic Plan.

We value . . .

- Students as our top priority
- High expectations for student achievement
- Respect for and appreciation of human diversity
- Excellence in teaching, leadership, and service
- School, community, and family partnerships
- Responsible planning and management of resources
- Education as the foundation of a strong community

Source: Adapted from Whitewater Unified School District, January, 2013.

Figure 9.2: Whitewater Unified School District's core values.

The ultimate success of our collective efforts will rest on the degree to which we can agree on and act in accordance with shared values. Core values guide the conduct of the people within the school. When we live and work according to our core values, they become the driving force behind our actions. Therefore, they need to be explicit and operationally defined so that schools can measure decisions and actions against them. If a plan, decision, or set of actions is contrary to or inconsistent with the values of the people within the school, frustration, conflict, and uncertainty prevail. Conversely, when plans, decisions, and actions align with our values, there is energy, commitment, and focus. Anyone visiting our school should see the values at work; they are observable to even an untrained eye.

Vision

A vision is a compelling picture of a preferred future that motivates us to act. Some refer to vision as a hope or a dream. However, vision is more than that. It might start as a hope or a dream, but it doesn't become a vision until there is some specificity about what that dream will look like in reality. What distinguishes a dream from a vision is the detail of the vision in action, something people can see or envision themselves doing. That is what makes a vision compelling. That is why vision motivates us to act—sometimes in ways that are very different than we ever would have imagined.

Vision is the manifestation of our stated values. When groups create their visions, it helps if they start with their value statements. The vision is the best possible future that can be achieved when we focus on our most valued priorities and behave in ways that are consistent with our core beliefs.

Shared vision answers the questions, Where do we want to be in the future? How great can we become? What do we want to create together? Shared vision captures the collective imagination of everyone in the school. It is a vivid picture of a place that could potentially be very different because the school community has collectively committed to creating it together.

How to Develop a Shared Vision

Too often, groups begin the visioning process by trying to write a vision statement. Though this task is not impossible, it is a more difficult way to begin because people have not had the time to think, interact, and dream together. What typically happens in these situations is that groups become mired in the words and ultimately lose sight of the purpose —to develop shared vision.

The vision statement is a communication device that is best created after a group has engaged in the process of visioning (such as the use of collaborative methods to evoke images of a new reality and to explore scenarios of possible futures). It is the visioning process that causes people to think differently, to be creative, and to design a future that is consistent with their values and purpose.

In setting the stage for visioning, it is important for people to think about the future as something potentially quite different from today. The key is to create opportunities and to provide time and structures for people to talk about their hopes and dreams.

There are a number of processes for creating shared vision. The best ones:

- Keep people focused on a key question about the future
- Involve a diverse mix of stakeholders

- Build in time for discussions in both large and small groups

Although there are no hard-and-fast rules for how many people to involve in developing a vision, it is important to involve those who will be in a position to lead or influence others, those who will bring fresh perspectives, and those whom peers highly regard. We suggest involving individuals from the following stakeholder groups.

- **The community:** Parents, community members, and business and political leaders
- **The district:** Board members and central office administration
- **The school:** Principals, teachers, other school staff, and students or graduates where appropriate

The key to effective visioning is helping people get out of their current way of thinking and acting. This is not to suggest that the current way is bad or wrong, but if we are to create a new vision, we need to be able to see a different picture. Sometimes the existing structures, systems, and even facilities are so limiting that people can't see a different future. That is why we suggest using processes that are not typically how a group, staff, or community works together. For the same reason, it's also a good idea to conduct the visioning activities in locations other than your existing school if at all possible.

Teams can generate vision statements in many ways. Here are some examples.

- **Blue sky scenarios:** If you could create the school of your dreams, what would it look like? This is an entrepreneurial approach—ignore all that was or is and create something totally new from scratch. Imagine that there is no school building and that there are no existing rules, contracts, or policies. There are no limitations of resources nor mandates from the district, state, or federal government. Now, review your mission and values.
- **Forecasting scenarios:** This is what some refer to as reality-based visioning—attempting to predict

the future by analyzing trends and then designing around those predictions. What are the big trends in education? What impact will technology, standards-based reforms, and the accountability movement have? What will be happening with our financial resources in the future? Our human resources? Our demographics? Have groups use the same facts to develop separate scenarios and share them with each other. Take the best and most likely elements from each to craft your vision.

- **Time warp:** Take an imaginary trip through time, ending up somewhere in the future (for example, five to ten years out). Turn on the evening news. What are the stories they're telling about your school? Begin the dialogue with, "What will you be proud to hear them saying about us?" Or, "Imagine it is five years from now. Our school has just received the Blue Ribbon Schools of Excellence Award. This award is given to only a select few schools in the United States. Recently visitors from all over the United States have been visiting to learn what is going on to make our school so outstanding." Describe this award-winning, ideal school. What kinds of things do you see? What does the school look like? What is happening with the students, staff, parents, and community?

- **Mapping:** Map out the assets of your community and how each relates to the others. What are your human assets? Your technology assets? Your financial assets? Your geographic assets? Which emerge as natural connections? Which needed connections are missing?

- **Role playing:** Have people return to their statements of core values and beliefs and then create a way to communicate those values to the rest of the group. One rule: there are no rules. They can use any form of expression they like—a skit, dance, poem, rap, newscast, song, or picture. Then, allow five minutes for each group to perform or share its vision of the future.

- **Pictogram:** Have people create a visual representation of the future. Give each small group a large piece of chart paper, poster board, or butcher paper, plus boxes of markers, some sticky dots, construction paper, glue, stickers, or even small toys or light objects that it can attach to the picture. The task is to create a visual image of the future as a group. There are two rules for creating a pictogram: (1) everyone must be involved in the actual creation, and (2) the group may not use words—only symbols—to express its ideas. Share the individual pictograms with the large group and identify common themes and patterns.

These processes are designed to get people thinking creatively about their future and to actively involve all the participants in the creative process. The most important part of this is the conversations that go into creating the vision itself, not the document, skit, or picture. You may need to reassure people that artistic talent is not the point. It's the shared dream that really matters.

Once a group has had the opportunity to create a vision together, writing the statement becomes an exercise in capturing the ideas and energy that the vision generated. This may take anywhere from a couple of hours to a day or two, depending on the process selected and the number of people involved.

Characteristics of Vision Statements

The vision statement, like the mission statement, should be concise and compelling. The words are very important because they must convey meaning beyond simple understanding. They must be inspirational, communicate promise, and create an image of something that cannot be seen today but is possible tomorrow. Vision statements:

- **Are concrete**—Have observable, detectable qualities
- **Focus on ends, not means**—Communicate what, not how
- **Are achievable and compelling**—Are believable, but beyond what is

Tips for Writing Vision Statements

- Have a larger group (an entire staff or a mix of staff and parents) generate some sample statements. You may want to divide the group into small mixed subgroups (each smaller group represents the diversity of the entire group as much as possible).

- Designate a team to write an initial draft of a vision statement. First, use a walkabout process in the large group to see the breadth of sample statements and clarify any confusion. Post statements on the wall. Have everyone walk around and silently read the statements. Members can make comments by leaving sticky notes with suggestions, compliments, and requests for clarification. Then have members return to their statements, read through the comments, and incorporate any changes they would like to make.

- Afterward, the team writes a draft statement that incorporates the ideas from the larger group and circulates its draft to all staff for comment (not just those who were included in the initial work).

- **Manifest the mission and values**—Live the values of the school and accomplish its mission well

Figure 9.3 shows sample school vision statements.

- We are committed to successful learning, student by student.
- Every student is a promise—we will be a community of learners and leaders united in our goal to enrich the lives of all our students through learning.
- We will be a safe place to learn and work, where our collective energy and resources are directed toward the unique and diverse learning needs of all.

Figure 9.3: Sample school vision statements.

The conversation about the vision doesn't stop when the stakeholders have agreed on the wording of the statement. It's important to keep the vision conversation going and return to it often. Three factors contribute to the necessity of sustaining the vision conversation.

1. As new people (staff, students, and families) enter the school community, they will need to become acquainted with and committed to the vision.

2. By its very nature, a vision is not physically present; it is in the hearts and minds of those who created it. Therefore, it must continually be shared if it is to become reality.

3. The vision will reform and reshape itself as it evolves into reality. Desire, not default, should guide that reformation.

How to Keep the Vision Alive

Writing a vision statement is not what creates successful districts and schools. The visioning process is a journey, one kept alive by the way that everyone in the school community frames each and every conversation and in the way the school supports actions in pursuit of the vision.

Through modeling, reinforcement, and recognition, schools keep a vision alive and build its momentum. Teachers and school leaders need time to imagine what the future will be like in this vision and how their personal lives will be different. It is especially important for leaders to share what the vision means to them, revealing their personal thoughts about the vision and how they see it unfolding. It is important that leaders write and talk about how they see the vision connecting to the mission and values of the school.

To keep the vision alive, ask stakeholders (teachers, students, parents, staff, and community members) what they think.

- "Do you think the vision is feasible?"
- "Is it something you are willing to commit to?"
- "Does it reflect what you want?"

Listen respectfully to their answers, exploring what they have to say through dialogue. Invite comments and incorporate those comments into the emerging vision statement. This will help create a sense that everyone truly shares this vision. The conversations centered on these questions provide a context for reinforcing a vision.

You can reinforce a vision by:

- Continually encouraging people to dream and hope beyond the day
- Using planning and goal-setting sessions that include visioning
- Providing time to pursue the vision and goals

When people partake in actions that will lead to or enhance the vision, bring those actions to the forefront to help everyone see how he or she contributes to the development of shared vision. When school leaders engage stakeholders in these ongoing, vision-enhancing practices, individuals throughout the school are able to internalize the vision so that it becomes a part of their daily behavioral repertoire.

Mission

A school's mission answers the question, "What is our purpose?" or "Why do we exist?" That may seem like an obvious question with an obvious answer, but when you get right

What If We're Not Ready to Create a Vision?

Sometimes a school has been through so many changes and so much strife that it really isn't ready as a community to start dreaming about the future. In this situation, it may be helpful to conduct the historygram process (see page 233). Make sure each storyboard includes a list of values from the past that participants want to carry into the future. Then use these values as a springboard for visioning and creating shared values for the future of the school.

down to it, there are many possible missions that any single school might pursue. If you polled individuals from inside and outside your school and asked, "Why does this school exist?" the many different responses may surprise you, such as:

- "To prepare students for the world of work"
- "To instill the joy of learning"
- "To develop basic skills in the areas of reading, writing, and arithmetic"
- "To meet the academic, social, and emotional needs of students"
- "To prepare students for college"
- "To have as many students graduate as possible"
- "To ensure that all our students know and can pursue their personal dreams"

None of these purposes are either right or wrong. However, depending on which one (or any number of other possible missions) your school chooses, your course of action and choice of curricula and instructional practices will differ.

The only way to truly know the mission of your school is to talk about it and decide what best defines the purpose you want. The mission evolves out of community discourse and consensus building. It's much more than just a compelling statement. It is the reason we choose to work and learn at this particular school.

A clear statement of purpose that teams develop collaboratively will create cohesiveness, commitment, and understanding. The mission gives meaning to our work. When we know why we exist, we can be better at choosing how we will work and what work we choose to do. That is the essential value of a mission.

How to Create a Mission Statement

The mission statement should communicate the essential aim of the school in a concise and memorable way. Once teams create a mission statement, they must continuously engage in dialogue about what the statement means and how they will use it.

Creating a statement from scratch can be done in a variety of ways. If possible, include all staff and faculty and a representative group of parents in drafting a statement. If everyone cannot participate in every step due to the size of your staff or timeline limitations, appoint a small group to take the lead in creating a draft statement and then use various methods for involving others in reacting to, making suggestions for, or revising the draft statement.

If you've already created a mission statement, the key is to keep it alive and present for all. One way to do this is to ask individuals to consider the *blinking words* in the mission statement—the words that speak to them or resonate with them and why. Use this technique as a check-in for a kick-off meeting at the beginning of the year.

You also may want to evaluate your current mission statement against the checklist in figure 9.4.

> When schools are unable to coordinate teachers' diverse aims for students into a curricular mission focused on high-quality student learning, it is difficult for even the most gifted teachers to make a positive difference for students.
>
> —Fred M. Newmann and Gary G. Wehlage

Our Mission Statement

☐ Is clear and understandable

☐ Is brief enough for most people to remember and say in one breath

☐ Clearly specifies the school's fundamental purpose

☐ Has a primary focus on a single strategic thrust (such as learning)

☐ Reflects the distinctive competence and culture of this particular school

☐ Is broad enough to allow flexibility in implementation, but not so broad as to create a lack of focus

☐ Will help school personnel, parents, and community members make decisions

☐ Is energizing and compelling

What changes would improve our mission statement?

Figure 9.4: Checklist for evaluating a mission statement.

*Visit **go.solution-tree.com/schoolimprovement** for a reproducible version of this figure.*

Ask new staff members to form a team and review the statement using the checklist. If they feel there are items that need improvement, have them identify how they would improve the statement. Circulate the suggestions to all staff, offering everyone an opportunity to revisit the purpose of his or her work.

How to Brainwrite a Mission Statement

Sometimes it's useful to provide a structure and a process for stakeholders to use to develop the mission statement. *Brainwriting* is a collaborative idea-generating process that encourages creative thinking around a set of defined parameters or elements of the mission statement. Using a structured technique like brainwriting ensures that the essential parts of the statement are included. It also helps build consensus among individuals working in small groups. Figure 9.5 provides a mission statement format.

Mission Statement

Our mission as a school community is _____.

                                                Aim or Action

We do this by _____.

                                Actions

We do this so that _____.

                                Reason or Purpose

Figure 9.5: Mission statement format.

Using this format, a school develops the following mission statement.

> Our mission as a school community is to challenge our students to reach their academic potential. We do this by teaching them new knowledge and skills and respecting them for who they are. We do this so that they are prepared to meet future challenges with confidence and expertise and so that they experience the absolute joy of learning throughout the rest of their lives.

The sample statement describes a noble and worthy purpose. However, it is likely to have different meanings to different audiences, such as the phrase "reaching academic potential." Therefore, it is important to start with a draft statement and then have everyone in the school discuss

---

Using Another School's Mission Statement

If you have found a mission statement from another school that you would like to use or modify, be sure to discuss the statement with stakeholder groups. In the end, the conversations about what the statement means are more important than the words on the page.

what it means to them. Share the mission with parents, try it out on students, and get their reactions.

The materials you'll need for a brainwriting activity are the following.

- Markers of three different colors
- Flipchart paper
- Tape
- Colored dots

Consider the following ten steps for a brainwriting activity.

1. Divide your group into three smaller groups of no more than eight people (if you have a very large group, break the group into six or nine smaller groups), all seated around tables.

2. Label three sheets of flipchart paper (or large pieces of butcher paper) with the following titles (one per page).

    - **Aim:** What are we here to do?
    - **Action:** How will we accomplish our aim?
    - **Audience:** Who do we exist to serve?

3. Review the rules of brainstorming (page 112).

4. Give each table one of the three papers and a colored marker (a different color for each group). Tell the participants they have two minutes to generate responses to the question on their page. They should write brief phrases or words and number them as they go.

5. At the end of two minutes say "switch." The groups pass their paper (not their markers) to another table. Be sure that once the rotation starts, all papers go in the same direction each time. Give the groups one minute to review what the previous group wrote and two minutes to add more ideas.

6. The process of switching and timing continues until each group ends up with their original paper. (That is, each group has worked on all three sheets.)

7. Have the groups review the final lists together. People may ask questions for clarification wherever

they do not understand what another group meant (or can't read their writing). Here's where the colors are useful—if there is a question about something written in blue, the group knows where to find the answer. If you are working with more than three small groups, those groups with the same question (all papers labeled "Aim," for example) should work together to reduce duplications and come up with one list that includes all ideas. Once the team has cleaned up the lists, post the papers on the wall for everyone to see.

8. Use the multivoting process (page 118) to narrow the number of ideas. The objective is to develop a targeted list of words and phrases that most closely match the group's sense of what the school's mission ought to be. This, then, is the pool of ideas that will help to create the mission statement.

9. Develop draft mission statements. Because group writing can be time consuming, and, for some people, downright painful, divide the whole group into two or more smaller groups. Have each group write a statement, using the words and phrases from the list.

10. Share and compare statements as a whole group. Frequently, one or two will emerge as clear favorites, or there will be parts of one or two that everyone will like.

How to Use the Mission to Maintain Focus

A mission statement is most worthwhile when schools use it daily. Many schools print their mission statement on their walls, stationery, business cards, refrigerator magnets, and the like. That's a good way to keep people aware of it, but these strategies alone won't guarantee its proper use. Here are some ideas for using your mission statement to help your school stay focused on its true purpose.

- Begin faculty meetings by reviewing the agenda against the mission: "How will this decision or discussion help us fulfill our mission? How is this consistent with our mission?"

- When you introduce a new program or initiative, create some time to have people discuss its relation to the mission.

- When deciding about new curricula or determining what not to teach, use the mission as your guide.

- Have people reflect on what they are currently doing or would do differently in light of the mission statement.

- Budget decisions are a good test for a mission. Are you allocating your resources in support of your mission?

- Professional learning should support the mission as directly as possible.

Core values, vision, and mission statements belong to everyone in the organization. They have galvanizing qualities especially when those who work, learn, and believe in the organization have created them together. Most importantly, by asking the question, "Where do *we* want to be?" we are signaling that we all share responsibility for behaving in ways that will move us toward our desired future.

Core Question Two: Where Are We Now?

This question helps the school community *reflect* on the current situation to get a data-based view of what its school really looks like. In answering this question, school members gather baseline data to identify both strengths and weaknesses. The resulting picture helps point the way toward improvement priorities.

Gathering and analyzing data on which to base a school's improvement plan and evaluating results may require a wide variety of qualitative and quantitative tools, balanced with a good share of intuition and common sense about what all the data mean. Previous chapters describe various types of tools you can use to collect and analyze diverse information.

In addition to the tools we presented in previous chapters, there are two specific strategies that are particularly helpful in answering the question, Where are we now?—(1) needs assessment and (2) friendly observers. When used together, these strategies generate high-quality, in-depth information your school can use to understand where it is today.

Needs Assessment

When we think about improving student learning, we tend to focus only on student academic or behavioral indicators. Research shows, however, that many other factors affect student learning, such as parent and community involvement and support, school climate, classroom instructional activities, curriculum alignment, professional community, pedagogical and assessment practices, equitable access to curriculum and instruction, teacher quality, professional development, leadership capacity, resources, and so on (Lezotte & Snyder, 2011; Marzano, 2003; Shannon & Bylsma, 2007). To fully understand a school's current performance, teams need to assess a variety of factors and dimensions.

A comprehensive needs assessment is a tool for assessing a diverse set of factors. The process engages teachers schoolwide in identifying areas they want to learn more about, organizing themselves into teacher-led study teams to research those areas, and bringing that information back to the school community as a whole. This strategy has proven to be a powerful method for discovering change, learning, and improvement.

There are at least six major areas of study that any school will want to take a look at when conducting a thorough needs assessment.

1. **Community:** Two groups form the school community. The people *inside* the school's walls are the students, teachers, paraprofessionals, support staff, and administrators. The people *outside* the school's walls include parents, families, community-based organizations, local businesses, labor unions, religious leaders, central office staff, school board members, and others.

2. **Order, discipline, and climate:** The school's internal functioning involves these factors, specifically policies, procedures, and systems for ensuring safety and a positive learning environment.

3. **Achievement:** Classroom and district assessments as well as standardized tests measure and define students' academic skills, knowledge, and capabilities.

4. **Teaching and learning systems:** Students' opportunity to learn is influenced by processes for identifying and assisting underachieving students, staff development practices, methods of identifying and incorporating best practices into the school, integration of technology as a tool for learning, and the amount of collaborative inquiry that occurs throughout the school.

5. **Curriculum and instruction:** Processes for developing and improving curriculum, methods for evaluating outcomes against standards, and the array of teaching and assessment practices are central to effective curriculum and instruction.

6. **Resources:** This is a catchall category that includes not only the school's use of time and money but also faculty and staff qualifications and competencies, administrative capabilities, organization of the school, the school's ability to translate goals into actions, and communication systems, as well as the depth and breadth of skillful leadership throughout the school.

The full staff should brainstorm with these questions: What do we want to know about these areas, and how can we find out? These questions lead to the use of a wide range of measures to find the answers. In addition to gathering information in these six areas, schools will want to get a clear picture of their student demographics—age, gender, race, ethnicity, mobility, socioeconomic status, special education status, and so on. When students' academic status (per grades, test scores, and other measures) is disaggregated for

Principles of Collaborative Inquiry

Many schools have adopted the following principles of collaborative inquiry to assist in creating an environment that supports shared, continuous learning.

- We are in this together to make a difference for students' learning.

- People are basically good and want to do a good job.

- All people deserve to be treated with dignity and respect.

- Bringing multiple perspectives and skills together adds value to the team.

- All of us are learners; all of us are leaders.

different subgroups, often the resulting picture is an eye-opening impetus for improvement.

Friendly Observers

Feedback from a team of friendly observers, experienced educators, and other experts who observe your school at work and provide their own commentary and insights augments the needs assessment process. More specifically, friendly observers should provide constructive feedback about the school's teaching and learning system, teachers' use of best practices, and the overall climate for leadership and learning.

For the friendly observer process to work well, it is important that the staff—particularly teachers—be fully involved in the process of selection and recruitment, as well as have significant input into what the observers are looking for. A staff that is open to looking in the mirror and really *seeing* what is there has taken a powerful first step toward making improvements.

To engage staff so that they are fully aware of and committed to the process and the feedback that it generates:

1. Have staff brainstorm a list of questions they would like answered about your school.

2. Have staff develop criteria for selecting the friendly observers, such as the following.

    - Knows our district or school

    - Has deep knowledge of reading literacy

    - Has deep knowledge of mathematics literacy

    - Understands poverty and learning issues

    - Has curriculum, instruction, and assessment experience

    - Holds central office position

    - Holds university position

    - Is a colleague or peer

3. Review the criteria, and then ask staff to brainstorm names of potential friendly observers. The candidates should be people who are highly

credible and trusted. As a whole, they should represent a variety of perspectives and areas of knowledge. These brainstormed names become your recruiting list.

4. Create a lead team to work on recruitment and final selection and to organize the logistics (planning their visit, clarifying expectations and needs, designing the process, and so on).

   • Try to recruit five to ten observers.

   • Prepping the observers should include a reminder that their role is to uncover strengths as well as opportunities for improvement because the school will need to build on those strengths to achieve its improvement goals.

5. Have the observers visit your school.

   • Schedule the visit over a period of several days, during which they observe classrooms and interview staff, students, parents, and the principal.

   • To create a safe environment for the friendly observer process, allow teachers to opt out when they need uninterrupted teaching time. One option is to have teachers post a sign that says "Pass" on their classroom door. The observers will be instructed to avoid rooms with such signs.

6. Have the observers meet off site to compare notes and compile a final report highlighting the school's strengths and opportunities for improvement.

7. Share this report among the staff.

The friendly observer process grew out of comprehensive school improvement work. Table 9.1 (page 256) contrasts the friendly observer process and the *instructional rounds process*. Instructional rounds are an adaptation of medical rounds, which medical schools and teaching hospitals use (City, Elmore, Fiarman, & Teitel, 2009). While the two processes are similar in nature, they differ in some significant ways.

Table 9.1: Friendly Observers Versus Instructional Rounds

	Friendly Observers	Instructional Rounds
Purpose	Improve teaching and learning system, use best instructional practices, improve overall leadership and learning climate.	Use protocols and routines to develop common practice (City et al., 2009).
Focus	School site and classrooms	District, schools, and classrooms
Leader	Principal	Central office
Observation Team	Experienced, diverse group of educators	System-level and school-level leadership teams
Observation Team Recruitment	Teachers	Administrators
Time Frame	Ad hoc group disperses after observations and report.	Ongoing learning network

Knowing the size and the nature of the gap between where we want to be (core question one) and where we are now (core question two) provides valuable information about the magnitude of the work that needs to be done to close the gap. (On pages 304–306 in appendix B, you will find "The SMART Schools Self-Assessment," which is a useful, iterative assessment of where you are now.) The next core question helps us determine the focus of the collaborative work that will be required to close the gap.

Core Question Three: How Will We Get There?

This question engages the school community in identifying and prioritizing goals with supporting rationale and improvement activities. This is where the school community turns to educational literature and best practice research to identify instructional strategies, curriculum, programs, and structures that they want to try out in their school. Benchmarking against successful schools with similar demographics and resources is another practice that can help focus improvement ideas. Of course, staff development that develops teachers' skills and knowledge in the targeted improvement area is key to building the school's capacity to achieve its goals.

By this point in your schoolwide improvement process, you will know where you *want* to be (core values, vision, and mission); you'll also know where you are now (data from your needs assessment and friendly observers). The next question is how you will get to where you want to be. The planning process begins by translating your mission into concrete steps to identify SMART goals and action plans that will help your school improve student achievement. We refer to this set of steps as the SMART school improvement process because it helps close the gap between where your school is now and where you want it to be.

The SMART School Improvement Process

The SMART school improvement process is built on a progression of collaborative steps that embed theory, research, data, professional learning, and continuous improvement. We refer to this as the *data-logic chain*; the interaction of thinking around or analysis of empirical results informs each step, which then fuels the progression of further thinking and data gathering. Figure 9.6 illustrates the data-logic chain.

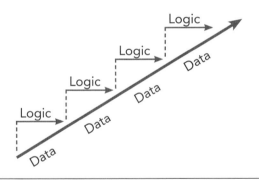

Figure 9.6: The data-logic chain.

Each step on this chain has a series of meetings and between-meeting work that the SMART leadership team leads and the entire staff carries out. Using the turbo meeting agenda format (see page 94), teams can accomplish the meetings in a highly engaging and efficient manner. Figure 9.7 (page 260) is an illustration of how the meeting process maps onto the data-logic chain.

Above the improvement line are the meetings that take place around a specific purpose; below the improvement

> If you have more than three priorities, you have none.
>
> —Jim Collins

> The lack of clear goals may provide the most credible explanation for why we are still only inching along in our effort to improve schooling for U.S. children.
>
> —Mike Schmoker

> When an organization has multiple immeasurable priorities, there's lots of activity, but not much really gets done, and results are slow to come or nonexistent.
>
> —Dennis Sparks

Alignment of SMART Goals

District Level

- All students will be reading at grade level by the end of third grade.

- All students will demonstrate proficiency in all tested areas (reading, language arts, mathematics, science, and social studies) by the time they graduate.

School Level

- By (three years out), 90 percent of our students will meet or exceed literacy standards.

- By the end of the year, 85 percent of our eighth-grade students will pass the mathematics and science standards assessment the first time.

- All students will demonstrate a minimum of 10 percent growth in all academic areas by the end of the third quarter.

Classroom Level

- By the end of the semester, we will achieve a 20 percent increase in the number of students demonstrating advanced proficiency in second-grade reading.

- By the end of the school year, 80 percent of first and second graders will be able to identify

Continued➔

line are the between-meeting tasks that provide the essential data for taking the next step. The entire process incorporates the PDSA continuous improvement cycle (see page 4). Early steps produce data-informed plans (P) that are carried out (D) and then studied (S) and adjusted (A) so that improvements continue to occur. Refer to appendix A (page 290) for the SMART school improvement process chain and complete planning guide for the SMART school improvement process.

The SMART school improvement process is a collaborative effort that develops in five steps: (1) isolating the need, (2) identifying the school's SMART goal, (3) selecting strategies, (4) developing action plans, and (5) analyzing and refocusing.

Step One: Isolating the Need

The needs assessment to answer core question two—Where are we now?—informs this step. In addition, the first meeting provides an opportunity for staff to share their perceptions and experiences related to the academic standards and skills they know their students struggle with most often. This is the thinking that drives additional data collection and analysis focused specifically on academic concerns, which is at the heart of the SMART school improvement process.

Meeting one utilizes the affinity process (see chapter 5, page 116). The outcome of this meeting is a plan for gathering any additional data the team needs to verify and further defining the nature of the challenges students are having academically. Team members gather additional data and organize them by a small group of individual volunteers between meeting one and meeting two.

Step Two: Identifying the School's SMART Goal

SMART goals are *gap closers* toward the vision. They move us toward the vision in ways that are both actionable and attainable. They refine the direction the vision provides into more specific and measurable outcomes and communicate expectations for improvement in ways that can be tracked over time.

SMART goals have unique qualities that differentiate them from other types of goals. In addition to their adherence to the SMART acronym (page 5), they help organize and propel improvement efforts because they are the basis for what teams research, implement, and learn along the way.

Process and Results Goals

Most goals in education are process goals; they focus on the activities, programs, strategies, and methods that educators want to engage in. Process goals aren't bad; they're just not particularly useful as a way to achieve and measure a particular outcome. Checking a process goal means seeing if the school implemented the program, strategy, method, or activity—that is, whether the process was changed. However, knowing a process changed doesn't tell you whether the school achieved the desired outcome or result.

The problem is not that we use process goals—we need good processes to build capacity. The problem lies in having only process goals with no goals that measure the effectiveness of the processes we put in place (results goals).

Results goals answer the "so what" question: So what if we did all these things? What actual improvement would we expect or want to see? To be useful tools for measuring performance and progress, goals *should* be results-oriented rather than process-oriented. They should identify what is desired in terms of performance after, or as a result of, putting new processes in place or improving existing processes. Table 9.2 summarizes the differences between process and results-oriented goals.

Table 9.2: Contrasting Process and Results-Oriented Goals

Process Goals	Results-Oriented Goals
Means	Ends
Inputs	Outputs
Capacity improvements	Productivity
System interventions	Outcomes
Improvement activities	Improvement targets
Function	Purpose

The bottom line is we need both good processes and results. SMART goals focus on student learning results,

musical instruments by ear using a textbook's pre- and post-tests.

- By the end of the school year, student attendance will increase by 50 percent for students who have been absent seven days or more since the beginning of the school year.

Student Level (Standards or Assessment-Based Statements That Reflect "I Can")

- I will achieve level three or better on our four-level rubric for each six-week performance assessment in mathematics.

- I will be able to write an eighth-grade essay with 95 percent accuracy using the 6+1 traits of writing criteria (Culham, 2003).

- I will exceed my growth targets in literacy by 50 percent.

Figure 9.7: SMART school improvement process chain.

Examples of Differences Between Process and Results Thinking

Process: Integrate mathematics and science curricula

—so that—

Result: Students are better able to apply mathematics and science concepts to real-life tasks

Process: Hire star-quality teachers

—so that—

Result: Student achievement improves

Process: Budget additional time for staff collaboration and professional development

—so that—

Result: Staff are more focused on and skillful in improving student results

which, in turn, inform us about the processes we need to engage in to achieve them.

Greatest Area of Need (GAN)

The power of SMART goals comes from the laser-like focus that teams develop when they compute and build their goal around the school's *greatest area of need* (GAN). This process incorporates three different views of the data that teams gather between meetings one and two. The three views are: (1) accountability gap, (2) proficiency gap, and (3) change-over-time gap.

The *accountability gap* is the difference between where the school is now (for example, 65 percent of the students are proficient readers) and where some official authority says the school ought to be (for example, 90 percent proficiency). We sometimes refer to this as the *compliance gap* because schools are expected to comply with certain standards and levels of performance. In this case, the gap is 25 percent.

The *proficiency gap* is the difference between where the school is now (for example, 65 percent of the students are proficient readers) and all students being proficient (for example, 100 percent proficiency). We refer to this as the *commitment gap*, because it is what we, as educators, aspire to in the end. In this case, the gap is 35 percent.

The *change-over-time gap* is the difference between where the school is now (for example, 65 percent of the students are proficient readers) and where it started out based on past data on the same measure or assessment (for example, 40 percent proficiency five years ago). What this tells us is that the improvements that have been put in place are working. The gap has closed by 25 percentage points over the past five years.

When teams examine all three views of data together, looking across all tested subject areas, the GAN emerges. The subject area with the largest accountability and proficiency gaps or the least amount of improvement over time becomes the focal point for the school's SMART goal. Further analysis of the specific standards within that subject area provides additional specificity for building the SMART goal tree.

SMART Goal Tree Diagram

The *SMART goal tree diagram* is a planning tool that helps collaborative teams think through, organize, and monitor improvement efforts using multiple measures and incremental targets toward the goal. It is a graphic organizer that keeps teams focused and ensures the team includes all five SMART criteria in the goal. Figure 9.8 (page 262) shows a SMART goal tree diagram.

Each box in figure 9.8 represents a critical property of the goal. The connectors between the boxes define a pathway from the results goal all the way to the targets, which are incremental, smaller steps toward the end goal.

The indicators are the specific standards or skills that represent what the data show are the greatest areas of need within the subject of the goal. For example, if the results goal is focused on reading, the indicators would be those components of reading that are most problematic for the students (for example, comprehending complex text, drawing conclusions, or making inferences).

One useful tool for determining which indicators to focus on is the cause-and-effect diagram (see chapter 7, page 164). Before you begin to plan solutions, dig into the causes of the problems or issues highlighted in the needs assessment data in order to understand underlying reasons. Use a

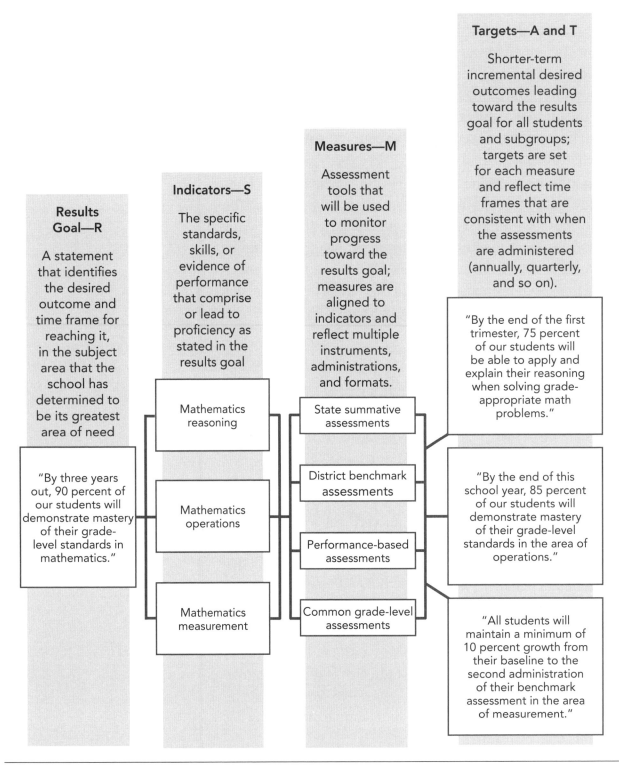

Results Goal—R

A statement that identifies the desired outcome and time frame for reaching it, in the subject area that the school has determined to be its greatest area of need

"By three years out, 90 percent of our students will demonstrate mastery of their grade-level standards in mathematics."

Indicators—S

The specific standards, skills, or evidence of performance that comprise or lead to proficiency as stated in the results goal

Mathematics reasoning

Mathematics operations

Mathematics measurement

Measures—M

Assessment tools that will be used to monitor progress toward the results goal; measures are aligned to indicators and reflect multiple instruments, administrations, and formats.

State summative assessments

District benchmark assessments

Performance-based assessments

Common grade-level assessments

Targets—A and T

Shorter-term incremental desired outcomes leading toward the results goal for all students and subgroups; targets are set for each measure and reflect time frames that are consistent with when the assessments are administered (annually, quarterly, and so on).

"By the end of the first trimester, 75 percent of our students will be able to apply and explain their reasoning when solving grade-appropriate math problems."

"By the end of this school year, 85 percent of our students will demonstrate mastery of their grade-level standards in the area of operations."

"All students will maintain a minimum of 10 percent growth from their baseline to the second administration of their benchmark assessment in the area of measurement."

Figure 9.8: SMART goal tree highlighting the SMART elements.

cause-and-effect diagram to help you define where to start for improvement. Conducting a cause analysis will help in the next step, which is to plan specific strategies for improvement. See figure 7.1 on page 166 for an example analysis of the causes of poor reading and writing performance and a process for conducting a cause analysis. Another approach for narrowing the focus of the broader results goals would be to conduct a Pareto analysis (page 182).

Each of the indicators on the goal tree is measured using multiple assessments of various types and formats (for example, summative, formative, performance-based, multiple choice, and so on). One type of assessment may be more useful for measuring comprehension, which is why the measures attach directly to the indicators. It is also possible that the same measure works for all of the indicators. It is still important to connect a measures box to each one because the targets will most likely differ depending on the baseline performance differences for each indicator.

Table 9.3 (page 264) summarizes the key terms associated with the SMART goal tree diagram along with some examples of each component.

Short-term targets that provide the information needed to monitor progress toward the results goal are the final component of the SMART goal tree. Targets express the amount of improvement that the team desires within a particular time frame. They represent the team's best estimate of what is attainable, communicate the team's expectations with regard to increased student performance, and are motivational in that they are expressions of confidence that what teachers do makes a difference. Figure 9.9 (page 265) shows how targets fit in the SMART goal tree.

Once teams have created the SMART goal, the staff turn their attention to figuring out what they need to do to achieve it. The work done between steps two and three of the SMART goal process prepares the staff to examine their current practices against the most recent, relevant research in the goal area. Based on interest and experience, individual staff members select various schoolwide practices they would like to research in the areas of curriculum, instruction, assessment, and classroom climate.

Table 9.3: Key Terms Matrix

Key Terms	Definition	Key Questions	Examples	Nonexamples
Results Goal	The results goal describes a specific desired result. It includes the overall amount of improvement desired and the time frame.	What specific result do you want to see in student learning or behavior?	Within three years, 85 percent of students will be proficient writers at their grade level.	By 2015, all teachers will participate in staff development in writing.
Indicators	Indicators are evidence we look for to see if we are achieving our results goal. They include the standards or components that are the weakest within a greatest area of need.	What specific skill areas or learning objectives do you want your students to know or be able to do? Which are the greatest areas of need?	We will evaluate student writing for: • Organization • Mechanics • Conventions	• Writer's workshop • Writing portfolios
Measures	Measures are the assessment tools you use to gauge progress on your indicators.	What data sources will provide us with the best information to measure our progress for each indicator?	We will draw on these measures of student performance: • Annual state test • Quarterly school writing assessment • Monthly writing samples with rubric scores	• Attendance rosters • Number of teachers who teach writing
Targets	Targets are the incremental steps toward reaching a longer-range goal.	• For our five-year goal, what is it that we want to achieve in year one, two, and so on? • For a course or unit goal, how much progress do we want to make each week?	We define these targets: • By the end of year one, 65 percent proficient • By the end of year two, 75 percent proficient • By the end of year three, 85 percent proficient	• By the end of year one, 100 percent proficient • All students will pass.
Strategies	Strategies are your plans for *how* you will accomplish your goal. They include implementing professional development and effective practices.	What approaches or strategies can we use that will best help us achieve our goal?	Provide staff development in a writers workshop. All teachers implement writing portfolios.	Try to teach writing skills at least once a week.

Source: Adapted from personal communication with Christy Reveles, November 6, 2012.

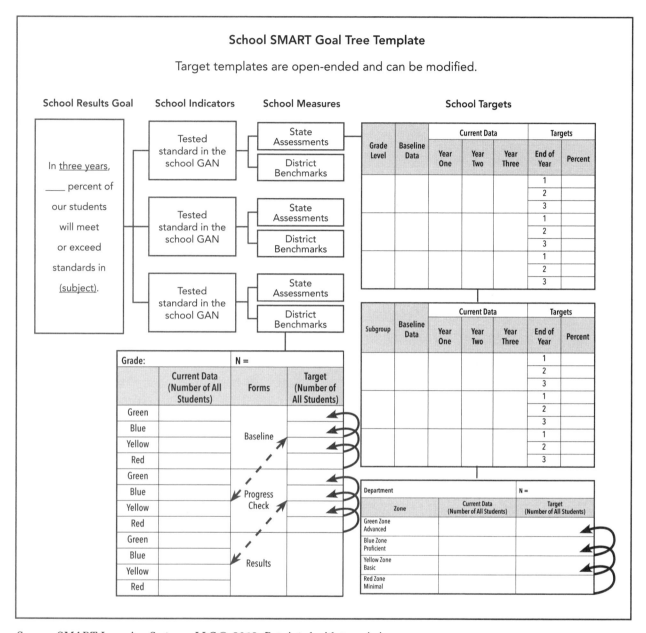

School SMART Goal Tree Template

Target templates are open-ended and can be modified.

Source: SMART Learning Systems, LLC © 2013. Reprinted with permission.

Figure 9.9: SMART goal tree with targets.

Step Three: Selecting Strategies

During this step in the process, staff take an inventory of their current practices in the goal area, how they apply their current practices, and their effectiveness in promoting better learning for students. They also identify their levels of understanding and use of the practices that emerged from the research conducted between steps. By cross-referencing the two, they are able to see that some of the things they are

The 3-2-1 Rule

SMART schools focus on no more than two or three goals at a time. Use the 3-2-1 rule when choosing the goals. If you opt for three goals, at least two of them should be student academic results goals with one focused on a contributing process or area of need for the adults, such as parent involvement, professional development, school culture and climate, collaboration time, and so on.

currently doing are considered best practice. They are also able to see that some of the things they are doing have no basis in the research and, by their own assessment, have not been particularly effective in practice. Finally, some of what they will learn from the research will be new to them—they either do not know about or use the best practice in their school or classrooms.

After reviewing all of the results, staff members use a multivoting technique (see chapter 5, page 118) to select three to five most promising practices to focus on as a school. Teams then plot this information onto a decision matrix, like the one in figure 9.10. Each individual places a sticky dot in the column that best describes his or her current level of use or knowledge. For those who have tried or are currently applying the strategy in some way, the final column is used to capture what they have learned and whether the impact of the strategy was evident. Figure 9.10 shows what one row of the matrix might look like. For instance, the strategy or practice selected by the team might be, "implementing word walls to improve vocabulary across the curriculum." If a teacher has tried this once or twice, he would put his dot in the middle column and add a note in the last column to indicate that it was moderately successful but difficult to sustain.

By the end of this step, the school has selected a few promising strategies for schoolwide implementation. Teams also know which, if any, staff members have been using these practices. The information gained from engaging in this step provides the launch pad for identifying the professional learning needs and methods that will build schoolwide capacity for change.

Between steps three and four, teams conduct a second round of research. This time the focus is on professional learning opportunities associated with the schoolwide strategies selected for implementation.

Creating Knowledge

This book begins with a discussion of learning communities —SMART schools where everyone is involved in acquiring new knowledge as well as contributing to the generation of new ideas, applications, and innovations in teaching.

Best Practice Aligned to Your School SMART Goal	Levels of Use					What Was the Result?
	Never heard of it	Have heard about it	Have started trying it in my classroom	Have been using it for a while in my classroom	Have modified or adapted its use in my classroom	

Source: SMART Learning Systems, LLC © 2013. Reprinted with permission.

Figure 9.10: Assessing current levels of use of best practices.

Although workshops and outside consultants certainly have their place, we know that most learning occurs when staff work with their colleagues in ways that help them examine their professional practice more deeply. In-service programs that don't connect to strategic school improvement priorities are scheduled at the end of exhausting teaching days, are delivered to the faculty as a whole, rely on outsiders who rarely know the school well, and are far less effective in building capacity for improved results than we often care to admit.

When professional learning focuses on the school's strategic priority areas for improvement, when staff are involved in determining how they want to learn, and then given time to process and make sense of what they're learning in community with others, then the goals of a school's improvement plans become reality. As staff become collectively skilled and share a common knowledge base, they grow in their capacity to move swiftly and decidedly into new arenas of learning and growing. Effective implementation of the methods,

Twelve Qualities of Powerful Professional Learning

Powerful professional learning has the following twelve qualities.

1. Arises from and returns benefits to classrooms

2. Focuses on real data from student work and teaching

3. Focuses on what really helps students learn

4. Thrives on buy-in

5. Leads directly to application in classrooms

6. Is part of a process of continuous improvement

7. Honors teachers' professionalism, expertise, experiences, and skills

8. Is content-rich

9. Is collaborative

10. Establishes a culture of quality

11. Fosters reflection and slows the hectic pace of schools

12. Gives heft to professional learning communities

Source: Adapted from Easton, 2008b.

tools, and school improvement plans described in this book relies, to a great extent, on the professional learning plans that support them. Additionally, the process schools use to implement professional learning is every bit as important as the plans themselves.

Putting Staff in the Driver's Seat

When teachers are given the opportunity to select the ways they want to learn, they feel more ownership over and commitment to the learning process. Putting them in the driver's seat enables them to control to a certain extent the inevitable vulnerability that arises when we stretch into our discomfort zone. The most effective professional learning is job-embedded (Learning Forward, 2011); for example, learning happens in the context of professional practice.

There are a number of different job-embedded designs to choose from for professional development. We highlight eight that are particularly powerful: (1) action research, (2) curriculum development, (3) student work analysis, (4) immersion, (5) model lessons observation, (6) student shadowing, (7), lead or master teacher shadowing, and (8) study groups.

1. **Action research:** This is a form of disciplined inquiry. One individual or a group can conduct it, but the learning is more far-reaching when a group engages in a question together. An action-research process with a focus on improving student learning often follows these steps.

   a. The individual or team raises a question about how to improve an instructional practice. The team collects data to verify the problem that generated the question.

   b. The team reviews educational literature and conducts research for best practices or visits model classrooms or programs.

   c. The team selects and implements a strategy or approach. Several strategies or approaches might be chosen, with plans to monitor the results of each.

d. The team collects data to assess the effectiveness of the strategies or approaches.

e. The team shares the results with others in the school or district.

Throughout the process, the team learns a great deal about subject content, teaching methodologies, problem-solving and research skills, and one's own power to improve practice. When coupled with a SMART goal-setting process, action research can provide a powerful way to target improvement efforts. (See appendix B, pages 302 and 316, for the reproducible "Template for Organizing Staff Research Findings" and "Collaborative Action Guide.")

2. **Curriculum development:** There is an increasing recognition in the field that teachers should be involved in collaboratively aligning, redesigning, and developing curriculum in more integrated ways (Udelhofen, 2005). With growing pressure to teach more while also helping students achieve higher standards, teachers can no longer afford to either "do what I've always done" or simply adopt textbooks wholesale. The process of working together to understand the standards and designing curriculum that works in one's unique school setting builds capacity to meet and exceed those standards.

3. **Student work analysis:** The practice of bringing teachers together to examine student work is quickly catching on as an important way for teachers to sharpen their practice to improve student learning. Before embarking on this strategy, however, a school should first be sure teachers are already using standards so they have some framework within which to assess student work. Second, teachers need time to do this work together. Third, at least in the beginning, it's helpful to bring in an outside facilitator who has expertise in this process.

Action Research Steps

Step One: Define the Research Project

- Identify improvement area.
- Develop SMART goal.
- Gather support from others for working on the project.

Step Two: Analyze the Situation

- Establish baseline data.
- Identify unique student characteristics.
- Develop hypotheses about causes of performance and potential solutions.

Step Three: Identify Strategies

- Agree on a few instructional strategies to try.
- Agree on how to measure effectiveness of strategies.
- Create a plan for implementing and evaluating new strategies.

Step Four: Try Solutions and Check Results

- Try strategies for several months.
- Assess results against baseline.
- Adjust until goal is achieved (or revise original project).

Step Five: Capture Lessons Learned

- Document results in graphs and narrative.

Continued➔

4. **Immersion:** One of the most critical findings emerging from educational research is the fact that a teacher's subject-matter expertise has an enormous impact on students' achievement (Danielson, 2007). A teacher's competence can make as much as a three grade-level difference in student progress. Additionally, new knowledge, particularly in the fields of mathematics and science, is emerging daily. Unfortunately, most teacher certification and recertification programs still do not require teachers to demonstrate up-to-date mastery of the subject areas they teach. As states and districts seek to understand and implement the Common Core State Standards, teachers need to actively seek out immersion opportunities—such as subject-related jobs, internships, and specialized training—to gain firsthand experience in their subject areas.

5. **Model lessons observation:** In Japan, teachers collaboratively develop model lessons with their colleagues, which they then demonstrate live with their students while other teachers (from their own school, from neighboring schools, or from other districts) observe (Lewis & Tsuchida, 1998). After the lesson, the teachers gather to share notes, dialogue about what they observed, and discuss applications to their own practice. Although very time-intensive, planning, conducting, and evaluating instruction promise rich learning for teachers. The observers become aware of new approaches to teaching and learning and assess these against what might work with their own students. The model teachers sharpen their own instructional practice as they carefully think through the logic and value of their lessons.

6. **Student shadowing:** Although time-intensive, the process of following a student and systematically recording his or her instructional experiences provides a rich base of understanding about the link between pedagogical practices in the classroom

and student performance. This approach requires a deep sense of trust between the observer and his or her colleagues and between the observer and the student. The purpose is not to play "Gotcha" but to use the experience as an opportunity for further dialogue, reflection, and school improvement.

7. **Lead or master teacher shadowing:** Another professional development approach is to allow teachers to shadow each other throughout the day. This is common practice with student teachers but not so common with licensed teachers. When a teacher has a wealth of skills, knowledge, and expertise, there is tremendous value in teaming him or her with another teacher for a day or more, with time for collaborative reflection and dialogue. The observing teacher need not be new to the profession; the process of watching and reflecting with those who exhibit masterful skills can be a powerful learning practice for anyone interested in continuous improvement of his or her professional practice.

8. **Study groups:** Study groups provide a venue for teachers or administrators to come together to learn more about a particular topic such as discipline, brain-based learning, balanced literacy, accelerated curriculum, and so on. The groups usually meet at least every other week to review the literature, visit model programs, and discuss the potential of the practices or program for their school or classrooms.

Step Four: Developing Action Plans

This step begins the ongoing cycle of PDSA (see page 4)— plan—within the broader cycle implicit in the SMART school improvement process. Armed with a multitude of methods for learning and specific strategies for content, you are ready to put action to the plans. In this step, all the research comes together with teacher intention and shared commitment to learn.

There are two parts to this step. First, it is important that teachers have selection in both the content and the process

- Share what was learned about making improvements in this system.
- Share what was learned about student learning.
- Develop ways to maintain the gain.
- Identify possibilities for next research focus.
- Celebrate!

Criteria for Evaluating Staff Development

- Do teachers change the way they work with students as a direct result of the professional development?
- Do students behave differently as a result of changes teachers make?
- Is there improvement in student achievement per anecdotal evidence, student work, test scores, and graduation rates?

Source: Adapted from Easton, 2008a.

of their professional learning. Additionally, along with a healthy respect for the individual learner is the explicit understanding that individuals exist within a community of learners. That means that there is an expectation that one teacher's learning will inform the learning of others. Every member of the staff is expected to be both a learner and a teacher, as the professional development planning matrix in figure 9.11 shows. Once the team gathers data, it is able to match people with content and learners with teachers, allowing for a highly customized schoolwide development plan.

Best practice focus:	
What do you want to know about this practice?	How do you want to learn about this practice?
What are you willing to share?	How do you want to share with others?

Source: Adapted from Abplanalp, 2007.

Figure 9.11: Professional development planning matrix.

Secondly, the whole staff or a representative group schedules the professional development. This group must take on the logistics that often present challenges to busy educators. It's always helpful to incorporate useful technology solutions when planning. Cloud-based tools such as document sharing and calendars can facilitate the process and punctuate the schoolwide approach. (Visit **go.solution-tree.com/school improvement** for examples.)

Figure 9.12 is an example of one school's plan.

SMART goal: Each year for the next three years, we will increase the proportion of students in each grade who score in the high category on the school writing sample and decrease the proportion who score in the low category.

Best practices and strategies associated with this goal:

- Plenty of opportunities for students to express themselves in writing
- Frequent and varied feedback to students on their writing
- Vocabulary lists of key words at each grade level; monitor use of vocabulary words in all writing tasks.

Action Steps (List each step on a separate line.)	Timeline (List month and year to start this step.)	Persons Responsible	Action Step Completed (List month and year this step was actually completed.)	Professional Development Method
All teachers attend the writer's workshop to learn effective instructional strategies for writing.	October to November 2013 One-third of staff to complete this year	Individual teachers and principal	October to November 2013 One-third of staff to complete this year	Workshop learning
Grade-level teams meet to create keyword vocabulary lists.	September 2013 Week two	Grade-level teams	September 2013 Week three	Curriculum development
Share vocabulary lists with other staff members. Align, reinforce, and reduce duplication.	September 2013 Week three	All teachers and principal	September 2013 Week four	Curriculum development
Create a checklist to monitor the number of writing opportunities students are getting and the number and types of feedback strategies teachers are using.	September 2013 Week four	Grade-level teams	October 2013 Week one	Curriculum development
Share results and chart schoolwide data on the number of writing opportunities and the number and types of feedback.	October 2013 Week two	All teachers and principals	October 2013 Week three	Curriculum development
Study best practice for writing.	November 2013 Week one	School staff	November 2013 Week two	Study groups
Implement new instructional strategies and monitor results.	November 2013 Week three	Grade-level teams	Monitor every six weeks.	Lesson study

Figure 9.12: SMART plan for professional development.

Step Five: Analyzing and Refocusing

Notice how the goal and the strategies provide the content of the plan in order to analyze and refocus—the days of "flavor of the day" professional learning are over. See also the reproducible "Template for Planning Professional Development" (page 303), "Sample School Improvement Annual Planning and Reporting Document" (pages 288–289), and the "SMART School Improvement Process Planning Guide" (page 290).

Core Question Four: What Are We Learning?

To answer this question, teaching teams and the school community as a whole use collaborative processes and data tools to periodically monitor the results of their implementation strategies, sharing what they're learning along the way and adjusting their approaches as needed. Implementation of professional learning plans provides the answer to this fourth core question.

Between steps four and five of the SMART school improvement process, teams implement professional learning plans with applications of the new learning along the way. This is the *do* and *study* part of the PDSA wheel. Teachers are learning new practices, and they are learning about their learning. The use of study teams and lesson studies takes place within the context of monitoring their students' progress on the goal targets, thus creating a direct link between professional learning and student results. Figure 9.13 shows that link.

The professional learning standards provide the link between teachers as learners and students as learners. In figure 9.13, the logic can move either clockwise beginning with box one or counter-clockwise beginning with box four. The following list provides descriptions of what occurs at each phase of the cycle.

1. When professional learning is standards-based, it has greater potential to change what educators know, are able to do, and believe.

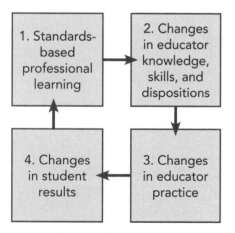

Figure 9.13: The relationship between professional learning and student results.

2. When educators' knowledge, skills, and dispositions change, they have a broader repertoire of effective strategies to use to adapt their practices to meet performance expectations and student learning needs.

3. When educator practice improves, students have a greater likelihood of achieving results.

4. When student results improve, the cycle repeats for continuous improvement.

This cycle works two ways. If educators are not achieving the results they want, they determine what changes in practice are needed and then what knowledge, skills, and dispositions are needed to make the desired changes. They then consider how to apply the standards so that they can engage in the learning needed to strengthen their practice. (Learning Forward, 2011, p. 16)

As your school begins to implement its plans, you can use collaborative inquiry to make sure you capture lessons you've learned along the way. Collaborative inquiry is the process of looking at your data, asking penetrating questions of one another, and deciding what you are learning about your students, the instructional strategies and approaches you are using, and your professional practice. Teams operationalize the data-logic chain (page 83) using collaborative inquiry.

Collaborative inquiry guides people in asking good (logical) questions, letting data provide the answers, and having data lead them to the next set of logical questions. This way, teams have a thorough understanding of the current situation before solutions are put in place. A culture of collaborative inquiry requires the school to observe certain fundamentals to maintain an environment of dignity, trust, and respect. People will be much more inclined to be open and honest about results when they feel assured, through words and deeds, that a continuous learning environment exists.

Tips for Conducting Effective Collaborative Inquiry

- Use the advocacy and inquiry method (see chapter 3, pages 61–62, chapter 5, page 114) in staff discussions to help uncover people's understanding and interpretation of the outcomes from your plan.

- Gather both perceptual and numerical data to assess performance as you implement your plan. Measure before-and-after results, as well as ongoing progress.

- Many of the snapshot tools from chapter 7 can help. If you have data that might help you explore cause-and-effect relationships, use a scatterplot (page 184) to correlate results with an intervention or activity. Scatterplots are a particularly useful tool for assessing the impact of improvements.

- You can use moving picture tools to monitor ongoing progress and to assess whether the plan is taking effect over time.

Standards in Practice

This method provides a way to analyze and improve instructional quality. Small teams of teachers, guidance counselors, and parents get together bimonthly to examine assignments, student work, and standards.

Time: 90–120 minutes

Directions:

1. A volunteer teacher brings in student work along with the assignment.

2. Team members do the assignment themselves in order to experience the task given to the students.

3. Team members identify the state, local, or national standards that align with the assignment.

4. Without looking at the student work, the team constructs a scoring guide (rubric) for this specific assignment. Scores go from 4 (highest proficiency) down to 1 (minimal proficiency). The rubric includes detailed descriptions of what successful work looks like.

5. The team uses the scoring guide to score the student work.

6. The team summarizes the insights it gained during the session and creates a plan of action.

Source: Mitchell, 1999.

Learning is a key driver of change. Learning in a community is what transforms organizations. This question "What are we learning?" is what makes a team or a school more than just a collaborative group. It is what transforms the organization into a professional learning community (DuFour & Eaker, 1998). Essentially, this entire handbook is about providing the tools, methods, processes, and resources needed to answer this question.

Core Question Five: Where Should We Focus Next?

Teams ask this question at the completion of each learning cycle. When an approach or strategy is found to work well, it is incorporated into the ongoing functioning of the school so that all students, teachers, and families can benefit. Then new priorities and goals are established based on new data gathered from results.

As you implement your plans (core question three) and learn from the results (core question four), you will generate improvements that begin to shift your priorities. Once you've reduced or eliminated a problem or issue, you need to move on to the next priority or goal. To decide when to move on and where, continue to review school trends, compare your school to exemplary schools, and assess your results and processes against your ongoing results and theirs.

Re-establishing goals and strategies based on results involves creating new SMART goals, new professional learning plans, and new implementation strategies. Here again, use Pareto thinking to refocus on the new vital few. Use tree diagrams (see chapter 5, page 134, and appendix A, pages 284–287) to help in planning new goals; invite friendly observers back to help identify new opportunities for growth and improvement. Throughout this process, you can build confidence and support for schoolwide improvement efforts by inviting stakeholders (parents, community members, and others) from outside the school walls to be part of the ongoing learning process.

To emphasize the need to regularly review and revise your school's or district's goals, you may want to develop a calendar for review that occurs in conjunction with annual planning and budgeting processes. This can ensure that the school directs resources toward true priorities and that communication occurs throughout the entire school or district.

Schoolwide improvement involves teachers, staff, students, parents, administrators, and community members who participate in a variety of ways: providing input, participating on and leading teams, and making decisions collaboratively. Using community forums to gather and share information, team structures to organize and implement improvement work, and a skilled facilitator to help guide the process will contribute to expanding the school's capacity for improving results.

To make sure you reach all the stakeholders, use a variety of forums and communication methods for discussing your plans and results: the school website, emails, blogs, school newsletters, meetings with faculty, grade-level teams, department teams, parent-teacher conferences, curriculum meetings, and performance coaching reviews, as well as parent-teacher association, parent-teacher organization, and community meetings.

Final Check: A Schoolwide Improvement Process

It is our hope that the days of individuals sitting down to create schoolwide improvement plans without the full engagement of those who must implement them are over. Guided by five simple but significant questions that are answered collaboratively by all members of the school staff, school improvement planning becomes a focused and dynamic process that results in better learning outcomes for both staff and students.

Use the following checklist to ensure that your schoolwide improvement process is engaging and successful.

My team collaboratively:

- ☐ Involves a wide range of stakeholders
- ☐ Uses a mix of whole-group meetings and between-meeting work by subteams or individuals

☐ Builds each question on the answers that came before

☐ Uses the turbo meeting format described in chapter 4 to energize collaboration time and make it highly efficient

☐ Uses planning tools such as the affinity process (chapter 5, page 113) to gather ideas from everyone before deciding on a single solution or a specific strategy or solution

☐ Uses the SMART goal tree to organize the school's goal-setting and progress monitoring efforts

☐ Makes professional learning a daily endeavor by incorporating it into goal-directed practices and professional conversations about students and their learning

Tools for SMART Schools

This appendix includes examples, guides, templates, and tools to support the information in *The Handbook for SMART School Teams (Second Edition)*. The various items are referenced in the chapters of the book and are organized according to the chapter sequence.

Table A.1: Sample Size Chart 280

Table A.2: Gap Analysis Survey 281

High School Climate Survey 282

Table A.3: Runs Table 283

Figure A.1: SMART goal tree diagram for climate...........284

Figure A.2: SMART goal tree diagram for elementary reading. 285

Figure A.3: SMART goal tree diagram for middle school analytical thinking. 286

Figure A.4: SMART goal tree diagram for high school writing. 287

Table A.4: Sample School Improvement Annual Planning and Reporting Document.................................288

SMART School Improvement Process Planning Guide 290

Table A.1: Sample Size Chart

N	S	N	S	N	S	N	S	N	S
10	10	100	80	280	162	800	260	2,800	338
15	14	110	86	290	165	850	265	3,000	341
20	19	120	92	300	169	900	269	3,500	246
25	24	130	97	320	175	950	274	4,000	351
30	28	140	103	340	181	1,000	278	4,500	351
35	32	150	108	360	186	1,100	285	5,000	357
40	36	160	113	380	181	1,200	291	6,000	361
45	40	180	118	400	196	1,300	297	7,000	364
50	44	190	123	420	201	1,400	302	8,000	367
55	48	200	127	440	205	1,500	306	9,000	368
60	52	210	132	460	210	1,600	310	10,000	373
65	56	220	136	480	214	1,700	313	15,000	375
70	59	230	140	500	217	1,800	317	20,000	377
75	63	240	144	550	225	1,900	320	30,000	379
80	66	250	148	600	234	2,000	322	40,000	380
85	70	260	152	650	242	2,200	327	50,000	381
90	73	270	155	700	248	2,400	331	75,000	382
95	76	270	159	750	256	2,600	335	100,000	384

Note: "N" is population size

   "S" is sample size.

   The sample sizes in this chart are based on a 95 percent confidence level.

Source: Krejcie & Morgan, 1970.

Table A.2: Gap Analysis Survey

Importance	Section I. School Climate	Current Situation
How important is this? 5 = Extremely important 4 = Very important 3 = Somewhat important 2 = Not very important 1 = Not important NA = Not applicable DK = Don't Know	Rate the *importance* and your *agreement* with the following items.	What's your perception? 5 = Strongly agree 4 = Agree 3 = Neutral 2 = Disagree 1 = Strongly disagree NA = Not applicable DK = Don't know
5 4 3 2 1 NA DK	Expectations for student behavior are clear.	5 4 3 2 1 NA DK
5 4 3 2 1 NA DK	There are logical consequences for misbehavior.	5 4 3 2 1 NA DK
5 4 3 2 1 NA DK	Students treat each other with respect.	5 4 3 2 1 NA DK

High School Climate Survey

Grade: (circle one)   9   10   11   12

Gender: (circle one)   Male   Female

Directions: Please complete the following survey items *honestly*—your viewpoints are important and very helpful. This survey is entirely anonymous. Thank you!

1 = Never   3 = Frequently   5 = I don't know.

2 = Sometimes   4 = Always

Leadership:

	1	2	3	4	5
1. I see my principal as the leader of my high school.	☐	☐	☐	☐	☐
2. My principal is visible (outside of office, in classrooms, halls, at activities, and so on).	☐	☐	☐	☐	☐
3. I receive prompt and efficient service in the high school office.	☐	☐	☐	☐	☐
4. My principal works to make our school a better school.	☐	☐	☐	☐	☐

Table A.3: Runs Table

Number of Data Points Not on Median	Lower Limit for Number of Runs	Upper Limit for Number of Runs	Number of Data Points Not on Median	Lower Limit for Number of Runs	Upper Limit for Number of Runs
10	3	8	34	12	23
11	3	9	35	13	23
12	3	10	36	13	24
13	4	10	37	13	25
14	4	11	38	14	25
15	4	12	39	14	26
16	5	12	40	15	26
17	5	13	41	16	26
18	6	13	42	16	27
19	6	14	43	17	27
20	6	14	44	17	28
21	7	15	45	17	29
22	7	16	46	17	30
23	8	16	47	18	30
24	8	17	48	18	31
25	9	17	49	19	31
26	9	18	50	19	32
27	9	19	60	24	37
28	10	19	70	28	43
29	10	20	80	33	48
30	11	20	90	37	54
31	11	21	100	42	59
32	11	22	110	46	65
33	11	22	120	51	70

Source: Oriel STAT A MATRIX, The Team Handbook (www.teamhandbook.com). Reprinted with permission.

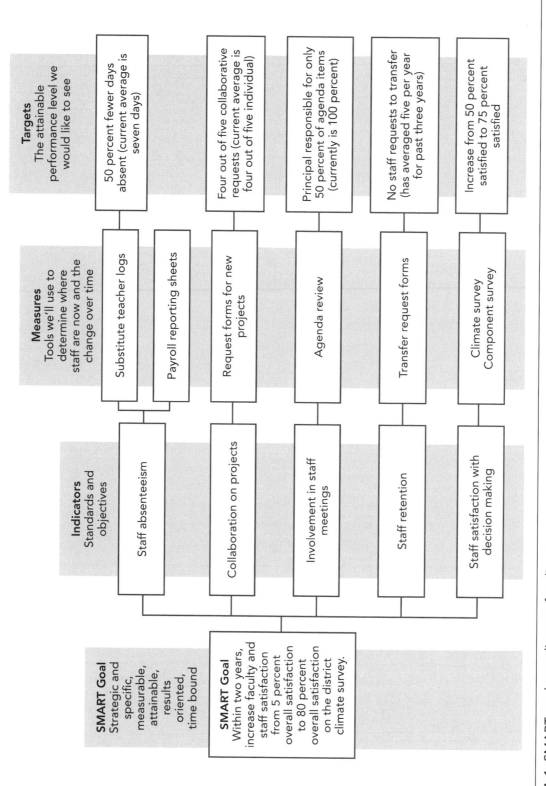

Figure A.1: SMART goal tree diagram for climate.

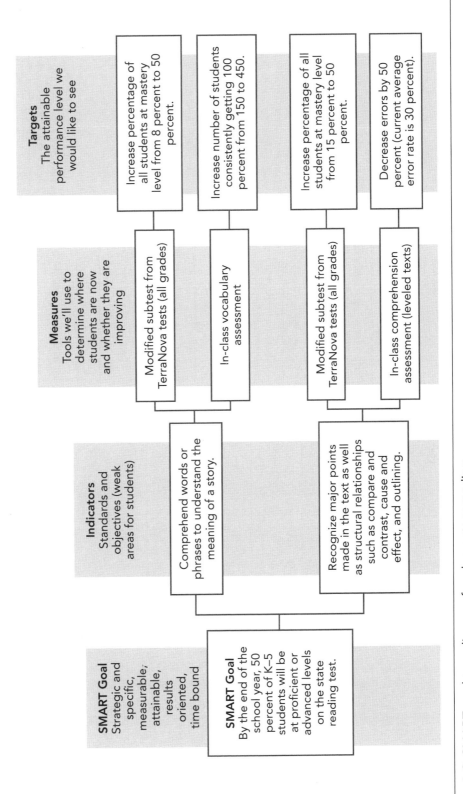

Figure A.2: SMART goal tree diagram for elementary reading.

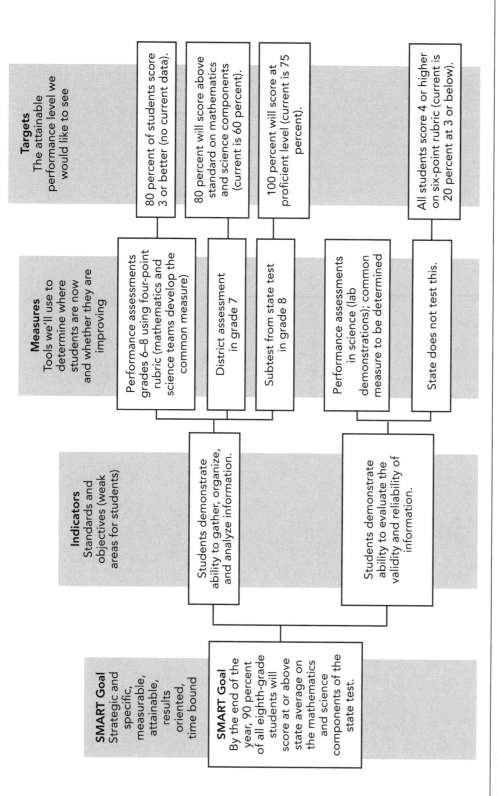

Figure A.3: SMART goal tree diagram for middle school analytical thinking.

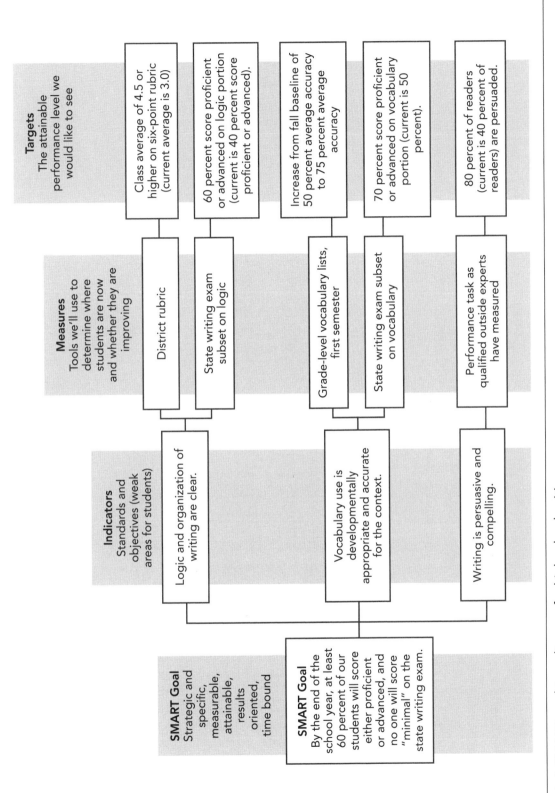

Figure A.4: SMART goal tree diagram for high school writing.

Table A.4: Sample School Improvement Annual Planning and Reporting Document

School: Eagle Ridge Elementary School School year: 2013–2014	Date of plan: August 2013
I. District Strategic Priorities We address three district priorities in this plan. 1. Improving student achievement 2. Offering challenging, diverse, and contemporary curriculum and instruction 3. Ensuring a safe, respectful, and welcoming learning environment	**II. School-Based Achievement Gaps** (Provide evidential data and rationale.) Our school data show achievement gaps in reading and writing. Only 13 percent of our students scored in the high category of the school writing sample while 24 percent scored in the low category over the past two years. Twenty-two percent of our third graders and 32 percent of our fourth graders fell below the proficient category on the state reading tests with specific weaknesses in comprehension. School behavioral referrals have risen by 25 percent over the last two years.
III. Building-Level SMART Goals 1. Each year for the next three years, we will increase the proportion of students in each grade who score in the high category and decrease the proportion who score in the low category on the school writing sample. 2. Increase by 5 percent each year the number of third graders and fourth graders who move into the proficient range on the statewide reading assessments. 3. Reduce by 25 percent per year, over the course of the next three years, the number of behavioral referrals received for disciplinary action.	**IV. Implementation Plan: Use** **SMART goal:** Each year for the next three years, we will increase the proportion of students in each grade who score in the high category and decrease the proportion who score in the low category on the school writing sample. **Best practices and strategies associated with this goal:** • Plenty of opportunities for students to express themselves in writing • Frequent and varied feedback to students on their writing • Vocabulary lists of key words at each grade level—monitor use of vocabulary words in all writing tasks

Continued→

Action Steps (List each step on a separate line.)	Timeline (List month and year to start this step.)	Persons Responsible	Action Step Completed (List month and year.)	Professional Development Method
All teachers attend the writer's workshop to learn effective instructional strategies for writing.	One-third of staff to complete each year	Individual teachers and principal		
Grade-level teams meet to create key word vocabulary lists.	September 2013	Grade-level teams		
Create a checklist to monitor number of student writing opportunities and number and types of feedback strategies teachers are using.	September 2013	Grade-level teams		
Implement new instructional strategies and monitor results.	Third week of September 2013; monitor every six weeks.	Grade-level teams		
Share vocabulary lists with other staff members. Align, reinforce, and reduce duplication.	Third week of September 2013	All teachers and principal		
Share results and chart schoolwide data on number of writing opportunities and number and types of feedback.	Sixth week of school	All teachers and principal		

SMART School Improvement Process Planning Guide

This planning guide describes the steps of the SMART school improvement process, as shown in figure A.5.

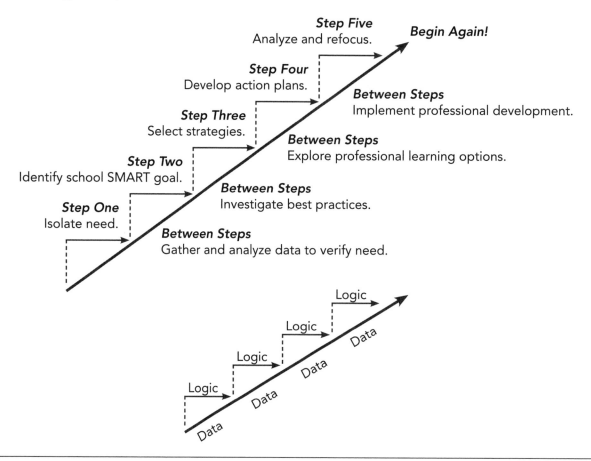

Figure A.5: SMART school improvement process and the data-logic chain.

Step One: Isolate Need

1. Review school mission, vision, values.
2. Establish and review data trust rules.
3. Gather individual data perceptions.
4. Create a data plan.

Purpose:

The purpose of this step is to identify perceptions of student learning needs. It serves as a way of bringing assumptions to the surface, which builds ownership for examining the actual data.

Who to involve:

Whole faculty, either collectively or in smaller learning teams

What to do:

Set the stage by reviewing your school's vision, mission, and values. If we're already a good school, what would it take to be great? If already great, how can we get better? What are our commitments to our students and to each other?

Present focus questions for brainstorming, such as "Where do we think our students struggle academically? Which standards are the weakest across the school? Which learning outcomes are the weakest in each grade or subject? What do we think we'll see when we look at the data?"

When to do it:

Ideally, at the beginning of a new school year

Guidelines for success:

- Use effective meeting skills.
- Work in small groups of five to six within the larger group.
- Use a template or graphic organizer to plan what data will be gathered, by whom and by when.

Between Steps One and Two: Gather and Analyze Data to Verify Need

1. Assign a small group to gather data.
2. Generate data-rich questions.
3. Identify available data and sources.
4. Collect and analyze data.
5. Display data using graphs.
6. Determine school's greatest area of need.

Purpose:

The purpose of this step is to create a data picture of students' academic needs that will help the groups develop SMART goals at the school, grade, or department levels.

Who to involve:

Individuals who have skill in collecting, analyzing, and organizing data (and using data technology if applicable)

What to do:

Gather achievement data in all subject areas or grade levels showing achievement over time. Analyze the data at the standards, objectives, and items levels. Disaggregate the data by subpopulations. Display the data in graphic format (versus lists of numbers). Based on presentation of data by subgroup, calculate the greatest area of need for the school.

When to do it:

Soon after step one so as not to lose momentum

Guidelines for success:

- Determine the vital few questions to answer before going out to collect data. Review the brainstormed lists from the larger group.
- Review multiple measures (state and local). Review multiple years, if possible.
- Use graphs to display data for group analysis and discussion.
- Prepare a presentation for the larger group that will engage members in the data inquiry cycle. Develop an engaging protocol.
- Set guidelines for looking at and using data in your school.
- Use a color-coding system to localize areas of need from key assessment results.

Step Two: Identify School SMART Goal

1. Interpret achievement data.
2. Review grade-level content expectations and standards.
3. Write a school SMART goal.
4. Write supporting grade-level or departmental SMART goals.

Purpose:

The purpose of this step is to provide specific, measurable direction to the actions, programs, resources, and practices of school personnel.

Who to involve:

School faculty works together to interpret student achievement data, establish results goals for the greatest area of need, and identify two to three standards, key measures, and targets. Grade levels or departments establish supporting SMART goals with indicators, measures, and targets by grade or department.

What to do:

Write a schoolwide results goal and complete the tree diagram for the school, with schoolwide indicators, measures, and targets. At the grade or department level, review school indicators and operationalize with grade- or department-level language. Then complete tree diagrams for each grade level or department to support the school tree.

When to do it:

Annually, based on the school's planning cycle

Guidelines for success:

- Keep number of school goals to a maximum of three with at least one in an area focused on student achievement.
- Goals are more robust when schools use both state and local measures.
- Use the tree diagram to make goals SMARTer.

Between Steps Two and Three: Investigate Best Practices

1. Analyze high-performing classrooms.
2. Assess own practices.
3. Study literature and published educational research.

Purpose:

The purpose of this step is to collect and organize information from a variety of sources about promising practices that can improve performance in the school SMART goal.

Who to involve:

Whole faculty, either collectively or in smaller learning teams, including special education and program specialists

What to do:

Focus the investigation on schoolwide strategies aligned with the school SMART goals. Consider curriculum, instruction, and assessment practices as well as climate and culture strategies aimed at improving student academic achievement. Observe master classrooms, read the literature, interview curriculum specialists, attend professional development workshops, review university-published educational research, and so on. Organize information for the larger group to review and digest.

When to do it:

Begin as soon as teams identify the greatest area of need.

Guidelines for success:

- Recognize the expertise already within the school and district.
- Develop a plan for gathering information from a variety of sources.
- Keep the end in mind—how will we organize the information so teachers can understand it?
- Organize information into themes but also provide enough specific details and examples that the practices can be envisioned by others.
- Share primary sources when possible. Use the Internet, Education Resources Information Center, professional associations, and so on.
- Consider the power of visual media to communicate ideas clearly—video, graphs, and so on.

Step Three: Select Strategies

1. Review the results of work done between steps two and three.

2. Assess current practices.

3. Decide which practices to learn first.

Purpose:

The purpose of this step is to raise awareness about promising practices in the goal area that the school may not currently employ, as well as those that the school is already implementing.

Who to involve:

Whole faculty, either collectively or in smaller learning teams

What to do:

Teachers review the new information from the subteam, review their own practices, and determine new practices they would like to learn in order to have a greater impact on the goal area.

When to do it:

Preferably summer, before school starts, or at the beginning of the year or soon after the team writes the SMART goal

Guidelines for success:

- Use a decision matrix (page 119) as a self-assessment to evaluate the extent to which teachers already know about and use these practices.

- Consider using friendly observers to gather information on what teachers are already implementing in classrooms.

- Use a decision matrix to engage staff in examining current best practices in relation to newly investigated strategies.

- Try a few of these methods at a time to see their effect.

Between Steps Three and Four: Explore Professional Development Options

1. Consider different needs of beginning versus experienced teachers.

2. Map out current professional development methods and schedules.

3. Analyze alignment to goal and newly selected strategies.

4. Explore additional or different goals.

Purpose:

The purpose of this step is to discover all the ways teachers could learn more about selected practices.

Who to involve:

Teams of classroom teachers, instructional specialists, and special education teachers

What to do:

Evaluate where teachers are in their understanding and skill in implementing the team-identified promising practices in the goal area.

When to do it:

Begin as soon as teams select new strategies.

Guidelines for success:

- Keep in mind that novice teachers have different learning needs than experienced teachers. Allowing teachers to select the method of learning that's right for them will ensure that they are in the driver's seat and will own the change.

- Use resources from experts within the school or district, especially proven masterful teachers.

- Peer coaching is one of the most powerful ways for teachers to learn. Structure plans so that master-level teachers are able to demonstrate what they do and reflect with the team about how they do it. Lesson study is another key feature of peer coaching.

- See also Learning Forward (www.learningforward.org) for standards of professional learning.

Step Four: Develop Action Plans

1. Assess own practices.

2. Select ways to learn strategies.

3. Develop a schoolwide plan for implementing and studying new practices.

Purpose:

The purpose of this step is to allow teachers to select how they would like to learn (and share), apply, and evaluate selected strategies in the classroom.

Who to involve:

Whole faculty, either collectively or in smaller learning teams, including special education and program specialists

What to do:

Provide a variety of ways teachers can learn about the agreed-upon practices. Allow teachers to self select how they want to learn about the selected professional development and how they will share their learning with their colleagues.

When to do it:

Immediately following the previous research step (can be part of the previous step if there is time)

Guidelines for success:

- Use decision matrices to select choices.
- Track professional learning team time that is occurring in the school.
- Refer to chapter 2 of *The Power of SMART Goals* (O'Neill & Conzemius, 2006) for ways to incorporate SMART goals into professional development planning.
- Build in time during faculty meetings for teachers to share their plans.
- Keep implementation strategies manageable—don't try to do everything at once.

Between Steps Four and Five: Implement Professional Development

1. Pilot new strategies on a small scale.
2. Establish support.
3. Monitor fidelity of implementation.
4. Gather data using common formative assessments.

Purpose:

The purpose of this step is to determine whether teams are achieving the SMART goal targets—whether instructional strategies are helping all students perform at higher levels.

Who to involve:

Whole faculty, either collectively or in smaller learning teams, including special education and program specialists

What to do:

Teams of teachers need dedicated time throughout the year to learn, apply, assess, and analyze their professional practice. Assign subteams to be responsible for ensuring that teachers get the support they need to learn and practice new strategies. Using the measures and targets from the SMART goal tree, teams of teachers analyze instructional and assessment results, share what is working well, and plan new strategies throughout the year.

When to do it:

Throughout the year with quarterly progress checks at a minimum

Guidelines for success:

- Keep implementation strategies manageable—don't try to do everything at once.
- Build in time during faculty meetings to allow professional learning teams to share strategies that are producing good results.
- Keep interim assessments targeted and meaningful but as simple as possible.
- The more frequent and rapid the feedback (such as data from assessments), the easier it will be to make adjustments and see ongoing improvements.

- Share progress during the year with the students and families.
- Create a standard protocol for supporting implementation via walkthroughs, feedback, and coaching.

Step Five: Analyze and Refocus

1. Analyze formative and summative results.
2. Adjust practices.
3. Decide whether to change goal focus.
4. Celebrate success!

Purpose:

The purpose of this step is to determine whether instructional or assessment strategies had the intended effect, how to sustain improvement, and whether to focus on a new greatest area of need or ontinue to focus on the current greatest area of need.

Who to involve:

Whole faculty, either collectively or in smaller learning teams plus broader community

What to do:

Convene a forum to review summative test results, compare to previous years, plan how the school will sustain improvement gains, and determine whether to continue with the current SMART goal or pick a new focus area.

When to do it:

At the end of the year or as soon as new summative assessment results are available

Guidelines for success:

- Assess progress on targets using the SMART goal tree.
- Disaggregate the data.
- Look for patterns of performance over time.
- Present data visually.
- Include the broader community in reviewing and celebrating success.

APPENDIX B

Reproducibles

Random Number Table...................................*300*

Template for Organizing Staff Research Findings...........*302*

Template for Planning Professional Development *303*

The SMART Schools Self-Assessment......................*304*

Team Charter *307*

Meeting Agenda Template *308*

Meeting Evaluation Form.................................*309*

Meeting Record...*310*

Meeting Skills Self-Assessment *311*

Decision Matrix *313*

Responsibility Matrix....................................*314*

Worksheet for Computing Control Limits *315*

Collaborative Action Research Guide......................*316*

Random Number Table

A random number table is a survey tool for helping select a sample from a population so that each member of the population has an equal opportunity to be selected. By using a random number table, you can have greater confidence that the results you receive from the sample are similar to those you would get if you sampled the entire population.

Directions

1. Decide how many you need in your sample (you may want to consult a statistician to determine the appropriate sample size based on your population and how confident you want or need to be that the sample represents the population as a whole).

2. Decide where you will draw the sample from (for example, staff directory, enrollment roster) and assign numbers to the entire set beginning with the first name, assigning it a "1."

3. Then select a cell from any column and row in the random number table. Use the number in that cell to begin selecting your sample. Select each subsequent number either by moving down the column or across the row or diagonally, but do not skip cells (unless the number in a cell doesn't apply to your set of names, in which case, skip the cell and move to the next cell). If there are 1–99 members in the population, use the last two numbers in the cells to select members; if there are 100–999 members, use the last three numbers; if 1,000–9,999, use all the numbers in the cell.

Example

We want to select ten families out of a total population of nine hundred families in our school. We use the school directory, which is alphabetized by last name, from which to draw our sample. We make sure that families that have multiple children are listed only once (to reduce the opportunity for over-sampling of one family). Each family is then numbered in the directory, 1–900. Because we are sampling from a population of nine hundred, we will use the last three digits in the cells.

We select row four, column four as a place to start—the number in that cell is 0.2638. Using just the last three numbers, this means the first family selected for our sample will be family number 638. We then move down a cell in the same column: 0.8405—so we select family number 405 as the second family in our sample. We proceed, working our way down the column and up to the next column, until we have completed our sample of ten families. Our final sample includes families with these numbers (we skip number 994 because that number is higher than our set of names): 638, 405, 467, 423, 183, 389, 627, 246, 444, and 516.

	1	2	3	4	5	6	7	8
1	0.7676	0.3167	0.8677	0.2342	0.9632	0.5291	0.5781	0.1489
2	0.7576	0.193	0.4166	0.7144	0.0719	0.8109	0.6874	0.5396
3	0.7635	0.9429	0.7015	0.7051	0.0164	0.1228	0.3966	0.4541
4	0.5705	0.8117	0.6033	0.2638	0.1578	0.5438	0.6836	0.5774
5	0.8637	0.7397	0.6554	0.8405	0.9351	0.0394	0.9147	0.5302
6	0.1985	0.5586	0.9588	0.8467	0.60	0.4007	0.8252	0.7829
7	0.2833	0.5231	0.1909	0.9423	0.2408	0.6079	0.7498	0.8159
8	0.5994	0.5298	0.13	0.183	0.2456	0.7644	0.8986	0.6278
9	0.9683	0.334	0.1977	0.3994	0.0891	0.9699	0.4013	0.1678
10	0.5599	0.5284	0.0624	0.3389	0.8004	0.9871	0.3657	0.3169
11	0.9567	0.1537	0.8563	0.3627	0.0158	0.7101	0.9796	0.1562
12	0.4396	0.2521	0.347	0.4246	0.7202	0.17	0.9671	0.3592
13	0.6546	0.2547	0.8725	0.4444	0.8648	0.793	0.0735	0.4079
14	0.5019	0.7787	0.3192	0.8516	0.5052	0.4754	0.6017	0.7394
15	0.1437	0.8561	0.3068	0.7349	0.0269	0.585	0.4837	0.4863
16	0.0118	0.6226	0.1932	0.3416	0.0957	0.6994	0.3828	0.8618
17	0.0086	0.209	0.3931	0.7363	0.2027	0.106	0.8662	0.9639
18	0.4973	0.7744	0.8074	0.0329	0.8665	0.6009	0.8186	0.0413
19	0.0401	0.6316	0.5995	0.5628	0.1518	0.0423	0.6101	0.7079
20	0.174	0.0698	0.0293	0.6006	0.9853	0.3564	0.6712	0.7989
21	0.7165	0.0924	0.0814	0.8343	0.9135	0.2701	0.4702	0.1825
22	0.377	0.3578	0.20	0.8596	0.2007	0.7491	0.5916	0.0735
23	0.1243	0.2708	0.758	0.3208	0.6268	0.9726	0.9281	0.75
24	0.1483	0.6169	0.2639	0.6042	0.3687	0.1393	0.1018	0.4156
25	0.4745	0.9524	0.0583	0.2908	0.1338	0.5646	0.4359	0.6868
26	0.3884	0.7946	0.9486	0.9847	0.2294	0.7557	0.7186	0.6235
27	0.9892	0.1696	0.9944	0.1819	0.0374	0.6021	0.3918	0.1692
28	0.1135	0.2734	0.7844	0.0304	0.4494	0.5873	0.2608	0.8112

Template for Organizing Staff Research Findings

Staff research occurs throughout the school improvement process. Use the template to organize and record the research and findings at each step, including sources and research findings. Identify the resource implications of the finding and ways the finding will be applied.

Check one box, and name the subject of this research (for example, Subgroup, Special Education or Skill, or Oral Presentations). ☐ Standard _____ ☐ Skill _____ ☐ Subgroup _____		Check one box. ☐ Curriculum and lesson planning ☐ Instructional design and delivery ☐ Assessments for learning and feedback ☐ Classroom climate and school culture	
Source	**Finding**	**Resources Needed**	**Specific Applications**

Source: QLD Learning, LLC © 2013.

Template for Planning Professional Development

Instructions: Use the template to lay out the appropriate professional learning in support of the best practices and strategies that address your SMART goal. Define the steps, timing, and those responsible; monitor completion of each step and record the method of professional learning involved.

SMART goal:

Best practices and strategies associated with this goal:

Action Steps (List each step on a separate line.)	Timeline (List month and year to start this step.)	Persons Responsible	Action Step Completed (List month and year.)	Professional Development Method

The SMART Schools Self-Assessment

Instructions: Complete the following survey, engaging several others from your school if possible. After each of the nine statements, circle the number that best indicates how you believe your school currently functions.

Focus

1. There is a shared vision for continuous school improvement that is focused on student learning.

1   2   3   4   5   6   7   8   9   10

We don't have a shared vision.

There is a formal vision statement but it is seldom referenced.

The school's vision for student success regularly guides our staff discussions and decision making.

2. School goals focus on improved student achievement.

1   2   3   4   5   6   7   8   9   10

We do not have written goals.

Our goals focus on process and program enhancement.

Our goals address student learning needs with regard to standards and learner expectations.

3. School goals are SMART.

1   2   3   4   5   6   7   8   9   10

Our goals are hard to measure.

Our goals are measurable but not very specific.

Our goals focus on student results and target needs based on a careful analysis of data on student performance.

Reflection

4. Staff, faculty, and administration reflect and dialogue together about professional matters that impact student learning.

1   2   3   4   5   6   7   8   9   10

We never meet to discuss substantive issues related to student learning.

We occasionally discuss student-centered issues focused on learning.

Our discussions focus on the quality of teaching and learning in our school.

5. Staff know how effectively current practices work and continuously seek to find new methods to improve student performance.

1   2   3   4   5   6   7   8   9   10

Staff do not talk about instruction, results, or improvements.

Staff occasionally look at how they're doing and make adjustments or improvements.

Staff regularly reflect on and assess the impact of their instruction and make revisions based on the results.

Collaboration

6. There is a high degree of trust among individuals.

1   2   3   4   5   6   7   8   9   10

Low trust and conflict characterize our school's working relationships.

We generally trust each other but are not always as open as we could be.

Trust and openness characterize the way we work.

7. The structures of the day and year provide flexibility and time for people to work together.

1   2   3   4   5   6   7   8   9   10

There are no specific arrangements made to create time for the school improvement team's interaction.

Time is arranged, but it is either inadequate or inconsistent.

The school day and year have been structured so as to make collaborative decision making and team learning the way we do business.

The Handbook for SMART School Teams © 2002, 2014 Solution Tree Press • solution-tree.com

Visit **go.solution-tree.com/schoolimprovement** to download this page.

Leadership Capacity

8. There is full participation in leadership. Staff, faculty, administrators, community members, parents, and students all have important and defined leadership roles.

1	2	3	4	5	6	7	8	9	10

There is one leader in the school.

Leadership is an assignment based on a specific task, committee appointment, or position.

All members of the school community take leadership action for improving school results.

9. Individuals have well-developed leadership skills and consistently use them in collaborative ways.

1	2	3	4	5	6	7	8	9	10

The development of leadership skills is limited to a few positional leaders.

Broad-based, skillful leadership is valued but not systemically developed.

Leadership skills are developed, valued, and consistently applied across a wide variety of stakeholders.

Total

Add the circled numbers, and record the total: _____

Strength areas to celebrate (ways that come close to what you want them to be):

Priority areas (biggest gaps between the way it is and the way you want it to be):

One step you can take that will address each priority area this year (preferably things over which you have direct control or influence):

Team Charter

Work as a team to define the scope of your team's task or project. If there is a decision maker who will need to be involved for critical decisions, bring that person into the conversation.

1. List all the members of the team.

2. Then define the purpose of the team's work; this is the team's mission. What is the team tasked to do? For whom? Why? By when?

3. Next, brainstorm the major tasks that will need to be accomplished in order to achieve the team's mission.

4. Finally, for each task, identify a start and end date. Consider using a Gantt chart (page 139) to complete this part of the team charter.

Team Members (List all members.)
Mission (Write a brief statement of purpose that includes specific end results or outcomes.)

Tasks to Complete (Sequentially list activities that the team will use to achieve the end results or outcomes in the mission.)	**Timeline** (List specific phases or timeline that the group will follow to achieve its mission. Ad hoc groups will most likely have a stated date for completion; ongoing groups will have a timeline that targets incremental progress within specified time ranges.)

Meeting Agenda Template

Instructions: Identify who will fulfill the responsibilities of each meeting role, and the purpose of the meeting. Complete the agenda to include all of your items of discussion or business as you see in the opening and closing items in the template. Fill in the middle rows with your own agenda items unique to your team.

Facilitator:

Timekeeper:

Recorder:

Other:

Meeting Purpose:

Estimated Time	Topic	Lead Person	Method	Outcome
Five minutes	Check-in	All	Round robin	We're all present!
Five minutes	Agenda review	Facilitator	Discussion	Agenda will be adjusted as needed.
Five minutes	Next agenda	All	Brainstorm	Brainstorm input for next meeting agenda.
Five minutes	Meeting evaluation		Write + or – on flipchart.	Decide meeting process improvements for next time.

Meeting Evaluation Form

The "Meeting Evaluation Form" provides an opportunity for feedback on the effectiveness of a meeting and insights about how your team can improve future meetings.

Date:

Time:

	Yes	No	Comments
1. Did the meeting start on time?			
2. Did we meet meeting objectives?			
3. Did we follow the agenda?			
4. Did the discussion remain focused?			
5. Were participants adequately prepared?			
6. Was the location appropriate?			
7. Did the meeting end on time?			
8. Have we sent a follow-up report?			
9. Did we adhere to ground rules?			
10. Was everyone involved?			

The strengths of this meeting were:

This meeting could have been improved by:

I could have assisted in making this meeting more effective by:

Meeting Record

Use the "Meeting Record" to summarize key team meeting activities, including decisions, actions, assignments, issues, and topics and ideas for subsequent meetings.

Team name:

Date: **Time:**   **Location:**

Members present:

Yes	No	Name	Facilitator	Timekeeper	Recorder	Other

Date: **Time:**   **Location:**
Date: **Time:**   **Location:**

Agenda for Next Meeting

Check-in:
Check-out:

Topic	Discussion Points	Decisions

Issues and ideas for future meetings:
Assignments:

What	Who	When

Meeting Skills Self-Assessment

Instructions: Each of the following statements represents a valuable meeting skill. Learning to identify, practice, and improve these skills is part of being a team member. Check the appropriate column for each statement indicating how often you practice that behavior. Your team may want to compare answers to find areas that the team as a whole should be working on.

Meeting Skill	I frequently do this.	I need to do more of this.
Goal Setting I help the group stay focused on the results we're working toward. I suggest interim benchmarks along the way.		
Resource Assessing I see the big picture of what will be required to get tasks done, and I share my thoughts with the group.		
Initiating I suggest methods, procedures, and plans as needed. I offer to take the lead on getting tasks done.		
Information Giving I offer facts, research, and background as needed.		
Opinion Sharing I contribute to the group's work by offering my thoughts, feelings, perceptions, and beliefs.		
Clarifying I help clear up confusion about the task by defining terms and offering additional information.		
Harmonizing I try to help group members find agreement in conflicting points of view; I help reduce tension by getting people to explore difficulties.		
Encouraging I am friendly, warm, and responsive; I celebrate successes; I validate others' points of view; I use nondestructive humor.		
Compromising I modify my thinking or position as appropriate by exploring other members' ideas rather than debating or defending each idea that comes up.		
Gatekeeping I create opportunities for others to participate in the discussion.		

page 1 of 2

Meeting Skill	I frequently do this.	I need to do more of this.
Regulating I point out when ground rules are being broken; I ask whether the group is satisfied with its progress.		
Summarizing I synthesize what's been said and then check the accuracy of my summary with the group; when I hear the group repeat itself, I help us close discussion and reach a decision.		

Decision Matrix

1. Decide which options you want to focus on. List these in the far left column.

2. Next decide the criteria you will use to evaluate each option. List these across the top.

3. Decide what your scoring system will be.

4. Each individual team member should then score each idea against the criteria, one criteria at a time (work down the column versus across a row). Add up the scores for each option.

5. Add up the scores for each option from all team members.

6. Discuss the vote results before making a final decision.

Options / Criteria						Vote Totals

Responsibility Matrix

1. Define the core processes for the organizational unit. Record these in the far left column.

2. For each core process, identify the Decision Maker, Process Manager, Backup, and Involved Stakeholders.

Name of the Core Process	Decision Maker	Process Manager	Backup	Involved Stakeholders
1.				
2.				
3.				
4.				
5.				
6.				

Worksheet for Computing Control Limits

Instructions: In preparation for creating a control chart, compute the control limits by recording appropriate data points in time order. Calculate the range between a data point and the previous data point recorded. Use the form to calculate the average of the data points and ranges. Plug these values into the formulas below the table for the upper (UCL) and lower (LCL) control limits.

Data and Time	Data Points in Time Order	Range
Sums		
Divided by	# of Data Points	# of Ranges
$\overline{X}$ or $\overline{R}$	Average of Data Points	Average of Ranges

Average of Scores   Average of Ranges

UCL = _____ + (2.66 ×_____) = _____

LCL = _____ − (2.66 × _____) = _____

Collaborative Action Research Guide

The purpose of defining the research project in step one is to focus improvement efforts on a particular area. The outcome of this step is the development of one SMART goal.

What improvement opportunity will you work on? There are a number of ways to identify a specific area. If at all possible, try to select an area where you already have some baseline data.[1] Examples:

- Analyze standardized test results to identify weak areas for students, or areas where all students are not achieving at the expected level.
- Analyze customized districtwide assessment data.
- Use information from your classroom assessments.
- Consider research that you have found that indicates areas of weakness or opportunity.
- Use your intuition to narrow and prioritize where to focus improvement efforts.

Improvement area: Analyze items on the assessments that your students are weakest in to further narrow, prioritize, and focus. For example, persuasive or expressive writing, mathematics problem solving or computation, capitals or punctuation, and so on. State the improvement opportunity as a gap to close, using SMART goal language:

SMART goal: Improve _____ by _____ by _____

Specific, measureable item   Attainable (how much)   Time bound (by when)

Example: "Increase by 10 percent the number of students achieving at 'meets standards' level in persuasive writing by end of February."

Plan for Collaborating With Others

Who will you use as a reality check to make sure you get feedback and advice on the direction and impact of your project? Who else will really care about this project? What will they care about? Who do you need help from in order to do this project? Develop a plan for involving them and communicating about this project.

Who I Plan to Involve	How I Will Involve Them	When I Will Involve Them

---

1   To identify the gap between what is and what should be, compare your students' results to standards, benchmarks, averages, and rubrics.

The Handbook for SMART School Teams © 2002, 2014 Solution Tree Press • solution-tree.com

Visit **go.solution-tree.com/schoolimprovement** to download this page.

References

Abplanalp, S. (2007). *Breaking the low-achieving mindset: A S.M.A.R.T. journey of purposeful change.* Madison, WI: Quality Leadership by Design.

Bailey, S. (2000). *Making progress visible: Implementing standards and other large scale change initiatives.* Vacaville, CA: Bailey Alliance.

Bailey, K., & Jakicic, C. (2012). *Common formative assessment: A toolkit for professional learning communities at work.* Bloomington, IN: Solution Tree Press.

Bellanca, J., & Brandt, R. (Eds.). (2010). *21st century skills: Rethinking how students learn.* Bloomington, IN: Solution Tree Press.

Bender, J. (1963). *How to talk well.* New York: McGraw-Hill.

Box, G. E. P. (1989). *When Murphy speaks—listen.* Madison, WI: Center for Quality and Productivity Improvement.

Chadwick, R. J. (2013). *Finding new ground: Beyond conflict to consensus.* Seattle, WA: CreateSpace.

City, E. A., Elmore, R. F., Fiarman, S. E., & Teitel, L. (2009). *Instructional rounds in education: A network approach to improving teaching and learning.* Cambridge, MA: Harvard Education Press.

Conzemius, A. E., & Morganti-Fisher, T. (2012). *More than a SMART goal: Staying focused on student learning.* Bloomington, IN: Solution Tree Press.

Cotter, M., Simmons, J., & Paris, K. A. (1997). *Administering a department: A guide for identifying and improving support processes in an academic department.* Maryville, MO: Prescott.

Culham, R. (2003). *6 + 1 traits of writing*. Portland, OR: Northwestern Regional Educational Laboratory.

Danielson, C. (2007). *Enhancing professional practice: A framework for teaching* (2nd ed.). Alexandria, VA: Association for Supervision and Curriculum Development.

Delehant, A. S. (2007). *Making meetings work: How to get started, get going, and get it done.* Thousand Oaks, CA: Corwin Press.

Deming, W. E. (1982). *Out of the crisis.* Cambridge, MA: Massachusetts Institute of Technology, Center for Advanced Engineering Study.

Deming, W. E. (1993). *The new economics for industry, government, education.* Cambridge, MA: Massachusetts Institute of Technology, Center for Advanced Engineering Study.

Drago-Severson, E. (2009). *Leading adult learning: Supporting adult development in our schools.* Thousand Oaks, CA: Corwin Press.

Drago-Severson, E., Blum-DeStefano, J., & Asghar, A. (in press). *Learning and leading for growth: Preparing school leaders to build capacity in our schools.* Thousand Oaks, CA: Corwin Press.

DuFour, R., DuFour, R., Eaker, R., & Many, T. W. (2010). *Learning by doing: A handbook for professional learning communities at work* (2nd ed.). Bloomington, IN: Solution Tree Press.

DuFour, R., & Eaker, R. (1998). *Professional learning communities at work: Best practices for enhancing student achievement.* Bloomington, IN: Solution Tree Press.

DuFour, R., & Marzano, R. J. (2011). *Leaders of learning: How district, school, and classroom leaders improve student achievement.* Bloomington, IN: Solution Tree Press.

Eaker, R., DuFour, R., & DuFour, R. (2002). *Getting started: Reculturing schools to become professional learning communities.* Bloomington, IN: Solution Tree Press.

Easton, L. B. (2008a). From professional development to professional learning. *Phi Delta Kappan, 89*(10), 755–759, 761.

Easton, L. B. (Ed). (2008b). *Powerful designs for professional learning* (2nd ed.). Oxford, OH: Learning Forward.

Frank, L. S. (1996). *The caring classroom: Using adventure to create community in the classroom and beyond.* Madison, WI: GOAL Consulting.

Garmston, R., & Wellman, B. (1999). *The adaptive school: A sourcebook for developing collaborative groups.* Norwood, MA: Christopher-Gordon.

Gibbs, J. (1995). *Tribes: A new way of learning and being together.* Sausalito, CA: Center Source Systems.

Hager, M. A., Wilson, S., Pollak, T. H., & Rooney, P. M. (2003). Response rates for mail surveys of nonprofit organizations: A review and empirical test. *Nonprofit and Voluntary Quarterly, 32*(2), 252–267. Accessed at http://philanthropy.iupui.edu/files/research /response_rates_for_mail_surveys_of_nonprofit _organizations_-_a_review_and_empirical_test.pdf on October 22, 2013.

Hargreaves, A., & Fullan, M. (2012). *Professional capital: Transforming teaching in every school.* New York: Teachers College Press.

Hipp, K. K., & Huffman, J. B. (Eds.). (2010). *Demystifying professional learning communities: School leadership at its best.* Lanham, MD: Rowman & Littlefield.

Hirsh, S., & Hord, S. (2012). *A playbook for professional learning: Putting the standards into action.* Oxford, OH: Learning Forward.

Honig, M. I., Copland, M. A., Rainey, L., Lorton, J. A., & Newton, M. (2010). *Central office transformation for district-wide teaching and learning improvement.* Seattle, WA: Center for the Study of Research and Policy, University of Washington. Assessed at www.wallacefoundation.org/KnowledgeCenter on November 11, 2013.

Hord, S. M., Roussin, J. L., & Sommers, W. A. (2010). *Guiding professional learning communities:*

Inspiration, challenge, surprise, and meaning. Thousand Oaks, CA: Corwin Press.

Johnston, P. H. (2012). *Opening minds: Using language to change lives.* Portland, ME: Stenhouse.

Juran, J. (1964). *Managerial breakthrough.* New York: McGraw-Hill.

Kanold, T. D. (2011). *The five disciplines of PLC leaders.* Bloomington, IN: Solution Tree Press.

Krejcie, R. V., & Morgan, D. W. (1970). Determining sample size for research activities. *Educational and Psychological Measurement, 30*(3), 607–610.

Learning Forward. (2011). *Standards for professional learning: Quick reference guide.* Oxford, OH: Author. Accessed at www.learningforward.org/docs/pdf /standardsreferenceguide.pdf on August 30, 2013.

Learning Forward. (2012). *Standards list.* Accessed at http://learningforward.org/standards/standards -list#.UhI6I9L2a4Q on August 19, 2013.

Lewis, C. C., & Tsuchida, I. (1998). A lesson is like a swiftly flowing river: How research lessons improve Japanese education. *American Educator, 22*(4), 12–17, 50–52.

Lezotte, L. W., & Snyder, K.M. (2011). *What effective schools do: Re-envisioning the correlates.* Bloomington, IN: Solution Tree Press.

Loehr, J., & Schwartz, T. (2003). *The power of full engagement: Managing energy, not time, is the key to high performance and personal renewal.* New York: Free Press.

Louis, K. S., Leithwood, K., Walhstrom, K. L., & Anderson, S. E. (2010). *Learning from leadership: Investigating the links to improved student learning.* Minneapolis, MN: Center for Applied Research and Educational Improvement. Accessed at www.wallacefoundation .org/KnowledgeCenter on November 11, 2013.

Markova, D. (1992). *How your child is smart: A life-changing approach to learning.* Berkeley, CA: Conari Press.

Marzano, R. J. (2003). *What works in schools: Translating research into action.* Alexandria, VA: Association for Supervision and Curriculum Development.

Mitchell, R. (1999). Examining student work. *Journal of Staff Development, 20*(3), 32–33.

Newmann, F. M., King, M. B., & Youngs, P. (2000, April). *Professional development that addresses school capacity: Lessons from urban elementary schools.* Paper presented at the annual meeting of the American Educational Research Association, New Orleans, LA.

O'Neill, J., & Conzemius, A. (2006). *The power of SMART goals: Using goals to improve student learning.* Bloomington, IN: Solution Tree Press.

Pareto, V. (1935). *The mind and society (Vol. 4).* New York: Harcourt, Brace and Company.

Senge, P. M., Kleiner, A., Roberts, C., Ross, R., & Smith, B.(1994). *The fifth discipline fieldbook: Strategies and tools for building a learning organization.* New York: Doubleday.

Shannon, G. S., & Bylsma, P. (2007). *The nine characteristics of high-performing schools: A research-based resource for schools and districts to assist with improving student learning* (2nd ed.). Olympia, WA: OSPI.

Shewhart, W. A. (1939). *Statistical method from the viewpoint of quality control.* Washington, DC: The Graduate School, U.S. Department of Agriculture.

Sweeney, D. (2003). *Learning along the way: Professional development by and for teachers.* Portland, ME: Stenhouse.

Tuckman, B. W. (1965). Developmental sequence in small groups. *Psychological Bulletin, 63*(6) 384–399.

Udelhofen, S. (2005). *Keys to curriculum mapping: Strategies and tools to make it work.* Thousand Oaks, CA: Corwin Press.

Weisbord, M. R. (1987). *Productive workplaces: Organizing and managing for dignity, meaning, and community.* San Francisco: Jossey-Bass.

Weisbord, M. R. (2012). *Productive workplaces: Dignity, meaning, and community in the 21st century.* San Francisco: Jossey-Bass.

Wellman, B., & Lipton, L. (2003). *Data-driven dialogue: A facilitator's guide to collaborative inquiry.* Sherman, CT: MiraVia.

Whitewater Unified School District (2013). *Strategic plan.* Whitewater, WI: Author.

Zmuda, A. (2010). *Breaking free from myths about teaching and learning: Innovation as an engine for student success.* Alexandria, VA: Association for Supervision and Curriculum Development.

Index

A

accountability gap, 260
action plans, developing, 271–274
action research, 268–269, 270–271, 302, 316
active listening, 62
    barriers to, 63
    strategies for, 63–65
ad hoc groups/teams, 33–37, 49
advocacy, 61
affinity diagrams, 113, 116–118, 152, 220, 258
agendas, 98, 99, 101, 308

B

Bailey, S., 200
bar charts, 170–172
bar graphs, 170
basic flowcharts, 126, 127
behavior
    guidelines, 46–49
    patterns of, 201–205
Bender, J., 199
bias, sampling frame, 145
bimodal distribution, 175, 176
blue sky scenarios, 241
brainstorming, 112–113, 115, 249
brainwriting, 248–250

C

Carlin, G., 49
cause-analysis tools
    cause-and-effect diagrams, 164–167
    five whys analysis, 162–164
    relations diagrams, 167–168
    role of, 161–162

cause-and-effect diagrams, 164–167, 261, 263
Cavafy, C. P., 233
change-over-time gap, 261
charter, developing a, 44, 45, 307
check-ins, 100–101
checkouts, 103, 104
coherence, 14
cohesiveness, 84–85, 86
collaboration
    barriers to, 22–25
    components of, 19–22
    defined, 8
    effectiveness of, 19
    inquiry, 254, 275
    people and, 19–20
    processes and, 21
    role of, 11–12
    structured, 27
    tasks and, 20–21
    See also teams/teamwork
Collins, J., 257
command decisions, 69, 72–74
commitment gap, 260
committees and task forces, 37
common cause variation, 187–188, 191
communication
    about meetings, 98–99
    active listening, 62–65
    dialogue, 61–62
    discussion, 60
    mental models and ladder of inference, 65–67
    role of, 58–59
    sharing, 59
    types of, 59
community members. *See* parents and
        community members

complexity, 223

compliance gap, 260

conflict management

    feedback, giving and receiving, 76–80, 81, 82

    techniques, 74–76

    tips, 74–75

Consensus Building on Profound Issues, 71, 75, 124–125

consensus decision making, 69, 70–71, 120–124

consensus round robin, 71, 122, 123

consultative decisions, 69, 72, 72

continuous improvement

    framework for, 8–14

    linking learning and, 3–5

    PDSA model, 4–5

    sample planning and reporting document, 288–289

    use of term, 3

control charts, 191–193, 202

control limits, computing, 193, 315

core values, 236–239

correlation, 185–186

Cotter, M., 47, 219

Cotter Question, 47–48

curriculum development, 269

customer needs, identifying, 223

customer, use of term, 220

D

data

    cause-analysis tools, 161–168

    collection rules, 80

    -logic chain, 83–84, 214, 257, 260, 275

    numerical data tools, 168–194

    use of term, 11

    See also perceptual data collection

decision making

    authorization to make decisions, 68–69

    command, 69, 72–74

    consensus, 69, 70–71, 120–124

    consultative, 69, 72, 73

    forums, 94, 95

    matrices, 71, 119–120, 121, 217, 313

    process, 67–74

    voting, 69, 71

Deming, W. E., 4, 81, 83, 128, 187, 219

deployment flowcharts, 44, 46, 128–131

detailed flowcharts, 131–134

dialogue, 61–62, 112, 113, 114

    dialogue sessions, 94, 95

disaggregation, 144, 147–148, 149, 170

discussion skills and examples, 60

distribution charts, 174–179

Dolan, P., 13

Drucker, P. F., 168

Dulles, J. F., 161

E

educational demands, 1–2

egg timer, use of, 93

80/20 rule, 10

85/15 rule, 206–207

Epictetus, 62

Erickson, M., 111

F

facilitators, 42–43

    at meetings, 93, 107–108

failing forward, 5

feedback, 14

    characteristics and examples of effective, 81

    from friendly observers, 254–256

    giving and receiving, 76–80, 81, 82

    guidelines for conducting, 77–79

    loops, 202–205, 225

    preparing to give, 76–77

    session, contents of, 79–80

    tips and example for receiving, 82

fist-to-five, 71, 122, 123

five whys analysis, 162–164, 214

flex item, 101

flowcharts

    basic, 126, 127

    deployment, 44, 46, 128–131

    detailed, 131–134

    problem solving using, 214–215, 221, 222, 224

    top-down, 127–128, 219

focus

    defined, 8

    groups, 153–155

    role of, 9–10

forecasting scenarios, 241–242

forming stage, 51, 52–53

Fullan, M., 226
functional analysis process
    core processes, identifying, 221, 223
    customer needs, identifying, 223
    flowchart, creating a, 221, 222, 224
    improvements, making, 224
    mission, values, and customers, identifying, 220–221
    prioritizing, 224
    responsibilities, identifying, 223
    results, checking, 224
    steps for, 219–220
functions, defining team, 41–43

G

Gantt charts, 44, 134, 139–141
gap analysis scales, 150, 151, 281
gap closers, 258
gaps, types of, 260–261
goals
    identifying team, 43
    monitoring, 43
    origin of, 43
    See also SMART goals
governance teams, 28–29
greatest area of need (GAN), 260–261
group process, defined, 112
group process tools
    affinity diagrams, 113, 116–118
    brainstorming, 112–113, 115
    consensus decision making, 120–124
    decision matrices, 119–120, 121, 313
    dialogue, 112, 113, 114
    multivoting, 118–119
    purpose of, 111
groups
    focus, 153–155
    See also teams/teamwork

H

histograms, 172–174
historygram, 202, 225, 233–235, 245

I

immersion, 270
improvement. *See* continuous improvement
incentives, 14
individuals chart, 192
information-sharing techniques, 59
inquiry, 61, 254, 275
inspection versus reflection, 11
institutional barriers, 22, 23, 24
instructional rounds process, 255–256
interviews, 150–153
issue bin, 92–93

J

Juran, J., 9–10

K

kinesthetic aids, 102–103

L

ladder of inference, 65–67
leaders
    coordinating functions of team leader and meeting facilitator, 107–109
    how they build leadership capacity, 13–14
    identifying role of, 41
leadership
    defined, 14
    guidelines for, 231–233
    link between learning and, 13
leadership capacity
    defined, 8–9
    role of, 12–14
learning
    link between leadership and, 13
    linking, and continuous improvement, 3–5
    organizations, 8
Learning Forward, Standards for Professional Learning, xix–xx, 230
Lipton, L., 61
listening
    active, 62–65
    barriers to, 63

M

mapping, 242
master teacher shadowing, 271
measures of central tendency, 177, 180
measures of dispersion, 177, 180
meetings
    action between, 104–105
    agendas, 98, 99, 101, 308
    check-ins, 100–101
    checkouts, 103, 104
    communicating about, 98–99
    coordinating functions of team leader and
        meeting facilitator, 107–109
    decision-making forums, 94, 95
    dialogue sessions, 94, 95
    evaluating, 103–104, 309
    facilitators, 93, 107–108
    functional roles, 106–109
    ground rules, 101
    how to keep participants engaged, 102–103
    logistics, 97–98
    managing, 106–109
    methods and tools, 93
    participants, 93, 108
    planning, 96–100
    process, 100–104
    purpose, 92, 97
    records, 105–106, 310
    skills self-assessment, 107, 311–312
    tangents, handling, 92–93
    timing, 93
    turbo, 94–95
    types of, 94
    who is responsible for planning, 91
members, team
    identifying, 38–40
    role of, 41–42
mental models, 65–67, 207
Millay, E. S. V., 201
mission
    defined, 236, 245–246
    identifying, 220, 245
mission statements
    how to brainwrite, 248–250
    how to create, 246–248
    maintaining focus with, 250–251

model lessons, 270
moving picture tools 186
    control charts, 191–193
    purpose of, 169, 194
    run charts, 188–191
    variation, 187–188
multivoting, 118–119, 220, 250, 266

N

needs assessment, 252–254, 258
Newmann, F. M., 247
non-normal curves, 177
normal curve, 177–178
normal distribution, 175, 176
norming stage, 51, 54–55
norm-referenced tests, 178–179
norms
    creating, 47–48
    topics and examples, 48–49
    uses for, 47
numerical data tools
    approaches, 168–169
    moving picture tools, 169, 186–194
    pictures, creating, 168, 169
    snapshot tools, 169–186

O

ongoing teams, 27–33, 49

P

paraphrasing, 64
parents and community members
    involvement of, 38–39
    logistics for, 39–40
    roles for, 39
    terms/language, identifying educational, 40
Pareto, V., 9
Pareto diagrams, 179, 181–183, 263
Pareto principle, 9–10, 11
Paris, K., 219
parking lot, 92–93
patterns of behavior, 201–205
PDSA model, 4–5, 85–86, 96, 134, 218, 258
perception checking, 64

perceptual data collection
    disaggregation, 144, 147–148, 149
    focus groups, 153–155
    interviews, 150–153
    quantifying, 144, 150, 151
    questioning, 144, 148–149
    research validity, 150, 152
    results generalizability, 150, 152
    results validity, 150, 152
    sampling, 144–145, 146–147, 300–301
    stratification, 144, 145–147
    surveys, 155–158, 284
performing stage, 52, 55–56
pictogram, 243
pictures
    creating, 168, 169
    See also moving picture tools
planning tools
    Gantt charts, 44, 134, 139–141
    PDSA model, 4–5, 85–86, 96, 134
    purpose of, 111
    responsibility matrices, 134, 138–139, 140, 314
    tree diagrams, 134–138, 284–287
probing, 64
problem-solving process, 211
    analyzing the problem, 214–215
    avoiding problems disguised as solutions, 212
    causes, verifying potential, 214
    for complex problems, 224–226
    goals, establishing, 215–216
    identifying and defining problem, 212–214
    implementation planning, 217–218
    implementation testing, 218–219
    monitoring and evaluation, 219
    solutions, identifying, 216–217
    steps for, 212
processes
    defined, 208
    differences between results thinking and, 260
    problem-solving, 211–219
    strategies for improving, 208–211
process improvement project groups, 35–36
process-mapping tools
    applications, 126

flowcharts, basic, 126, 127
flowcharts, deployment, 126, 128–131
flowcharts, detailed, 126, 131–134
flowcharts, top-down, 126, 127–128, 219
purpose of, 111, 125–126
professional development, 271, 274, 303
professional learning
    job-embedded designs, 268–271
    qualities of powerful, 268
    relationship between student results and, 274–276
professional learning communities (PLCs)
    role of, 2–3
    use of term, 8
professional learning teams, 31–33
proficiency gap, 260
Proust, M., 148

Q

quantifying, 144, 150, 151
questioning, 144, 148–149

R

random number tables, 145, 147, 300–301
rank order scales, 150, 151
rating scales, 150, 151
record keeper, 108
records, meeting, 105–106, 310
reflection
    assertion and, 61
    defined, 8
    inspection versus, 11
    role of, 10–11
relations diagrams, 167–168, 215
research validity, 150, 152
responsibility matrices, 134, 138–139, 140, 223, 314
results generalizability, 150, 152
results thinking, differences between process and, 260
results validity, 150, 152
role playing, 242
round robin, consensus, 71, 122, 123
run charts, 188–191, 202
runs table, 191, 283

S

sample size chart, 146–147, 280
sampling, 144–145, 146–147, 300–301
sampling frame bias, 145
scales, 150, 151
scatterplots, 183–186, 275
scheduling tasks, 44, 139
Schmoker, M., 257
school improvement/effectiveness teams,
    29–30, 235
scribe, 108
Senge, P., 37, 207
shared mission. *See* mission
shared vision. *See* vision
sharing, 59
Shewhart, W., 4
Simmons, J., 219
skewed distribution, 175, 176
small-scale test, 219
SMART goals
    alignment of, 258–259
    defined, 5–7
    identifying, 258–265
    tree diagrams, 134–138, 261–265, 276,
        284–287
SMART leadership team, guidelines for,
    231–233
SMART meeting process, 96
SMART schools
    change, preparing for, 233–235
    framework for becoming a, 8–14
    goals of, 7–8
    improvement process, 257–274, 290–297
    other terms for, 8
    questions for, 235–277
    self-assessment, 256, 304–306
snapshot tools
    bar charts, 170–172
    bar graphs, 170
    distribution charts, 174–179
    histograms, 172–174
    Pareto diagrams, 179, 181–183
    problem solving using, 215
    purpose of, 169, 170
    scatterplots, 183–186
social barriers, 22, 23, 24–25

social systems, principles of, 204
Sparks, D., 257
speaking and listening, 61
special cause variation, 187, 188, 190–191
staff development, 271, 274, 303
stakeholders, identifying, 40
statistical measures, 177, 179, 180
steering committees, 33–34
storming stage, 51, 53–54
stratification, 144, 145–147
student results, relationship between
    professional learning and, 274–276
student shadowing, 270–271
student work analysis, 269
study circles, 34–35
study groups, 271
suboptimization, 207–208
surveys, 155–158, 282, 284
system, defined, 199
systemic structures, 205–207
system-level improvement teams, 30–31
systems thinking
    defined, 199, 201
    feedback loops, 202–205
    functional analysis process, 219–224
    mental models, 65–67, 207
    metaphor exercise to understand, 200–201
    patterns of behavior, 201–205
    problem-solving process, 211–219, 224–226
    strategies for improving, 208–211
    suboptimization, 207–208
    systemic structures, 205–207

T

tangents (meeting), handling, 92–93
T-Chart, 103
teams/teamwork
    ad hoc, 33–37, 49
    barriers to, 22–25
    committees and task forces, 37
    governance, 28–29
    ongoing, 27–33, 49
    processes, 21
    process improvement project groups, 35–36
    professional learning, 31–33
    role of, 12

school improvement/effectiveness, 29–30
   starting, 37–49
   steering committees, 33–34
   study circles, 34–35
   success of, factors that affect, 58–85
   supporting, 49
   system-level improvement, 30–31
   tasks, 20–21
   time consuming, 22–23
   when to consider, 27
   who make up, 19–20
   See also collaboration
teams/teamwork, growth and development
   forming, 51, 52–53
   norming, 51, 54–55
   performing, 52, 55–56
   stages for, 51–52
   storming, 51, 53–54
   transforming, 52, 56–57
teams/teamwork, starting
   assumptions, 46
   behavior guidelines, 46–49
   charter, developing a, 44, 45, 307
   functions, defining, 41–43
   goals, identifying, 43
   members, identifying, 38–40
   organization, importance of, 43–44
   roles and responsibilities, determining, 44, 46, 128
   scheduling tasks, 44, 139
   stakeholders, identifying, 40
   steps for, 37–38
3-2-1 rule, 266
timekeeper, 108
time plots, 190
time warp, 242
top-down flowcharts, 127–128, 219
transforming stage, 52, 56–57
tree diagrams, 134–138, 261–265, 276, 284–287
turbo meetings, 94–95, 257

V

validity, research and results, 150, 152
values, 3, 220–221
   core, 236–239
variables, independent and dependent, 184

variation
   common cause, 187–188, 191
   special cause, 187–188, 190–191
vision
   defined, 2–3, 236, 239–240
   how to develop a shared, 240–243
   how to keep the vision alive, 244–245
vision statements
   characteristics of, 243–244
   tips for writing, 244
voting, 69, 71

W

Wehlage, G. G., 247
Wellman, B., 61

More Than a SMART Goal
Anne E. Conzemius and Terry Morganti-Fisher
Setting data-informed, high-priority SMART goals is a critical step in school improvement that is widely acknowledged. However, goals themselves don't drive improvement; they must be aligned to the school improvement process, curriculum, instruction, assessment practices, mandates, and professional development. Understand how to properly use the SMART goal process to effect change and achieve real school improvement.
BKF482

The Power of SMART Goals
Jan O'Neill and Anne E. Conzemius
Help staff focus on results, and implement SMART (strategic and specific, measurable, attainable, results based, and time bound) goals to transform your school into a place where every student meets or exceeds standards. The authors present four success stories from real SMART schools and several frameworks for adult and student goal setting that lead to real results.
BKF207

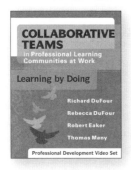

Collaborative Teams in Professional Learning Communities at Work™
Richard DuFour, Rebecca DuFour, Robert Eaker, and Thomas W. Many
This short program shows exactly what collaborative teams do. Aligned with the best-selling book *Learning by Doing*, the video features unscripted footage of collaboration in action. Learn how team norms are managed; how teams organize, interact, and find time to meet; what products they produce; and what team conversations about the critical questions of student learning "look like."
DVF023

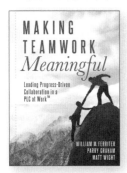

Making Teamwork Meaningful
William M. Ferriter, Parry Graham, and Matt Wight
Focus on developing people—not just improving test scores. The authors examine how staffing decisions can strengthen professional learning communities and explore actions that can help school leaders safeguard their schools against complacency. Collect tips and strategies that every teacher can adopt, and apply the professional development techniques that prove most useful.
BKF548